ENDO

Barry Callen has written a caref[...]cal pilgrimage of perhaps the most significant evangelical theologian [...] half of the twentieth century. By showing both how Pinnock's mind has changed and why, Callen provides a window on some of the more central theological issues of our day. This is a story that needed to be told, and Callen has done so with clarity, understanding, and grace.

> Henry H. Knight III, Saint Paul School of Theology. Author of *A Future for Truth: Evangelical Theology in a Postmodern World* (1997).

No twentieth-century evangelical thinker has been more controversial than Clark Pinnock. He has been lauded as an inspiring theological pilgrim by his admirers and condemned as a dangerous renegade by his foes. Yet no story of evangelical theology in the twentieth century is complete without the inclusion of his fascinating intellectual journey from quintessential evangelical apologist to anti-Augustinian theological reformist. For this reason, Barry Callen's intellectual biography of Pinnock is not only "must reading," but also an insightful guide for Clark's supporters and detractors alike.

> Stanley J. Grenz, Carey Theological College and Regent College. Author of *Revisioning Evangelical Theology* (1993), *Theology for the Community of God* (1994), and co-author of *20th Century Theology* (1992).

Barry Callen's intellectual biography of Clark Pinnock reveals that the evangelical theologian many have labeled a "moving target" is in fact a pilgrim on a consistent journey. Biography and theology are inseparable. Pinnock's life story and the story of his consistent, single-minded path toward a reasonable, faithful, and contemporary interpretation of Scripture are shown to be one story in this fascinating account. Even those of us who disagree with some of Pinnock's conclusions understand better how and why he has arrived at them because of Callen's superbly critical and sympathetic portrayal of the man and his journey.

> Roger E. Olson, Truett Theological Seminary, Baylor University. Co-author of *20th Century Theology* (1992) and author of *The Story of Christian Theology* (1999).

At the height of the "battle for the Bible" that boiled within American evangelicalism in the 1970s, fundamentalist leader Harold Lindsell bitterly remarked of Clark Pinnock, "his pilgrimage has been inexplicable." In this detailed and sympathetic intellectual biography, Barry L. Callen admirably shows otherwise. Drawing on his ample research, including his revealing interviews with the subject, Callen offers a vivid account of Pinnock's theological journey from a Reformed-determinist fundamentalism to an open-ended, narrative-oriented, Arminian evangelicalism of Word and Spirit.

> Gary Dorrien, Kalamazoo College. Author of *The Remaking of Evangelical Theology* (1998) and *The Barthian Revolt in Modern Theology* (1999).

Since biographies have been published on evangelical luminaries who have not produced near the volume of substantial theological work that Clark Pinnock has, it is good to see this book come forth. The conservative side of evangelicalism is already well represented; now it is time for a retelling of the intellectual pilgrimage of a man who has embodied so much of the theological development of evangelical theology since the 1960s. In Pinnock's interaction with conservative evangelicalism, pentecostalism, Wesleyanism, process thought, Eastern Orthodoxy, and Roman Catholicism, one sees the vision of an open and generous evangelical theology which still remains true to evangelical distinctives.

> John Sanders, Huntington College. Author of *No Other Name* (1992) and *The God Who Risks* (1998).

In this engaging biography of Clark Pinnock, Barry Callen presents the inseparability of the man and his message by skillfully weaving together the stories of his personal, theological, and spiritual development. The reader is taken on a journey which not only serves as a lively introduction to Pinnock's important theological contributions, but through it models a challenging way of doing theology by risking the tension between openness and evangelical commitment. This book will resonate with people at many different levels: as a celebration of Pinnock's life and work; as a journey which might awaken, convert, or confirm the instincts of many in the evangelical community; and as reminder that theology is best done both on one's knees and walking in the Spirit.

> Philip R. Meadows, Garrett-Evangelical Theological Seminary. Editor of *Windows on Wesley: Wesleyan Theology in Today's World* (1997).

Barry Callen has done the church a great service by displaying the work of one who, having prayed his head into his heart, finds more to revelation than fundamentalism and inerrancy, unravels Reformed scholasticism in search of a more dynamic theology, revises classical theism to allow for a God mercifully present, and, in a confluence of Eastern, Wesleyan, and Pentecostal streams, discovers new depths of biblical meaning. Here is a distinctive integration of theology and spirituality. It is an important resource for college and seminary courses in theology, spiritual development, and especially the doctrines of revelation, Trinity, Scripture, theological method, and salvation.

Steven J. Land, Dean, Church of God Theological Seminary. Author of *Pentecostal Spirituality: A Passion for the Kingdom* (1993).

In many respects Clark Pinnock's fascinating theological pilgrimage illustrates the sometimes strained diversity of theological options which comprise contemporary evangelicalism. To understand the journey of this one brilliant thinker is to better understand the nature of contemporary evangelicalism, and Callen's masterful work succeeds at helping us to do both.

Gregory A. Boyd, Bethel College and Seminary. Author of *Cynic, Sage or Son of God?* (1995) and *God At War: The Bible and Spiritual Conflict* (1997).

Barry Callen's work is essential reading for anyone who wants to know what the future of Evangelicalism might look like. Clark Pinnock's work encapsulates many of the debating points of evangelical theology, including the openness of God and the inclusiveness of Jesus Christ, the authority and interpretation of Scripture, and spirituality and the role of Christianity in the world. Through his careful tracking of Pinnock's personal theological pilgrimage, Callen reveals what lies behind the several course corrections and provides insight into the joy and pain that some of these changes have brought.

Ray C. W. Roennfeldt, Avondale College (Australia). Author of *Clark Pinnock on Biblical Authority* (1993).

CLARK H. PINNOCK:
JOURNEY TOWARD RENEWAL

An Intellectual Biography

Other books by Barry L. Callen and
published by Evangel Publishing House

GOD AS LOVING GRACE:
The Biblically Revealed Nature and Work of God

FAITHFUL IN THE MEANTIME:
A Biblical View of Final Things
and Present Responsibilities

SEEKING THE LIGHT:
America's Modern Quest for
Peace, Justice, Prosperity, and Faith

RADICAL CHRISTIANITY:
The Believers Church Tradition in
Christianity's History and Future

CLARK H. PINNOCK:
JOURNEY TOWARD RENEWAL

An Intellectual Biography

by Barry L. Callen

Published in Cooperation With
The Wesleyan Theological Society

Evangel
Publishing House
Nappanee, Indiana

Toll-free Order Line: (800) 253-9315
Internet Website: www.evangelpublishing.com

Publisher's Cataloging-in-Publication
(Provided by Quality Books, Inc.)

Callen, Barry L.
    Clark H. Pinnock : journey toward renewal : an
intellectual biography / by Barry L. Callen — 1st ed.
    p. cm.
    Includes bibliographical references and index.
    LCCN: 00-101021
    ISBN: 1-928915-02-7

    1. Pinnock, Clark H., 1937- —Religion.
2. Theology, Doctrinal. 3. Evangelicalism—Biography.
4. Christian college teachers—Canada—Biography.
I. Title

BR1643.P56C35 2000   280'.4'092
                                       QBI00-258

Printed in the United States of America

1 2 3 EP 5 4 3 2 1

Dedication

To Ethan Alexander, my beloved grandson who has just begun the journey of life. Given this world of ours, there will come times when he will need renewal that can open a fresh path to lead him toward truth, peace, and joy. May something in these pages become light and encouragement along his way. Above all, may he never choose to walk alone, but always draw on past wisdom and follow faithfully the way of God's loving Spirit.

Table of Contents

Foreword xiii

Introduction xvii

Chapters

1. Joining the Journey 1
   Why This Particular Journey?
   Destabilizing the Status Quo
   A Place To Begin

2. Formative Contexts 15
   Roots of a Rigorous Faith
   A Canadian Abroad
   Out of the Arid Desert
   Time To Teach and Write

3. The Certainty of Revealed Truth 41
   No Diluted Christianity
   Affirming and Revising Inerrancy
   Claiming Middle Ground
   The Place of Piety

4. Unraveling Reformed Scholasticism 87
   Toward A More Dynamic Theology
   The Results of Reciprocity
   A Pilgrimage in Political Theology
   Reason Enough

5. Open and Unbounded 127
   An "Open" Way of Doing Theology
   Revising Classical Theism
   The God Who Risks the Process
   A Wideness in God's Mercy

6. Walking With the Spirit 175
    Into the Eastern and Wesleyan Streams
    Interpreting Theological Change
    Flame of the Spirit
    New Dimensions of Biblical Meaning
    Invitation to Celebration

Appendixes:
    Selections from the Writings of Clark Pinnock and
    Pinnock's 1999 Comments on "How My Mind Has Changed"

    A. What Is a Baptist? (1968) 219
        Pinnock: How My Mind Has Changed
    B. A Rich Selection of Christian Evidences (1971) 225
        Pinnock: How My Mind Has Changed
    C. Biblical Inspiration and Authority (1984) 231
        Pinnock: How My Mind Has Changed
    D. Revising the Doctrine of God (1989) 239
        Pinnock: How My Mind Has Changed
    E. High Christology and a Pluralistic World (1992) 245
        Pinnock: How My Mind Has Changed
    F. On Theological Method (1996) 253
        Pinnock: How My Mind Has Changed
    G. The Evangelical Big Tent (1998) 263
        Pinnock: How My Mind Has Changed

Afterword by Clark H. Pinnock 269

Bibliography: Select Works by and about Clark Pinnock 273

Index: Subjects and Persons 285

Foreword

Clark Pinnock has been one of the most prominent and provocative theological voices in North Atlantic evangelical Christianity since the 1960s. His long and distinguished career has found him present in and greatly impacting the evangelical scenes in Canada, the United States, England, and the European continent. His special status is grounded in his responsible scholarship and his ability to communicate Christian theology with clarity and cogency. But his influence also has been heightened because he has been ever ready to engage contested theological issues within evangelicalism and to revise his views on these issues when he found the evidence for change compelling. In the creative and sometimes turbulent process, he has helped to clarify what is at stake in the debates and has scouted a way forward for others who share his evangelical background and his questions about certain reigning assumptions within this large and diverse Christian movement known as evangelicalism.

Of course, one person's "scout" is another person's "drifter." Change in one's central convictions is not always viewed positively, particularly within the theological academy. Since the truth we deal with is grounded in and concerns the steadfast God, there is a subtle temptation to view negatively any change in our conceptions of this truth. Ironically, this temptation is as prevalent among Protestants—who emerged with a call to continually reform inadequate theology—as anywhere else. But whatever its object, the discipline of theology is fundamentally a human enterprise, and our human fallibility makes change not only possible but often desirable. The legitimate concern is not whether there is change, but whether this change is only mindless drifting or the mere pursuit of novelty instead of an honest and faithful quest for better understandings of Christian truth.

If there is one thing that this book makes clear, it is that Clark Pinnock's entire adult life has been devoted to such an honest and faithful quest. This is reflected in the book's very form as an "intellectual biography" rather than a systematic survey of Pinnock's theology. It is reflected as well in the coherence that Barry Callen demonstrates within the changes he chronicles. In fact, one could argue that there is more real coherence found in the journey of Clark Pinnock than exists in some (supposedly) systematic theologies! But the most striking thing that emerges from this study is the holistic nature of Clark's quest. He has not limited his search to merely a better understanding of key theological issues. He recognizes that Christian faith involves more than just *right belief*—it also necessarily involves that overall orientation of the person that we call the *heart* and the *actions* toward God and others that flow from and nurture this orientation. As Callen has aptly titled it, Pinnock's life as a theologian has been a "journey toward renewal." Those who read this book will not only learn much about Pinnock's specific theological proposals; they also will be challenged to consider what such a journey might look like for themselves.

To be sure, not all Christians will be (or have been) happy with the direction that Clark's journey has taken. Some in the evangelical community can view it only as a lamentable deviation from his original "orthodoxy" within the fold. This has been particularly true for those who take classic Princetonian Reformed theology as the exclusive standard for "evangelical" theology. But many others within the broader evangelical tent—Anabaptists, Wesleyans, Pentecostals, and the like—have long protested this standard and have argued the biblical warrant for their alternative stances on such issues as predestination, general revelation, and the nature of biblical authority. As Callen shows, some of the most significant moves Pinnock has made (based particularly on his reconsideration of Scripture!) are toward positions long affirmed by these "other" evangelicals. As one of these "others," Callen provides a chronicle of Pinnock's journey that is sympathetic while remaining very reliable.

In effect, Pinnock's insistence on Scripture as the primary basis for reconsidering some of the assumptions that framed his earliest theological work soon embarked him on a journey into the broader Christian community of biblical interpretation. It led him to appreciate other dimensions of persons who were already important to him, like F. F. Bruce, C. S. Lewis, and Sir Norman Anderson. It led him to consider the broader "Arminian" wing of evangelicalism. It led him to engage the renewed emphasis on the person and work of the Holy Spirit in the Pentecostal and Charismatic renewal movements. It led him to an appreciative dialogue with "liberal" theology. And it led him into the recently renewed appreciation of some of the distinctive theological emphases of Eastern Christianity. Overall, it has led him into becoming an "ecumenical evangelical" who now weds a strong commitment to the importance of the gospel with a recognition of the importance of listening to, and learning from, how others read this shared gospel.

We in the Wesleyan tradition have often characterized John Wesley as an "ecumenical evangelical." Many of us in the evangelical wing of this tradition have watched Clark's long journey with great interest. Having a prominent evangelical voice publicly shift toward positions for which we have taken much chiding from the evangelical establishment has been refreshing, to say the least. But it can also pose a temptation toward unholy smugness. The best way that we Wesleyans can welcome a fellow journeyer who has come to share some of our deepest convictions is to be willing to listen to, learn from, and dialogue with him when he poses thoughtful challenges to our traditional framing and application of these convictions. I am thinking particularly of his insightful and provocative work on the possibility of truth and salvation in other religions, the nature of God's relationship to temporality, and the need for restoring pneumatology to a fully equal role within our theology.

Clark laments at one point in this volume that his journey might have been easier if he had started out as a Wesleyan. While that may be true, there are sufficient examples of Wesleyans now caught up in the militant rationalist apologetics that Pinnock has struggled to transcend to show that it is not inevitable. In any case, I for one have been instructed and enriched as a Wesleyan theologian by Clark's work precisely because of the specific journey he has taken, and the integrity and grace with which he has taken it. His story, as told here, is an especially valuable one for any serious Christian ready to listen and learn.

Randy L. Maddox
Seattle Pacific University
Past President of the
Wesleyan Theological Society

Introduction

The issues, risks, and possibilities are all great. The body of Christ's people is facing the urgent need for renewed integrity as it pursues its divinely-appointed mission in today's world. Will the church find the renewal it needs to truly be Christ's people in a "post-Christian" and "post-modern" environment that is data rich yet peace starved, consumer-oriented yet poor in the most basic of ways, tolerant of anyone's "truth" yet in need of a coherence of meaning and the comfort of a community that can enrich and satisfy human life? Thinking particularly of the large "evangelical" Christian community of North America, what needs for renewal does it have, and are they being faced honestly and constructively?

This intellectual biography of Clark H. Pinnock is an attempt to highlight the needs and point toward promising solutions. The means used is the story of the eventful career of one key player in the contemporary evangelical community of scholars and church leaders. Narrating the stages and struggles of Pinnock's own journey is judged an excellent way to name the issues and point in good directions. His experiences and thoughts may not be the last word, but at the least it is a committed, informing, stimulating, and sometimes inspiring word. To miss his word is to miss much indeed.

Christians are pilgrims, resident aliens in this world, exodus people who by divine grace are on the way to God's future. Traveling under the guidance of God's Spirit, committed believers seek the full reign of God, not kingdoms for themselves. They love and learn as they go. To really love and learn requires remaining open to what has not yet been, but what is becoming possible because of God. The eyes of those who journey must remain fixed on the amazing God who loves much and is with them on their way. As they journey together with God, these new creations in Jesus Christ become closer to each other as brothers and sisters in the growing family of God. Their ever-widening discernment of God's truth and purposes emerges only in the midst of the constancy of their faithfulness and the authenticity of their mutual relationships with God and each other.

Assumed here is a thesis of Roger Olson who has recently written a helpful guide to the whole history of Christian theology. The wonderful fact is that "God works in mysterious ways to establish his people in truth and to reform theology when needed."[1] This present book focuses on a recent chapter in "reformation" theology. It is presented as an "intellectual biography," or the tracing of the widening discernment of truth by one Christian traveler who has remained open to the guiding God and to the community of pilgrims who have surrounded him on the way. This traveler bears the marks of being a divinely inspired catalyst for reform in the Christian theology of the last half of the twentieth century and now into that of the twenty-first. He has been a very faithful, if not always a perfect traveler; one in whom, in God's mysterious way, there have emerged at least key signposts guiding Christians toward a fresh establishment of God's people in divinely revealed wisdom and intended mission.

There is in these pages a minimum of detail about the personal life of Clark H. Pinnock. Included is only what is judged essential to set the several contexts in which his intellectual journey has proceeded toward theological renewal for one man personally and for the Christian community generally. Pinnock's personal and family lives are admirable models of what a seeking and growing Christian walk should be. Even

---

[1]Roger Olson, *The Story of Christian Theology: Twenty Centuries of Tradition and Reform* (Downers Grove, Ill.: InterVarsity Press, 1999), 21.

so, personal and family information is not the central focus here. The core concern lies with his intellectual and theological journey, with the resulting body of teaching that is instructive for what Christians should believe, with how such beliefs are best determined, with how openness, humility, and community can lead to growth in thought, with how the rational side of believing should relate to personal transformation, and with how believers should relate to the contemporary work of the Spirit of God. In these regards, the subject of this work is the wisdom to be gained from the path of a Christian pilgrim now long on the faith journey.

The trail of Pinnock's thought is unusually self-reflective, sometimes experimental, occasionally daring, and frequently fresh and fruitful. From time to time it doubles back on itself. Finally, the judgment rendered in these pages is that the end result is full of wisdom, clearly worthy of careful review. Pinnock's trail leads through the roots and ideals, traditions, inflexibilities, and increasing diversity of contemporary evangelicalism. Eventually it comes to a fresh opening that offers biblical Christians a way to be both faithful and relevant. There is in process today a paradigm shift in evangelical thought. The change offers new hope and includes lurking danger. Following the intellectual journey of Pinnock is an excellent way to understand the change and clarify the boundaries between real progress and unacceptable innovation. It may even be a way to help bridge the ancient West-East divide within Christianity in a constructive way that is renewing to Christian theology worldwide and enabling to Christian mission.

Like Pinnock's own commitment, this present tracing of his journey has sought to be "open." I have read extensively and listened intently. In a series of taped interviews done especially for this book, Clark Pinnock and others have shared freely with me. Several insightful theologians have invested significant time in critiquing the initial draft of the volume. It now is hoped that they have been heard properly and reported fairly. My sincere appreciation is extended to Gregory Boyd, Delwin Brown, Anthony Campolo, Gary Dorrien, Stanley Grenz, Henry Knight, William Kostlevy, Steven Land, Randy Maddox, Philip Meadows, Roger Olson, Grant Osborne, Ray Roennfeldt, John Sanders, Douglas Strong, and others who saw value in this research and writing and provided helpful assistance whenever asked. It surely says something about the widespread influence of Clark Pinnock that such a significant group of accomplished scholars, representing a wide range of universities, seminaries, nations, and Christian traditions, all hold Pinnock in high regard and were pleased to help with this publishing project.

Sincere appreciation is expressed to Dorothy Pinnock for graciously hosting me in their culturally-rich Canadian home and to Clark Pinnock himself, who has willingly invested many hours interviewing with me in various settings in Canada and the United States. He promptly answered numerous telephone and e-mail inquiries between visits. His spirit truly reflects that of his Master. A gracious and generous Christian man, he never pled for mercy in my writing, only that I be careful with the facts and fair to all people in my eventual judgments. After all, the well-being of the church and the health of the Christian theological enterprise and mission in the world are finally more important than how any of us is remembered and evaluated. In this regard, Pinnock, while certainly sensitive about how he is perceived, nonetheless exhibits a disarmingly vulnerable selflessness in his pursuit of ideas and in his acceptance of both criticism and praise. He is a persistent pilgrim who admits to a certain personal shyness. Despite all of his credentials and scholarly accomplishments, at times his human frailty reminds him that he is only an unworthy servant. He aspires to reflect, both in his strength and weakness, a Christlikeness that he very much knows is enabled only by the work of God's gracious Spirit.

In these pages the reader will find more than the usual footnotes, index, and bibliography—all important and certainly here. Found also are interactive features that continue the dynamic nature of Clark Pinnock's own work and increase the instructional usefulness of the book. There are several appendixes that together provide a small "Pinnock Reader." After each is fresh writing by Pinnock himself, done specifically for this book, on "How My Mind Has Changed." There also is an "Afterword" by Pinnock in response to this book as a whole (he did not read the manuscript until it was done). The Foreword by Randy Maddox reflects something of the high regard in which this Christian theologian is held in numerous Christian traditions, in addition to his own Baptist heritage. It also represents one of the several ways in which the Wesleyan Theological Society was able and anxious to assist in this biographical work.

Pinnock has become a contemporary bridge between Christians of the East and West, between Calvinists and Wesleyans, and between conservative Evangelicals and the more dynamic worlds of Pentecostal and Process thought and experience. He has proven to be a creative, provocative, and interactive Christian pilgrim. His eyes have remained fixed on God and his heart committed to the centrality of biblical revelation for proper understanding of God. He has journeyed with courage and faith, persistently pursuing his two deep hungers: to be an effective Christian scholar/apologist and to be a man full of Christ's love. The latter of these two has become especially prominent for Pinnock in recent years as he has de-emphasized viewing evangelicalism as a set creed and rather has conceived of it more as a spirituality at heart, a particular way of being Christian, a style of religious experience that makes Christ central and has a passion for spreading the good news.

Following Pinnock's theological trail is not a smooth journey at all points, but it is a trip well worth taking for any Christian who is serious about the faith's integrity, mission, and transformative power in the twenty-first century. What Stanley Grenz has said about Donald Bloesch may well be said of Clark Pinnock. He "belongs to a select group of pioneers whose example has given younger conservative thinkers permission to explore new vistas while self-consciously maintaining their moorings within the evangelical movement."[2] Grenz judges as follows in his endorsement statement for this current volume: "No twentieth-century evangelical thinker has been more controversial than Clark Pinnock. He has been lauded as an inspiring theological pilgrim by his admirers and condemned as a dangerous renegade by his foes [as

---

[2]Stanley Grenz, "'Fideistic Revelationalism': Donald Bloesch's Antirationalist Theological Method," in *Evangelical Theology in Transition: Theologians in Dialogue with Donald Bloesch*, ed. Elmer M. Colyer (Downers Grove, Ill.: InterVarsity Press, 1999), 36.

he has pursued] his fascinating intellectual journey from quintessential evangelical apologist to anti-Augustinian theological reformist."

Contrary to the fixed theological mindset of many evangelical theologians, Pinnock thinks of evangelical theology as "in progress."[3] He recently reflected on the nature and meaning of his own theological work, seeing it as "an effort to overcome [evangelical] forgetfulness and indicate the contemporary relevance of neglected insights."[4] Thinking, then, of Pinnock as one who has been seeking to keep evangelical theology remembering and constructively in progress, Daniel Strange detailed this way Pinnock's impact on the path of progress in the final decades of the twentieth century:

> [Pinnock] has often become the figurehead (perhaps not intentionally) of many of the controversial issues which have confronted Evangelicalism in the last two decades: the authority of Scripture (as a "limited inerrantist"); the role of other religions (as an inclusivist); the nature of hell (as an advocate of annihilationism); the charismatic renewal and the place of spiritual gifts (a strong advocate); and the doctrine of God (as a free-will theist).[5]

The church must find renewal through faithfulness to God's Word and transformation by God's redeeming presence. Authentic Christian life is available only by and in God's Spirit. As Clark Pinnock has innovatively and courageously sought to do since the 1950s, may these pages make some modest contribution toward the greatest of all ends: being transformed into the image of Christ by hearing rightly the Word of God; receiving humbly and transformingly the grace of God; then through God's Spirit faithfully living the full implications of the presence and mission of God today.

---

[3]This is a focus of the chapter Pinnock contributes to Roger Badham's *Introduction to Christian Theology* (Westminster John Knox Press, 1998).

[4]Clark Pinnock, "Response to Daniel Strange and Amos Yong," *The Evangelical Quarterly*, 71:4 (October 1999), 354.

[5]Daniel Strange, "Clark H. Pinnock: The Evolution of an Evangelical Maverick," *The Evangelical Quarterly*, 71:4 (October 1999), 325.

1

Joining the Journey

Life is essentially a journey. It is of the essence of reality that it should be process, and it is of the essence of our life that we should walk. We have many dangers as we walk, for the bypaths are many and some of them lead to dead ends. It is very hard to know whether we are veritably on the high road, and that is why we must help one another. Each, as he journeys, keeps asking the way and watching for hints dropped by those who may have walked the same path, either long ago or in recent times. Sometimes we are forced to retrace our steps and frequently we find the pathway rough.[1]

The above quote by the beloved Quaker theologian D. Elton Trueblood says it quite well. We humans are all on a journey. Included in the ongoing quest of life is the journey of faith. This particular journey does have its doubts and dead ends—it is, after all, *by faith*. All who choose the journey of faith seek the high road and soon learn that there are many bypaths, rough places, and the clear need for the wisdom available from other travelers who have walked that way before and may have dropped guiding hints along the way. One such traveler is Clark H. Pinnock. This contemporary theologian has been on the faith path for several decades now, has tested many of the bypaths, and

---

[1]D. Elton Trueblood, *The Life We Prize* (N.Y.: Harper & Brothers Publishers, 1951), 213.

certainly has left many hints of learned wisdom about the high road for those of us just now coming along. He would not claim final answers (the theological journey always continues), but his current faith hypotheses are well-tested and worthy.

The chapters that follow seek to retrace Clark Pinnock's walking and to retrieve the hints that he has left behind. The twin tasks of responsible Christian theology require a constant reassessment of both the faith's formative sources, especially the Bible, and of its current cultural contexts. One focus seeks reassurance that the faith is remaining authentically Christian; the other focus seeks to maximize the effectiveness of the faith's witness to people of a given time and place. Pinnock has come to speak of responsibility to both biblical text and contemporary context. Consequently, it is the case that the good theologian in some ways is always on a journey—to the Word of God and to the world of God. For the sake of enhancing the always necessary biblical vision and mission preoccupation, it is well worth the time to join the especially eventful journey of theologian Clark Pinnock. Retracing his steps and rethinking his thoughts prove provocative, raise many of the right questions, and often point in fresh and wholesome directions for Christian believing and living in the twenty-first century. We choose to join his journey.

Why This Particular Journey?

Two questions focus the remainder of this first chapter. The first is: At what point in time do we join the intellectual faith journey of Clark Pinnock? The answer is, the opening year of a new century and millennium, and in the sixty-third year of this theologian's life (born in February 1937). Probably more important than Pinnock's exact age at the time of this writing is the fact that he already has journeyed far and may be nearing the peak of his thinking and writing career. Even more important is the larger picture of the journeying of the whole church in its ongoing quest for renewal and relevance. This bigger story, told well by Roger Olson, includes Martin Luther rediscovering the gospel of faith, Anabaptists returning to the roots of Christianity, Arminians reforming Reformed theology, Pietists renewing Lutheran theology, and Methodists reviving English theology. Olson concludes:

It is a story of the gradual growth of tradition—a firm
foundation of basic Christian beliefs that guide and regulate
Christian discipleship. It is also the story of amazing reforms
within that tradition that continually called God's people back
to the sources of divine revelation and forward to new light
breaking forth from it. If the story continues to unfold with
great coherence and surprise—two necessary ingredients of any
good story—it will be because Christians continue to value the
twin principles of tradition and reform by drawing on deep
wells continually being refreshed by new springs.[2]

This surely is where Clark Pinnock comes in. He values these twin
principles highly and seeks always to be refreshed by new springs of
insight and life. The "evangelical" community of the late twentieth and
early twenty-first centuries has been on its own journey of renewal. It is
in the midst of this broader journey that we pick up Pinnock's renewing
trail.

The second question addressed by this chapter requires much more
space to answer. We also must ask: Why is this particular theologian's
journey singled out for so much attention? Regarding the significance
and timeliness of this intellectual biography of Clark Pinnock, at least
two things are clear and are basic assumptions of this volume. First, the
religious and social lives of North American society in the last half of the
twentieth century have been influenced significantly by the Christian
movement known popularly as "evangelicalism." Second, the story of the
theological journey and work of Clark Pinnock both traverses this half-
century in ways that track helpfully the larger story of evangelicalism and
reflects significant impact on it at many points. This impact has been
nothing short of his encouraging a theological paradigm shift for
evangelicalism—a shift which Pinnock first experienced personally and
now has shared widely through his teaching, extensive writings, and
lecturing.[3] Ever a loyal Baptist, he nonetheless belongs and speaks to the
whole church. He has been especially influenced by and active in

---

[2]Roger Olson, *The Story of Christian Theology* (Downers Grove, Ill.: InterVarsity
Press, 1999), 612-613.

[3]Gabriel Fackre titled his review article on two of Pinnock's recent works, "An
Evangelical Megashift? The Promise and Peril of an 'Open' View of God" (*Christian
Century*, May 3, 1995), 484-487.

evangelical parachurch organizations, sometimes even thinking of his special love, InterVarsity Christian Fellowship, as "my real ecclesial home."

Prominent evangelical leader Timothy George has said it well: "When the history of evangelical theology in the last half of the twentieth century is written, the intellectual biographies of Clark Pinnock and Tom Oden will loom large. Like two ships passing in the night, they have crisscrossed the theological landscape with abandon."[4] Oden's is one important story for which we wait. The time now has come, however, for the work on Clark Pinnock. His may not be the whole of the story of contemporary evangelicalism, but his journey takes one into virtually every aspect of the larger tale, introducing one to nearly all players in and dimensions of the drama of evangelicalism since the 1940s in Canada, England, Switzerland, and the United States. His dramatic story is an especially valuable window into the whole evangelical scene, including its internal struggles and its intersections with other Christian traditions (e.g., the Process, Pentecostal, Believers Church, and Wesleyan/Holiness traditions). If Millard Erickson is right in anticipating that one day the story of Thomas Oden will serve as "something of a parable" of evangelical Christianity's engagement with "postmodernism,"[5] it surely also is the case that Clark Pinnock's story is a parallel and pivotal parable worthy of careful study.

Which of the following questions is most appropriate? Is Clark Pinnock the one who unfortunately departed significantly from evangelical orthodoxy? Or is he the one who fortunately took real risks to bring new life and relevancy to the orthodoxy that he staunchly refused to leave to the fate of its own limitations? Both questions are explored here, with the eventual judgment that the latter question is the more appropriate.[6] As he concludes his distinguished career and the

---

[4]Timothy George, "A Theology to Die For," *Christianity Today* (Feb. 9, 1998), 49.

[5]Millard Erickson, *Postmodernizing the Faith: Evangelical Responses to the Challenge of Postmodernism* (Grand Rapids: Baker Books, 1998), 43.

[6]John Sanders has observed that often Pinnock is "seen as a threat by the evangelical doorkeepers." In large part this may be because evangelical theology, rather than being innovative and theoretically reflective and self-critical, often operates more like the practice of accounting in the business field—it insists in proceeding only by pre-approved rules and fixed formulae and formats (interview with Barry Callen, September 22, 1998).

chaotic twentieth century is left behind, Pinnock remains in the forefront of positioning evangelical Christianity for the rigors of what lies ahead. If conservative Christianity, as Delwin Brown maintains, is "essentially an insistence on the central importance of the Christian past [especially the Bible] for the Christian future," and if such a tradition in changing circumstances inevitably generates from within a self-critical creativity for the sake of its current credibility and mission, then we agree with Brown that among contemporary evangelicals "the work of Clark Pinnock represents this exploration in its most compelling form."[7]

Pinnock is probably the most prominent pioneer of a fresh mood, maybe even a fresh movement in contemporary North American evangelical theology. Roger Olson has called it "postconservative" and characterized it as a gathering of those who "no longer make their chief role that of defending historic orthodoxy—especially Reformed scholasticism—against the 'acids of modernity.'"[8] For the ten years before the mid-1970s, Pinnock "had produced one aggressive book after another that made the case for inerrancy doctrine and evidentialist apologetics.... But in the mid-1970s he began to question whether the cause of inerrancy was worth all the turmoil and hostility it was causing in the evangelical movement."[9] He began to pioneer another way. Formally educated in Canada and England, Pinnock was tutored early in his long career by Francis Schaeffer, F. F. Bruce, and many others. Soon he came to play a key role in the early stages of the conservative resurgence in the Southern Baptist Convention in the United States, and then shifted course to lead a new "open" school of evangelical thought into a largely uncharted future marked by both theological faithfulness and innovation.

Pinnock would come to argue that the Christian theological enterprise is bipolar, simultaneously about the two tasks of (1) reaffirming the foundational truths of Christianity and (2) rearticulating

---

[7]Delwin Brown, "Rethinking Authority from the Right," *Christian Scholar's Review* 19:1(1989-90), 66.

[8]Roger Olson, "Postconservative Evangelicals Greet the Postmodern Age," *Christian Century* (May 3, 1995), 480.

[9]Gary Dorrien, *The Remaking of Evangelical Theology* (Louisville, KY: Westminster John Knox Press, 1998), 129, 131.

these truths in fresh ways that are both consistent with the foundations and creatively sensitive to contemporary culture. The coordinate questions are: What is the Christian "good news"; and How can it be communicated best to today's world? Theology, as Pinnock has come to understand it, is at the same time *stable* in its historic rootedness and *fluid* in its structures of thought and forms of expression. Both this stability and fluidity are crucial for the effectiveness of the Christian mission. One assures that there is an authentic message to be shared; the other attempts to be sure that the message is delivered understandably and persuasively. There are sturdy roots of the faith that can enable and encourage the formation of new flowers of evangelistic expression in each spring of cultural change.

Viewing his career as a whole, Clark Pinnock has worked vigorously and creatively on these coordinate tasks. He now knows that most Christian theologians occasionally change their minds, usually in modest ways, but sometimes significantly. It is, he judges, "better to change one's mind than to continue on a wrong path." After all, the theological issues at hand involve the greatest questions and mysteries that can be addressed by humans. So Pinnock does "not apologize for admitting to being on a pilgrimage in theology, as if it were in itself some kind of weakness of intelligence or character.... We are fallible and historically situated creatures," he insists, "and our best thinking falls far short of the ideal of what our subject matter requires."[10] The resulting openness and willingness to search, change, and innovate have come to create for him a place in the evangelical community that has been described in ways ranging from staunch defender of the faith against the liberal disaster, to cautious biblical pioneer, to a dangerous and sophisticated carrier of subtle heresy into the contemporary faith. As the editors of a prominent Pentecostal academic journal reported in 1998, Pinnock "has produced several ground-breaking (and ground-shaking!) studies in evangelical theology."[11] Since the 1960s his courage and style have

---

[10]Clark Pinnock, "From Augustine To Arminius: A Pilgrimage in Theology," in *The Grace of God and the Will of Man*, ed. Clark Pinnock (Zondervan, 1989, rev. ed., Minneapolis: Bethany House, 1995), 15-16.

[11]*Journal of Pentecostal Theology*, 13 (1998), 3. Pinnock had been invited to function as a special dialogue partner for this journal issue in which appeared two substantial and appreciative review articles on his 1996 book *Flame of Love*.

tended to gain a wide hearing and generate many responses of varying kinds. He is loved and feared. He is a man of simplicity and complexity, a tall man whose substantial intellect and warm heart have challenged evangelicalism's status quo and set numerous persons and places aglow with the flame of God's Spirit. He surely has cared deeply, spoken forthrightly, and made quite a difference.

Yes, Clark Pinnock has been on a pilgrimage. "More like a pilgrim than a settler," he says, almost echoing St. Paul, "I tread the path of discovery and do my theology en route."[12] By his own admission, he has had to introduce "course corrections" and "listen more carefully to what the Scriptures actually say and teach." When venturing forth, every step can be something of an adventure. He has had "to reduce certain emphases and experiment with others."[13] But there has been a sturdy consistency in the midst of the ongoing pilgrimage. Since the 1970s he has remained on the path of seeking to be a liberator (not a "liberal"), freeing the evangelical Christian community from its shackles of Reformed scholasticism and hellenistic and other cultural accommodations. Pinnock's pilgrimage has influenced many other evangelicals to reassess where they are at various points, small and large, and sometimes to join him on the road to what may be a more biblical view of the Christian faith. Others have resisted his counsel, judging him an uncertain and sometimes impulsive guide. Regardless, Pinnock continues to serve as a prophetic voice and has sought to be a bridge, a unifying force, a catalyst for renewal and relevance in the evangelical community.

Here is the story of one Christian theologian who has been seeking to minister to an evangelicalism now full of diversity, but still largely defined by a rational theological system whose adequacy is increasingly in question. In his judgment, conservative Christians who insist on conserving in ways reflective of past thought traditions and cultures more than of biblical thought and true Spirit life are at risk of stagnating—losing the vitality of the Spirit's witness to biblical meaning—and

---

[12]Clark Pinnock, "A Pilgrim On the Way," *Christianity Today* (Feb. 9, 1998), 43.

[13]Clark Pinnock, "A Response to Rex A. Koivisto," *Journal of the Evangelical Theological Society*, 24 (1981), 153-154.

thus undercutting the crucial mission of Christ in this increasingly pluralistic world. His passion is strong because his career-long journey has convinced him that the stakes are so high for the church.

Destabilizing the Status Quo

James McClendon, Jr., notes rightly that "the character we investigate in a biographical study is always character-in-community."[14] In the case of Clark Pinnock, the general "evangelical" community is the key context in which he is to be understood, and is the community on which, from the inside, he has had great impact. He once said: "Relating my own pilgrimage would not be of much importance if it did not represent the experience of other evangelicals also, but I think it does."[15] We readily agree. In fact, the number represented is increasing steadily. A new generation is arising that fears missing God's will and way for today's church more than they fear the criticism of colleagues who refuse to consider the possible necessity of any theological changes.

The significance of Pinnock's life and thought was highlighted in 1988 as the prominent career of Carl F. H. Henry waned with age. While it was then too early to name Henry's successor as the new "Dean" of evangelical theologians, Robert Price thought that "it would not be surprising to see the name of Clark H. Pinnock rise to the top" and that "to understand Pinnock's theology may well be to understand the evangelical theology of the coming generation." Why? Price judged:

> As the [Evangelical] movement has grown and developed in the last decades, Pinnock has been there in the thick of it, a participant-observer who has come to see both that the voice of

---

[14]James McClendon, Jr., *Biography as Theology: How Life Stories Can Remake Today's Theology* (Nashville: Abingdon Press, 1974), 202.

[15]Clark Pinnock, "From Augustine to Arminius...," 26. In an e-mail letter to me on April 2, 1998, Pinnock expressed a certain hesitancy about a biography of him being researched and written, partly out of a natural shyness and partly out of a genuine sense "that I am only an unworthy servant." This is not a contrived public face for him, but a true characteristic of his Spirit-filled nature. Even so, with only a little reluctance, he agreed to submit to the research process leading to this book in the hope that the telling of his story would prove helpful to others, and especially to the all-important mission of the church in today's world.

Evangelical Christianity needs urgently to be sounded in the modern world, and that it has little chance of being heard and heeded unless it speaks in the idiom and to the concerns of "modernity."[16]

Pinnock himself certainly has not sought this kind of elitist recognition and certainly has not received it universally—in fact, he is subtly shunned by some establishment evangelical leaders who judge that he threatens "the truth" as they understand it. Rather than seeking recognition (he is neither an administratively manipulative nor politically inclined person), Pinnock has wanted only to be a creative catalyst, a biblically faithful bridge person both within the evangelical community and between the evangelical and other Christian theological traditions. He has worked for increased understanding and unity on behalf of effective mission. Extremes in any direction are always his likely targets. He disturbs the complacency of lifeless establishments ("orthodox" or not), but also cautions that overreactions, his or anyone else's, can easily lead to even worse ends. The wisdom of the Spirit is always crucial.

After years of theological searching, Pinnock placed himself in the "moderate" category of theologians. His intention has been to function between the "conservatives," who concentrate heavily and sometimes almost blindly on what they see as the unchanging biblical revelation, and the "progressives," who seek, sometimes without proper limits, to update Christian foundations by so connecting them to today's issues and experiences that they become almost unrecognizable as distinctively Christian. He has hoped for a proper balance of these "text" and "context" poles and has been unwilling to choose between a crisis of Christian *identity*—violating biblical authority—and a crisis of *intelligibility*—being captured and controlled by an agenda not emerging from the Christian gospel itself.[17] There must be both continuity with the ancient apostolic faith of Christians and effective communication of

---

[16]Robert M. Price, "Clark Pinnock: Conservative and Contemporary," *Evangelical Quarterly* 60 (1988), 157.

[17]See Clark Pinnock, *Tracking the Maze: Finding Our Way Through Modern Theology From an Evangelical Perspective* (San Francisco: Harper and Row, 1990), 54-75.

that faith in biblical terms and in current cultural circumstances. Continuity keeps one anchored; communication keeps one thinking, translating, and journeying. This is Pinnock's heart and has become his perennial task.

Positioned intentionally in this dynamic middle, Pinnock has been on an experimental journey toward his own renewal and that of the church and its mission in our time. The trip has not always been comfortable or in a straight line, however it has been intentional and persistent across four decades so far. There has been a pattern of loyalty to his biblical faith and Baptist roots. He has chosen to "stay home," work for needed change from within, and survive whatever becomes momentarily uncomfortable for the sake of the bigger agenda and the longer haul. Working for change has had its risks. He has observed that his own story comes down to this: "Some evangelicals think I am just what is needed, while others fear I am nearly a pagan."[18] Renewal has its risks and its price. Pinnock has been willing to risk and pay. Without question there are numerous evangelical leaders today who identify strongly with his struggle to be free of fundamentalism without compromising the essence of Christian faith itself, becoming captive to something even less reflective of true Christianity than was the older and rigid fundamentalism.

At the beginning of the twenty-first century, thousands of educated Christian leaders in numerous denominational traditions have on their shelves a large collection of books by Clark Pinnock and think of him as an inspiring and innovative model for their own theological journeys. Others, like his former student Adrian Rogers, think apprehensively of him as a brillant man who is on a "curious theological odyssey" that so far has yielded "ephemeral theological oddities."[19] Tracking the events and issues surrounding such dynamics and mixed readings is full of lessons for the believing community. At times it may be a little destabilizing, but always the process is worth the time and effort. Concluding his review of the book *The Openness of God*, in which Clark

---

[18]Clark Pinnock, Interview with Barry Callen, April 19, 1998.
[19]Adrian Rogers, in *The Proceedings of the Conference on Biblical Inerrancy*, 1987 (Nashville: Broadman Press, 1987), 106.

Pinnock was deeply involved, Roger Olson poses a penetrating question: "How do American evangelical Christians handle theological diversity? Have we come of age enough to avoid heresy charges and breast-beating jeremiads in response to a new doctrinal proposal that is so conscientiously based on biblical reflection rather than on rebellious accommodation to modern thought? This may be the test."[20] Indeed, a review of the whole theological career of Clark Pinnock is itself such a vital test.

One evaluator speaks of Pinnock's "stylistic stridency" which arises in large part from the intensity of his feelings, the depth of his biblical commitments, and the honest straightforwardness of his speaking and writing. A theologian once reacted this way to a Pinnock article: "Clark Pinnock has set forth his case bluntly. For this I am grateful. His honesty may have its risks, but it would be a sad day for all of us if interpretations of Scripture such as his could not be debated publicly."[21] Pinnock certainly has been honest, sometimes quite direct, frequently accepting risks, and usually willing to be perceived as premature or even naive in his immediate pursuit of a promising line of thought. He always has cared passionately about biblical authenticity and evangelistic credibility. His has been an energized and eventful journey toward Christian spiritual renewal for himself and the church at large. To not have had him in the middle of the evangelical mix of recent decades would have been to impoverish the self-critical creativity of the whole enterprise. He has been very much in the middle, however, with his many insights and his tendency on occasion to slightly destabilize a conservative tradition that often is too inflexible and not ready to listen unless someone of the stature of a Clark Pinnock raises his voice just a little!

So, why give such attention to the intellectual journey of this particular theologian? He is the one who has been the pioneer, the model and mentor to numerous others, the consistent catalyst for renewal in evangelical theology. He often has been there first and said it

---

[20]Roger Olsen, review of *The Openness of God* by Clark Pinnock et. al., *Christianity Today* (January 9, 1995), 30-34.

[21]David F. Wells, "Everlasting Punishment," *Christianity Today* (March 20, 1987), 41.

best. His may only be one journey, but it is one of special significance for Christians who care deeply about biblical faithfulness, theological sanity, life's transformation, and the church's current mission.

A Place To Begin

Where to begin is always a crucial question. For Christians, it is always good to begin with the Spirit.[22] Clark Pinnock did just that, centering his 1963 doctoral dissertation on the concept of the Spirit in the Epistles of Paul.[23] The Spirit of God, as promised, has been speaking to the churches (Rev. 3:22). Pinnock has been trying to be open, to listen carefully and fearlessly, and to speak, even when many others are not ready to hear. What he has heard and said is worthy of the attention, appreciation, and thoughtful consideration of any serious Christian who cares about the nature and mission of Christian faith in today's world. After all, here is one theologian who, in the midst of all his education, sophistication, and publications, has not lost touch with the personal and practical dimensions of Christian faith. Terry Cross is one who has noticed this. He sensed that Pinnock's book *Flame of Love* (1996) seemed to have been written more on the author's knees than at his desk.[24] Pinnock liked this observation by Cross. This book indeed had been "a bold attempt to place the Spirit at the center of a theological vision" and had been "informed by a vital experience of the Spirit."[25] Apparently, being on one's knees is a very good place for a Christian theologian to begin serious work on the meaning, potential, and demands of faith in Christ and life in Christ's Spirit.

To know any given theology well, one needs to understand the theologian. What was the setting, the community of meaning, the motivations out of which the theology arose? With such pivotal

---

[22]For elaboration of this assertion, see Barry L. Callen, *Radical Christianity* (Nappanee, IN: Evangel Publishing House, 1999), chapter two.

[23]Clark Pinnock, "The Concept of the Spirit in the Epistles of Paul" (Ph.D. diss., University of Manchester, England, 1963), done under his mentor, Dr. F. F. Bruce.

[24]Terry Cross, "A Critical Review of Clark Pinnock's *Flame of Love*," *Journal of Pentecostal Theology* (October 1998), 3-29.

[25]Clark Pinnock, "A Bridge and Some Points of Growth: A Reply to Cross and Macchia," *Journal of Pentecostal Theology* (October 1998), 49-50.

questions in mind, we now join the theological journey of Clark Pinnock. Geographically speaking, there are rich roots in England that soon led to Canada. The trail then leads from Canada back to England and Switzerland, then to New Orleans and elsewhere in the United States, and finally back to Canada. But geography is probably not of central importance, although it does add much color and interest and certainly some distinctive cultural flavors to the story. Most important intellectually is where the trail has led within the shifting world of "evangelicalism" and its relationships with other Christian traditions. Pinnock has traversed most of the existing territory, has personally planted several of today's prominent signposts, and has been a stimulating catalyst for reevaluation and change on various subjects over several decades.

Let us begin retracing this journey, not so much for its own sake as for the wisdom that it may bring to the journey that yet lies ahead for faithful believers in Jesus Christ.

2

Formative Contexts

Since the moment when I began to study theology…everything theological has been for me marvelously new…. Right down to the present day, theology has continued to be for me a tremendous adventure, a journey of discovery into a, for me, unknown country, a voyage without the certainty of a return, a path into the unknown with many surprises and not without disappointments. If I have a theological virtue at all, then it is one that has never hitherto been recognized as such: curiosity.[1]

Later in life Clark Pinnock would become very sensitive to the issue of context. Often he would speak of the *text and context* poles for Christians—the Bible base and the world setting. He would even say, "Who we are influences what we see."[2] He would come to realize that, in general, evangelical theology has not been particularly adept at relating constructively to world contexts. Consequently, he would insist that a key task of Christian theology is "to present the truth as a living reality for the present time" and he would observe that evangelicalism has been

---

[1]Jürgen Moltmann, *The Coming of God: Christian Eschatology* (Minneapolis: Fortress Press, 1996), xiii-xiv.

[2]Clark Pinnock, "From Augustine To Arminius: A Pilgrimage in Theology," in *The Grace of God and the Will of Man*, ed. Clark Pinnock (Zondervan, 1989, rev. ed., Minneapolis: Bethany House, 1995), 27. He says further that "every generation reads the Bible in dialogue with its own vision and cultural presuppositions and has to come to terms with the world view of its day" (27).

overly bound to its classic "rational" method. Such binding "makes us feel that we cannot afford to listen to what the Spirit is saying to the churches now." Being spiritually deaf is an intolerable faith disease.

Since from the very beginning of his spiritual life Pinnock was on a journey toward renewal in the Spirit, he could not long ignore the fresh voice of the Spirit. He determined to listen and then speak, taking whatever were the related risks to his own reputation and career. Like Moltmann (above), "curiosity" is a theological virtue Pinnock has always possessed. It would help him to listen, learn, and sometimes pioneer. The fact that the classic evangelical method of doing theology would come to be viewed by Pinnock as "relatively indifferent to issues of context" certainly had not rendered it immune to the influence of context. What evangelicalism became was less than appropriately "open to discovering the meaning of revelation for the present" and not adequately "thinking with the mind of Christ in relation to fresh challenges."[3]

Given Pinnock's sensitivity to the significance of context, it is both needful and desirable in the case of his own life and theological work that proper attention be given initially to early life context. For him, at least at first, aspects of his family, church, and educational settings aided in his coming to a life-changing Christian faith. It was a faith with a particular theological orientation that was bolstered by the personality and heart of a young man who had the determination to learn about, witness to, and defend that faith against the perceived erosions of modernity.

Roots of a Rigorous Faith

Born to a middle class family in southern Ontario, Canada, on February 3, 1937, Clark Harold Pinnock was heir to an important Christian faith tradition that reached him primarily through one particular family member. His paternal grandparents were Samuel and Madora Pinnock from the British Midlands. In the early 1890s these pious Methodist people went to Nigeria as British Methodist missionaries. They became Baptists by conviction while in Nigeria

---

[3]Clark Pinnock, "Evangelical Theologians Facing the Future: An Ancient and a Future Paradigm," *Wesleyan Theological Journal* 33:2 (Fall 1998), 17.

(change of view on baptism) and joined the U. S. Southern Baptist mission. Samuel soon was seeking increased Africanization of the leadership of this mission, a philosophy well ahead of its time and not surprisingly resisted by the mission leaders. Here was a hint of the progressive spirit of Samuel's yet-unborn grandson, Clark. After the Pinnock's mission service ended and they had immigrated to Canada in the 1920s, Samuel soon published two books, the grammar of a Nigerian dialect and one called *Romance of Missions in Nigeria.* The heritage they passed on to Clark would include a keen interest in international mission, genuine Christian piety, an appreciation for scholarship and writing, British roots, Canadian identity, and a Baptist affiliation. Even more, through Samuel's writing and the personal witness of Madora late in her life, Clark caught something of the "romance" of the Christian faith, the sheer honor and delight of being a child of God by the loving grace of God.

In the 1940s young Clark was reared in Park Road Baptist Church in Toronto, a congregation that he later referred to as "a liberal church [that] had forgotten both the truth and the reality of God pretty much. It was a bore."[4] While surely not theologically heretical, this congregation was experienced by young Clark as empty of much gospel and slowly losing its next generation, at least so far as a truly evangelical faith was concerned. This congregation, he later reported, was under the influence of the "progressive theological views which had swept through scholarly Baptist circles in North America in the first decades of the 20th century and were being disseminated at that time from the Canadian Baptist Seminary at McMaster University."[5]

His 1950 conversion to a personal and meaningful Christian faith came largely through the witness of his Bible-believing paternal grandmother, Madora, and a like-minded Sunday School teacher at the

---

[4]Clark Pinnock, "I Was a Teenage Fundamentalist," *The Wittenburg Door* (December 1982—January 1983), 18.

[5]Clark Pinnock, "Baptists and Biblical Authority," *Journal of the Evangelical Theological Society,* vol. 17 (1974), 193. Ironically, many years later Pinnock himself would become a controversial figure among Baptists and would accomplish much of his more mature biblical and theological work from the base of his extended faculty tenure at McMaster Divinity College in Hamilton, Ontario.

church. The teacher was Frank Elliott, a man troubled by the lack of sound biblical preaching in that congregation who determined to compensate for the lack, at least for his class of boys aged 12-14. The result was an instilling in young Clark of a love for God and a confidence in the Bible. This love and confidence would prove enduring. Probably even more significant than the influence of Elliott was the witness of Madora. She really "touched me" with the vibrancy of real Christian faith. Living out her final years in Toronto with Clark's parents, her son Harold and his wife Mable Clark Pinnock,[6] Clark was privileged to have long talks with her in the upstairs of the family home. She shared her faith with the boy, including many mission stories from Africa, and the transforming power of the Christian gospel. God convicted and encouraged Clark through her and he "accepted the Lord." His long and eventful spiritual journey had begun.

As a conservative evangelical teenager maturing in a "liberal" church setting, he became aware early of "the need to be alert to defections from the true faith and to maintain a theologically sound testimony."[7] The need for such alertness only increased when, at age fifteen and a Christian only three years, he attended a lectureship in one of the Toronto Baptist churches. The lecturer, a faculty member at nearby McMaster Divinity College, championed "higher critical theories" regarding the Pentateuch, the book of Daniel, and the Psalms. The audience was mostly laypersons, with some, including young Clark, judging that such teaching was "destructive to our confidence in the reliability of the Bible."[8] Bothersome as this was, as a high school student Pinnock was not particularly open about his faith. He read the Bible regularly, but proceeded rather quietly, feeling a little "odd" in a secular setting. Later that would change, although a natural shyness would never leave him.

---

[6]Harold Pinnock and his brother Carey had immigrated to Canada before World War I while their parents were still in Africa. Both returned to Great Britain to fight as Canadians in the war, with only Harold surviving. He returned to Canada and married Mable Clark in 1922. The Clark family was also from England originally.

[7]Pinnock, "Baptists and Biblical Authority," 193.

[8]Ibid.

His Christian nurture outside the family began coming through a Bible study group at the high school, literature he secured through the mail from the American Prophetic League, and several religious radio programs that he came to value. The programs were "The Old Fashioned Revival Hour" with Charles Fuller, "The Hour of Decision" with the young evangelist Billy Graham, the broadcast of Perry F. Rockwood, a fundamentalist pastor in Truro, Nova Scotia, and the dispensationalist Bible teacher Donald Grey Barnhouse of Philadelphia. He also began profiting from the local chapter of a particular parachurch group. Through an ad in the *Toronto Star*, Clark learned that a "Youth for Christ" group met regularly at Toronto's prominent Peoples Church pastored by Oswald J. Smith. This was an interdenominational Bible church with a strong missionary emphasis. He began attending there and found a network of young evangelicals who helped meet his felt need for a Christianity "that meant something."

Pinnock had begun his Christian life and theological formation in the context of post-World War II fundamentalism in North America, an ethos soon to be called "evangelicalism."[9] In part through being nurtured in Youth for Christ meetings in Toronto, his tendencies to be critical of "liberalism" and committed to Scripture's central place in Christian faith both were strengthened. He was hungry for quality Bible instruction and found it available to him nearby in Ontario. Needing a summer job while still in high school, he worked with a mining company one year and grasped the opportunity another summer to wash dishes at the Canadian Keswick Bible Conference.[10] His real purpose there was not the dishes, of course, but attending the rich

---

[9]Pinnock later reported this about himself: "I began my spiritual pilgrimage as a fundamentalist" ("Defining American Fundamentalism," *The Fundamentalist Phenomenon*, ed. Norman Cohen [Grand Rapids: Eerdmans, 1990], 39). Such was the beginning, but not the end. He indeed had embarked on a spiritual journey that had a long way to go yet!

[10]Such annual gatherings of evangelical Christians began at Keswick in England's Lake District with the Moody-Sankey revival of 1875. Counter to the Wesleyan/ Arminian view, Keswick conferences typically maintained that the Spirit of God limits but does not eliminate the inclination for humans to sin. Gatherings were for Bible study, prayer, instruction in practical holiness, and generating enthusiasm for Christian mission.

teaching sessions and learning more about the "deeper life" as biblically portrayed. He read books in the camp's bookstore, loved the special peach ice cream, and kept learning about evangelical theology in a life-transforming setting. Particularly significant, he met there some Wycliff Bible Translators. Thinking about his own future, they gave him a vision of entering the honors program in biblical languages at the University of Toronto to prepare to be a translator or missionary. Maybe he, like his grandfather Samuel, could be a linguist for the Lord.

During the 1950s Pinnock was introduced to some of the key institutions of North American evangelicalism. He attended an early Billy Graham crusade in Toronto and a large missionary conference in Urbana, Illinois.[11] He was encouraged to read evangelicalism's theologically "sound" authors. Going frequently to an InterVarsity bookroom in Toronto, he immersed himself in the staunchly Calvinistic writings of John Murray, Martyn Lloyd-Jones, Cornelius Van Til, Carl F. H. Henry, James I. Packer, and Paul Jewett. As a young Christian, Pinnock's attention was directed to Westminster and Fuller seminaries and, for safe and true formation in theology, to leaders like Kenneth Kantzer, John Gerstner, and Gordon Clark. Although hardly aware of it in the 1950s, Pinnock later would observe that at mid-century the "modern" period, with its emphasis on universal rationality, favored evangelical scholasticism. Accordingly:

> When I was "born again" into evangelicalism, I did not know its true character as a historically particular movement. I accepted it uncritically as it was and made it my tradition, not aware of its post-fundamentalist and Reformed texture. I just assumed it was the ideal form of Christianity and did not reflect on its deficits and peculiarities.[12]

A loyal Baptist, it nonetheless was the case that young Pinnock's primary ecclesial identity was parachurch in nature. He later reported

---

[11]The first InterVarsity Christian Fellowship Missionary Convention was convened in Toronto in 1946. In 1948 the convention moved to Urbana, Illinois.

[12]Clark Pinnock, "Evangelical Theologians Facing the Future: An Ancient and a Future Paradigm," *Wesleyan Theological Journal* 33:2 (Fall 1998), 11. Earlier he had observed: "Many like me began theologically as post-fundamentalists and developed into mainline evangelicals" (in *Christian Scholar's Review*, September 1993, 44).

that he and an increasing number of others found it natural to identify with and work within the "big tent" of evangelicalism—"we prefer its broad spaces to the more restrictive quarters of the denominations. We benefit from the fruitful interaction of a confluence of traditions."[13] Much later he would report his early attraction to and evaluation of parachurch evangelicalism this way:

> What I got swept up in was a religious movement that overflowed with vitality without being theologically defined beyond a few simple points. Spiritually and missiologically, it was and it is a powerhouse, but theologically there was and is only a simple set of convictions and not much inclination to deepen and broaden them.... Most people just wanted vital Christianity with a simple theology. This made it possible for members of many traditions to come together around the evangelical banner—Lutheran, Reformed, Wesleyan, Baptist, Dispensational, Pentecostal, Adventist, Campbellite, and more. It was possible because this was a movement, not a theology, and it was a piety that held it together, not a creed.[14]

InterVarsity Christian Fellowship was a key component of Pinnock's Christian nurture from almost the beginning of his faith journey. It had been founded in 1927 to further cooperation among the evangelical unions in the universities and colleges of Great Britain and probably was the most important single reason for the advance of conservative evangelicalism after World War II.[15] John R. W. Stott, rector of All Souls Church in London, had been involved in the worldwide ministry of this Fellowship since his own student days at Cambridge University in the 1940s. He was committed to it because it encouraged thoughtful evangelism, intentional discipleship, and indigenous principles that allowed relative freedom to the associated movements of evangelical students in many countries—a key reason, he judged, why by the 1980s

---

[13]Pinnock, "Evangelical Theologians Facing the Future," 8.

[14]Clark Pinnock, "Evangelical Theology In Progress," *Introduction to Christian Theology*, ed. Roger Bedham (Louisville: Westminster John Knox Press, 1998), 76.

[15]See D. W. Bebbington, *Evangelicalism in Modern Britain* (London: Unwin Hyman, 1989), 257-261.

so many Christian leaders in Third World and other countries had an IVCF background.[16]

Clark Pinnock of Canada was one such evangelical leader. He later would recall that as a young Christian he experienced the ethos of InterVarsity Christian Fellowship as a coherent whole, a single theological package of biblical commitment and evangelistic fervor, all in a Calvinistic framework.[17] For many years Pinnock readily accepted this theological model without serious question. Although hardly aware of it at the time, such Calvinist theology enjoyed an elitist position of dominance within postwar evangelicalism on both sides of the Atlantic. Accordingly, young Pinnock began his theological life "as a Calvinist who regarded alternate evangelical interpretations as suspect and at least mildly heretical."[18] Calvinism was understood to be evangelical Christianity in its purest form.

Later, Pinnock would speak graciously of Carl F. H. Henry's substantial autobiography, saying that in it the reader will discover "what he [Henry] knew and when he knew it in all sorts of important events and turning points in the history of post-war American evangelicalism, the fortunes of which he principally steered."[19] It was a grand venture in what was thought to be biblically based and doctrinally clear Christianity. For young Pinnock, however, all was not ideal. He

---

[16]John R. W. Stott, foreword to Keith and Gladys Hunt, *For Christ and the University: The Story of InterVarsity Christian Fellowship of the U.S.A., 1940-1990* (Downers Grove, Ill.: InterVarsity Press, 1991).

[17]See Mel Donald, "A Spreading Tree," an unpublished history of the InterVarsity Christian Fellowship of Canada, 1928-1988. Later Pinnock would define evangelicalism as less of a coherent theological package and more as "a conservative theological ethos" where there are "wide-open spaces" that allow creative theological work— including work outside a Calvinistic framework. By the end of the twentieth century it was his judgment that evangelicalism was "more like a distinctive spirituality than a precise theology" (*Wesleyan Theological Journal*, 33:2, Fall 1998, 10).

[18]Pinnock, "From Augustine To Arminius...," 17.

[19]Pinnock's review of Carl Henry's *Confessions of a Theologian* (1986) published in *Christian Scholar's Review* 17(1987-88), 211. Pinnock characterized this way Henry's significant academic leadership of the new Fuller Seminary in the 1950s: "He wanted Fuller to be the flagship of the neo-Reformed, postfundamentalist evangelical movement which was getting under way" (in *Christian Scholar's Review*, September 1993, 45).

experienced only a few exceptions to what later he would look back on and call "the context of North American conservative-evangelicalism with its strongly exclusivist temper." In this context of the 1950s "there were not many lines of inclusivist thinking coming my way as a young Christian."[20] But there were a few.

Pinnock particularly notes C. S. Lewis, whom he trusted as an orthodox thinker. Pinnock listened when Lewis said he could detect God's presence in other faiths and thus believed such people could be saved because God was at work among them. Lewis had imagination and mixed evangelical apologetics with "a liberal twinge" that made him a free thinker "who didn't worry about saying things that no one else was even thinking."[21] Much more than Pinnock realized in the 1960s, Lewis offered a complex model of Christian believer and apologist that in many ways would come to characterize Pinnock himself. This Lewis model has been described this way:

> He has a knack for captivating readers one moment and confounding them the next. His musings on mythology, purgatory and world religions trouble many conservatives, while his dogged defense of objective truth, the divinity of Christ and the miraculous exasperate many self-avowed liberals. He charms and alienates the extreme opposite elements of his audience with equal ease.... We must continually resist the impulse to stuff Lewis into a prepackaged system—liberal, conservative or otherwise. He defies this type of uncritical, superficial categorization.[22]

---

[20]Clark Pinnock, "An Inclusivist View," in *More Than One Way?*, eds. Dennis Okholm and Timothy Phillips (Grand Rapids: Zondervan, 1995), 107. Speaking of InterVarsity Christian Fellowship in Canada during the years of Pinnock's youth, John Stackhouse, Jr., reports: "From small, closed, theologically conservative denominations, these students would find in the howling wilderness of the university a haven where the familiar priorities (personal spiritual growth and evangelism) were taken for granted" (*Canadian Evangelicalism in the Twentieth Century*, University of Toronto Press, 1993, 90). While Clark Pinnock may not have come from such a sheltered background, spiritual growth and evangelism certainly were his personal priorities.

[21]Clark Pinnock, Interview with Barry Callen, April 18, 1998.

[22]Scott Burson and Jerry Walls, *C. S. Lewis and Francis Schaeffer* (Downers Grove, Ill.: InterVarsity Press, 1998), 121, 123.

As the years would come and go, such a characterization of Lewis would increasingly fit Pinnock rather well.

A similar openness to something other than standard and rationalistic evangelicalism was received from Pinnock's awareness of Sir Norman Anderson, a scholar of Islamic law and longtime leader of the InterVarsity Christian Fellowship in Great Britain. Pinnock also soon became aware of dispensational theology, very influential in conservative evangelical circles. He noticed in this theology the claim that God deals with people in more than one way, depending on their circumstances. For instance, Charles Ryrie spoke of a dispensation during which God accepted pagans like Job on the basis of their faith alone, although they had no knowledge of either Moses or Jesus Christ. He recalls: "I felt this was biblical and found it appealing. I remember thinking how helpful it would be if this arrangement were still true for today for people in the same situation."[23] Eventually he would come to believe that indeed it is true that God is "open" as people make decisions in radically differing circumstances.

Evangelical theologians like Carl F. H. Henry, John Warwick Montgomery, and J. I. Packer were helping to establish Pinnock in the usual rationalism characteristic of the evangelical mainstream. Increasingly, however, C. S. Lewis and soon F. F. Bruce of England would be moderating influences in this regard. The former group very early brought out Pinnock's ideological side. He readily agreed that Christianity stands on a divinely revealed base, is absolutely and everywhere true, and should be demonstrable to any serious seeker. The latter pair tended to bring out another dimension in Pinnock, tempering "what might otherwise have been the serious downsides of being a fundamentalist in the Reformed tradition."[24] He later would look back and admit readily to having a "naive enthusiasm" that had kept him on the theological journey. This natural openness, while sometimes getting him into trouble, kept fresh insight available to him that could reveal a new horizon of truth. People like Henry and Packer tended to remain firmly within the strict confines of their own beginning

---

[23]Clark Pinnock, "An Inclusivist View," 108.
[24]Clark Pinnock, Interview with Barry Callen, April 18, 1998.

presuppositions. Pinnock, however, has always had a pilgrim aspect to his mentality. If his mind or heart perceived something as right or beautiful, he was ready to receive and pursue it, almost with abandon, always understanding God as choosing to guide him in that direction.

For those theologians less daring and pilgrim minded, Pinnock later would conclude this in a discussion on the nature of divine omnipotence:

> It mystifies me why conservative thinkers are so reluctant to abandon the classical framework at this point but rather continue to struggle within it. For example, excellent theologians like Bloesch, Erickson, Fackre, and even Packer make concessions which require them to break with strong omnipotence in Augustine and Calvin, but they refuse to do so. I attribute this timidity to the privileged position Calvinism enjoys in what calls itself evangelicalism.[25]

Pinnock, however, was hardly bound by timidity when he thought that the well-being of the church was on the line. Although at first absorbing the whole theological ethos of the privileged position of Calvinism among evangelicals, he later would deal forthrightly with several related issues and free himself from much of this theological ethos.

A Canadian Abroad

High school graduation came in 1956 for Clark Pinnock. He received a scholarship and attended Victoria College, University of Toronto, near his home. Intending some form of a missionary ministry, probably Bible translation like his grandfather Samuel Pinnock and the Wycliff Bible Translators he had met, he pursued biblically-related ancient languages and was very active in the campus chapter of InterVarsity Christian Fellowship. He became aware of the new Fuller Seminary in California, studied its catalog, and found there an inspiring vision of a scholarly fundamentalism in the Princeton tradition. Studying Semitics and encountering teachers at the University of Toronto who had skeptical attitudes toward the Hebrew Bible, Pinnock

---

[25]Clark Pinnock, "God Limits His Knowledge," *Predestination and Free Will*, eds. David and Randall Basinger (Downers Grove, Ill.: InterVarsity Press, 1986), 154 (text and note 20).

later recalled: "I was thrilled at the possibility that one could actually study such subjects with orthodox Christians one could trust. Fuller Seminary was a beacon for me, affirming biblical inerrancy and offering the prestige of a conservative scholarly heritage."[26]

After four years Pinnock completed the B. A. with honors in the Ancient Near East Studies program. For his quality work in college and his obvious scholarly potential, he earned both a Woodrow Wilson Fellowship to Harvard and a British Commonwealth Scholarship to any university in England. Accepting the latter because it was England (the place of his family heritage) and his respect for F. F. Bruce, a noted international Bible scholar admired in InterVarsity circles as a true evangelical, Pinnock pursued Ph.D. studies at the University of Manchester. He focused the first year in Semitic languages (Old Testament) and then shifted to New Testament studies under the esteemed biblical scholar and apologist F. F. Bruce. Bruce was patient and highly disciplined, a great Bible scholar in the Brethren tradition who was not a crusader for the necessity of a doctrine of biblical "inerrancy." This doctrinal issue and irenic Bruce style would be important for Pinnock's future. He remained an active young churchman while a graduate student, but found the Baptists in serious decline in England. So he again turned to InterVarsity for a ready avenue of worship, learning, and witness, serving as president of the fellowship at the University of Manchester.

Bruce had come to Manchester as a professor in 1959. Beginning in 1961 he oversaw Pinnock's dissertation choice and development. After completing his dissertation in 1963 (see below), Pinnock remained with Bruce for two more years as an Assistant Lecturer in the Department of Biblical Criticism and Exegesis. Bruce recalls with pride the significant company of lecturers among which Pinnock was numbered.[27] Robert Kraft was a first lecturer in New Testament who had come to Manchester with an outstanding record from Wheaton and Harvard. After two years he accepted a professorship at the University of Pennsylvania and

---

[26]Clark Pinnock, in *Christian Scholar's Review* (September 1993), 45.

[27]F. F. Bruce, *In Retrospect: Remembrance of Things Past* (Grand Rapids: Eerdmans, 1980), 216.

was replaced by Clark Pinnock who stayed for two years before accepting his professorship at New Orleans Baptist Seminary. Following Pinnock would be Ralph Martin who stayed for four years and then was called to Fuller Theological Seminary in California. Bruce himself retired in 1978.

Immediately following completion of his dissertation and receiving his Ph.D. in 1963, Pinnock took the opportunity to sail home to Canada, part of the funding of the original scholarship. He was anxious to see his family in Toronto and was committed to assist with the teaching responsibilities of a summer "Campus-in-the-Woods" week sponsored by InterVarsity Fellowship in a rustic Ontario setting.[28] During this week he met Dorothy, a young woman also with significant InterVarsity experience (Madison, Wisconsin) who had taught on a military base in Germany and now was teaching in Harlem while living in the Village in New York. They fell in love and were married a few months later in England. As a young couple they managed economically for two years on Clark's meager Assistant Lecturer salary, even finding a way to journey each of the summers to help in an Italian orphanage and spend important time in Switzerland.

During the years 1961-1963 Pinnock first heard about Francis Schaeffer and found himself enthused about the idea of a modern Christian apologist effectively addressing secular culture. He corresponded with Schaeffer and one summer spent time as a student and worker at Schaeffer's L'Abri Fellowship in Huemoz, Switzerland. When married and back in England for two years immediately after the doctoral program, he and Dorothy would spend parts of those summers both in Italy and with Schaeffer in Switzerland. L'Abri is French for "the shelter," this particular one being a "spiritual shelter...especially [for] those seeking the answers to the basic philosophical problems with which all who care about finding a meaning or purpose in life have to struggle."[29] This rather isolated mountainside center was attracting, sheltering, and stimulating searching young intellectuals from many

---

[28]The first such Campus-in-the-Woods session was convened in 1946 on Fairview Island in the Lake of Bays, Ontario, Canada.

[29]Edith Schaeffer, *L'Abri* (Wheaton, Ill.: Tyndale House, 1969), 13.

countries and faith backgrounds (including some humanists and atheists).[30] Pinnock was a relatively young Christian convert looking for a more well-reasoned faith in the face of intellectual challenges being encountered on numerous fronts. He sensed that liberal revisions of classic Christianity were inadequate, but he needed an inspiring teacher like Schaeffer to reinforce and illumine his own basic theological instincts.[31]

Schaeffer was more insistent than F. F. Bruce on the importance of understanding the biblical text as "inerrantly" inspired, and thus he tended to "reinvigorate that root" already planted in Pinnock by his earlier reading of B. B. Warfield. Warfield "made me a theological rationalist in addition to being a pietist."[32] Schaeffer extended for him the cultural apologetic thrust of such rationalism. Only much later would Pinnock reflect back and observe that it was not until his own book *Reason Enough* (1980) that he came to see that Christian believers do not have or need evidence or proof of the rightness of their faith that is adequate to overwhelm modernist objections with its sheer rational weight. To even try such a cognitive overwhelming may itself be a wrong yielding to modern rationalistic assumptions about the essential nature and means of acquiring truth. See Appendix B, including Pinnock's own 1999 reflective comments on his shifts in epistemology.

In the fluid 1960s, evangelicalism in general needed more of something. Protestants who combined a "high" view of the inspiration and authority of Scripture with a Reformation-Puritan-Pietist understanding of the new birth in Christ were experiencing considerable

---

[30]In a *Christianity Today* cover story on Francis Schaeffer (March 3, 1997), Michael Hamilton emphasizes Schaeffer's influence on a "wildly diverse" cross-section of today's Christian leaders, including musician Larry Norman, Moral Majority founder Jerry Falwell, professional football player and national politician Jack Kemp, and theologian Clark Pinnock. It is Hamilton's conclusion that "perhaps no intellectual save C. S. Lewis affected the thinking of evangelicals more profoundly" (p. 22). Pinnock was impacted by both Schaeffer and Lewis.

[31]Clark Pinnock once referred to himself as "a co-worker and confidant of Francis A. Schaeffer of the L'Abri Fellowship" ("Defining American Fundamentalism," in *The Fundamentalist Phenomenon*, ed. Norman Cohen [Grand Rapids: Eerdmans, 1990], 39-40).

[32]Clark Pinnock, Interview with Barry Callen, April 18, 1998.

difficulty. According to James Packer, liberals "had given evangelicals a bad beating, leaving them sore and suspicious, anti-intellectual and defensive, backward-looking and culturally negative, enmeshed in ideological isolationism with regard to the world of thought, and lacking all vision for the future of the church save the defiant hope that a faithful remnant would survive somewhere."[33] Pinnock recalls this about Schaeffer's contribution to himself and such a troubled setting:

> Francis Schaeffer showed the young evangelicals who came to L'Abri that fundamentalism was intellectually respectable. He made orthodox Protestant theology live and have relevance in the twentieth century. Furthermore, he devastated liberal theology, not with the fiery rhetoric of the redneck preacher, but by means of intellectual analysis. He was a kind of evangelical Paul Tillich, moving back and forth between the questions of the culture and the answers of Christianity.... One of the points of appeal in Schaeffer for me was his claim to be able to vindicate conservative theology in dialogue with the best and the brightest in the liberal camp. There were exciting ideas at L'Abri and we flocked to hear the new scholar-prophet....[34]

Those who went to learn from Schaeffer encountered a man who appeared to have discerned the destructive spirits at work in the Christian theology of the time, including existentialism and "death of God" theologians. He tied critique of them into a larger view of the great cultural trends of the Western world. Pinnock later called those effectively challenged in the process of Schaeffer's vindication of Christian orthodoxy "neologians." The "neos" were the ones who had chosen as their destructive task "transforming Christianity into useful fiction, into existential symbols, themselves the products of man's own fertile imagination."[35]

— echo of Mc Fagues view of theology as 'fiction'.

---

[33]James I. Packer, "No Little Person," in *Reflections on Francis Schaeffer*, ed. Ronald Ruegsegger (Grand Rapids: Zondervan, 1986), 9-10.

[34]Clark Pinnock, "Schaeffer on Modern Theology," in *Reflections on Francis Schaeffer*, ed. Ronald Ruegsegger (Grand Rapids: Zondervan, 1986), 173-174.

[35]Ibid., 174. Schaeffer was a product of the "old school" Princeton theology of B. B. Warfield by way of Schaeffer's own teacher, J. Gresham Machen. In 1929 the Presbyterian Church approved a reorganization of Princeton Seminary that allowed

Pinnock had been exposed to Schaeffer before Schaeffer's books began rolling off the presses in great quantity and while Pinnock himself was still gaining the tools of sophisticated biblical and theological analysis. In later years Pinnock would speak at length and somewhat critically of certain aspects of Schaeffer's thought, once referring to his bold ideational critique of Western history as "pretentious."[36] Nonetheless, never would he denigrate the man's significance or impact on him personally. With deep gratitude he characterized Schaeffer this way:

> Here was a serious disciple of Jesus Christ, who paid a price for following his Lord and bore a courageous witness to the gospel. He was a godly man, a man of prayer, who wept and pleaded, intellectually and passionately, that people should heed the message of God's kingdom. He convinced me of the importance of keeping a balance of mind and heart and not backing down in the face of opposition whether from within the church or the culture. He cared about truth, and because he was not a prisoner to the establishment in any sense, he could speak out boldly on issues that mattered.... His influence as a thinker will not last long. But what is impressive and what will last...is not the thought but the total quality of the man in whose face the glory of God shone.[37]

In this characterization one can see much that Pinnock himself would come to emulate for decades to come. Truth is important for Christians. The Bible is basic and to be trusted as the revealed Word of God.

---

a more inclusivist approach. Soon Machen and others left to form Westminster Seminary in Philadelphia. By 1937 another split came that saw a departure from Westminster and the formation of Faith Seminary in Philadelphia, where Schaeffer chose to complete his own education. This latter and very vigorous "coming out" move on behalf of the purity of the church soon came to be represented by Carl McIntire who was an unyielding fighter for the rigid truth that he confidently affirmed. By the late 1940s McIntire was fighting the new World Council of Churches. At that time Schaeffer's family was located in Lausanne, Switzerland, beginning children's work in war-torn Europe and launching a campaign to warn the churches against liberalism. By 1953, McIntire was alienating almost everyone, including Schaeffer who finally broke with him. Then, in 1955, the L'Abri Fellowship was founded by the Schaeffers.

[36]Clark Pinnock, "Schaefferism as a World View," *Sojourners* 6:8(July 1977), 33.

[37]Clark Pinnock, "Schaeffer on Modern Theology," in *Reflections on Francis Schaeffer*, ed. Ronald Ruegsegger (Grand Rapids: Zondervan), 192.

Courage is needed to defend it in an unbelieving world. Challenging contemporary intellectual waywardness is a sacred duty, whether the waywardness comes from inside or outside the church. Beyond belief that has substance and standards, being a true Christian should involve passion, serious discipleship, and a warm heart as well as an informed head. Even when choosing to be loyal to an establishment, like North American evangelicalism, Pinnock would always refuse to be its prisoner. He would speak as a scholar-prophet when he judged it necessary for the well-being of the church and its mission in the world. Such speaking always gains attention, but not always respect and friends. No matter. The issues at stake are larger than any one man's reputation. Such was the legacy being gained by Pinnock while still a young Canadian abroad.

Out of the Arid Desert

During the years of doctoral study in England, the emerging legacy of young Clark Pinnock began to focus on the meaning and implications of the Spirit of God. In part this focus was motivated initially and rather straightforwardly by the academic need to choose a dissertation topic— one that hopefully could build on the undergraduate studies completed at the University of Toronto, be acceptable to his mentor F. F. Bruce at the University of Manchester, and be personally stimulating and pro- fessionally satisfying to Pinnock himself. The chosen topic was "The Concept of Spirit in the Epistles of Paul." Pinnock approached this topic first within perspectives already gained from his undergraduate Semitic studies in Toronto. He began from the "virile notion" of *ruach* in the Hebrew Scriptures, moved to awareness of the "two-spirits pattern" in the Dead Sea Scrolls,[38] and finally arrived at a broader study of the Spirit pattern found in the New Testament. He observed that most Hebrew writers in the centuries closest to the beginnings of Christianity had not given prominence to the *ruach* reality. The exception was the radical Qumran community that clearly sought to incorporate pneumatology into religious belief and practice. He judged that the

---

[38]This two-spirits pattern in the *Manual of Discipline* of Qumran depicts a moral duality in which there is a spirit leading people to do good and a spirit leading toward the wrong. St. Paul would call the latter "flesh" (Galatians 5).

role of this community was to serve as a bridge between the older and normative Hebrew tradition of the Spirit and the New Testament writers, especially Paul.

What did Pinnock learn in this study about the epistles of Paul and the subject of the Spirit of God? Paul's central concept was rooted deeply in his Hebrew heritage. It is best to understand Paul as a converted rabbi "whose conviction that Jesus was the Messiah assured him of the dawning of the eschatological age in which the Spirit of God was to act in a new way."[39] Therefore, seeking a presumed relevance of the philosophies and literature of the Greek world is hardly helpful since "their relevance to the Pauline concept alters in inverse ratio as the degree of hellenization increases."[40] Here is the beginning of what later would be Pinnock's significant faulting of certain aspects of "classic" Christian doctrine because of their excessive accommodation to non-Christian Greek thinking.

For Paul it is the person and work of Jesus Christ that is most crucial. Understanding the relation of the Spirit to Jesus Christ opens "large vistas into the divine redemptive plan." Having determined this, Pinnock then devoted one-third of his dissertation to the "all-determining significance" of the work of the Spirit in believers and in the church. The dissertation was completed and submitted to the Faculty of Arts in the University of Manchester in April, 1963, but pursuing its subject had only begun for this new holder of a Ph.D. degree. In the years to come he would continue to explore its depths in his own Christian experience and in his numerous publications. As he said in the dissertation's preface, this study was only "prolegomenon." The wider theological and pastoral implications could, and would, be clarified later.

Time would validate Pinnock's 1963 observation that, across its long history, the church has seldom taken full advantage of the doctrine of the Spirit in its thought, preaching, and life. For instance, in 1994 a very large volume appeared by Gordon Fee titled *God's Empowering*

---

[39]Clark Pinnock, "The Concept of Spirit in the Epistles of Paul," (Ph.D. dissertation, University of Manchester, 1963), iv-v.
[40]Ibid., vi.

Presence: The Holy Spirit in the Letters of Paul. It attempts an extensive study of Pauline pneumatology, citing on the first page Clark Pinnock's unpublished but foundational 1963 dissertation on the subject. Echoing Pinnock's general thesis, Fee argues that, for Paul, the Spirit of God "as an experienced and living reality" was the "absolutely crucial matter for Christian life, from beginning to end." Unfortunately, Fee concludes, today "the Spirit is largely marginalized in our actual life together as a community of faith."[41]

Pinnock, of course, was unaware at the time of his dissertation writing that in coming decades he would be one of the more prominent of all evangelicals worldwide in arguing such a thesis and in pursuing its implications. He would come to insist on crossing back over that Qumran-provided bridge to the older "virile notion" of the person, presence, and power of God's Spirit in the midst of God's people, now historically known as the Spirit of Christ. He would join the Apostle Paul in seeking to teach the church that to be "in Christ" through the presence and power of Christ's Spirit is essentially what it means to be a Christian. He would join Fee, whom he identifies as "himself a Pentecostal and a feisty fellow…[who] warns passionately that, unless we abandon watered down versions of Christianity and return to the dynamism of the New Testament, we will not count for much as Christians in mission in the coming years."[42] The call is to spiritual renewal, a necessary journey with the Spirit.

Time To Teach and Write

Coming out of an arid desert to the welcome waters of life in God's Spirit is an apt symbol of the prophetic ministry pursued by Clark Pinnock for the decades from the 1960s onward. This coming out first began in written form in relation to his role as president of the InterVarsity Christian Fellowship at the University of Toronto. As would often be the case in regard to perceived inadequacies in classic

---

[41]Gordon Fee, *God's Empowering Presence* (Peabody, MA: Hendrickson Publishing, 1994), 1.

[42]Clark Pinnock, review of *God's Empowering Presence: The Holy Spirit in the Letters of Paul*, by Gordon Fee, Pneuma 18:2 (Fall 1996), 230-231.

evangelicalism, Pinnock approached his 1960 IVCF annual report forthrightly. His candid appraisal was a lover's quarrel with a Christian organization which had wonderful intent, while the local chapter was experiencing only limited success. In his view:

> On the whole our IVCF chapter lacks clear understanding of InterVarsity's historical nature as an international movement. With this loss of perspective, certain dynamic principles of Biblical faith have been obscured, principles which undergird our existence as a student witness to Jesus Christ. The vision of interpreting the Good News to every student has been unconsciously modified to harmonize with our own relative strength, instead of being rooted in the greatness of God's promises.[43]

Where could the vision be found again? According to Pinnock, the treasure, the mandate to win university students for Christ, was to be found only as the local fellowship was "on its knees at the throne of grace." The point was not to perpetuate an organization, but to recapture and obey an evangelistic vision born of God. The Fellowship was not supposed to protect "spiritual saplings," but to facilitate Kingdom advance by networking students who already knew the power of God in their lives. If the InterVarsity Christian Fellowship expended its energy internally, "its certain (and desirable) end is suffocation." On the other hand, mere pietism was not adequate. Pinnock reported that under its masks "the sophisticated world of scholarship has a heart of flesh that yearns and longs for this [Christ's] gospel." Therefore, he pled for a recovery of creative Christian thinking in every academic discipline. According to his young prophetic voice in 1960, for too long evangelicals had been content to be "big frogs in little ponds" instead of examining God's Word with "the finest tools of learning"—always, of course, under the guidance of God's Spirit. The IVCF should be proud to declare "a body of revealed truth as the intellectual and spiritual point of reference and a sure foundation."[44]

---

[43]Clark Pinnock, "An IVCF President Reports," *HIS* (October 1960), 28.
[44]Ibid., 28-32.

The contexts of Pinnock's life would shift several times over the decades to follow. He would teach in several prominent institutions, move from England to the United States, then back to Canada, and write many books and articles, but he would remain a loyal Baptist and keep active contact with InterVarsity. Whatever the changes, he would be sensitive to them and allow them to direct what would become his very extensive and influential body of writings. For the most part, his context would be North American evangelicalism.[45] Within this context he would be an experimental frontiersman, an active apologist, and a critical and flexible but nonetheless faithful son of classic Christianity. Later he would look back and gratefully acknowledge the major effect that his early context had on him. He, of course, also would have had quite an effect on his context, usually by his persistent tendency to oppose vigorously all departures from what he understood to be the teachings of the Bible. He would emerge as a staunch defender of the faith and then move over the years from a combative champion of truth to more of an irenic theologian—no less convictional, but more dialogical. At the beginning of his career, however, he was aggressive and passionate about the certain truths of divine revelation that he was sure were available in an inerrant Bible. The issues surrounding such revelation, certainty, and biblical authority would dominate his attention for several years.

To these early years we now turn. The doctoral dissertation was done, the degree was in hand, and a strong evangelical identity had been established. Significant experience with F. F. Bruce and Francis Schaeffer had been gladly absorbed into his emerging self-identity. Now a deep concern about "liberalism" in the churches, and an apologetic fervor prepared to explain and defend the faith on biblical grounds and sometimes in alien environments were ready to be released. Pinnock's would be a beginning much like his later assessment of the beginning of

---

[45]It may be that British evangelicalism has been a more inclusive "big tent" than the North American evangelical scene, which has evidenced a strong correlation between Calvinism and evangelicalism. This difference would have a definite influence on the theological development of Clark Pinnock who, although educated at the doctoral level in England, was initially nurtured and then has spent his professional life in North American seminaries scattered across the United States and Canada.

his fellow Baptist theologian, Bernard Ramm. Reported Pinnock, Ramm "began boldly, as young scholars often do, full of confidence in their powers of reason to prove faith."[46]

One day the phone rang in the Pinnock's England apartment. On the line was Dr. H. Leo Eddleman, the president of the large Southern Baptist seminary in New Orleans, Louisiana.[47] Would Pinnock come to lecture and candidate for a faculty position in New Testament? Carl F. H. Henry had visited Pinnock in England, was impressed, and apparently had recommended him for this pivotal post back in the United States.[48] Pinnock's answer was positive. So the trip was made, and then came the decision to end the long and significant sojourn in England. He informed Dr. Bruce that he would leave his post as lecturer at the University of Manchester for a full-time appointment among the Southern Baptists in the United States. Bruce was disappointed, having hoped that he would stay much longer, but he understood and was supportive.

Much indeed lay ahead, including the 1967 birth of the Pinnock's only child, Sarah, in New Orleans[49] and an aggressive leadership role for Clark Pinnock in North American evangelicalism. In part the public prominence would begin because of the volatile circumstances of the Southern Baptist Convention in the late 1960s, a volatility which matched the skills and readiness of Pinnock to intervene on behalf of classic Christian truth. He apparently had been brought to this seminary to help "hold the line." That he surely would do. Carl Henry was well

---

[46]Clark Pinnock, "Bernard Ramm: Postfundamentalist Coming To Terms With Modernity," *Perspectives on Theology in the Contemporary World: Essays in Honor of Bernard Ramm*, ed. Stanley Grenz (Macon, GA: Mercer University Press, 1990), 20.

[47]Brought into being by the Southern Baptist Convention in 1917 and bearing the name Baptist Bible Institute until 1946, New Orleans Baptist Theological Seminary was the first theological institution birthed by the SBC. Dr. Eddleman, formerly president of Georgetown College in Kentucky, had become president of the seminary in 1959.

[48]In 1992, for instance, Carl F. H. Henry's book *The Identity of Jesus of Nazareth* cites Pinnock with appreciation (pp. 58-59), referring to Pinnock's article "The Many Christs of Current Theology," (*Christianity Today*, March 19, 1982).

[49]At the time the Pinnock's were living in the French Quarter. Sarah's birth address was 1111 Bourbon Street in the Slave Quarter. The family loved this place and thus were not, culturally speaking, living at the seminary.

aware of what he later would refer to as "the invasion of neo-orthodoxy into Southern Baptist seminaries [that] eroded emphasis on scriptural inerrancy." Henry was confident that young Pinnock had the skills and will to resist this invasion. Indeed, early in his career Pinnock had both the skills and the will.[50] Soon he was speaking vigorously and widely. In the summer of 1968, for instance, he was the primary teacher at a Reformed conference in Florida. His biblical focus was Romans 9-11, a prominent double-predestinarian text that he handled in the "high Reformed" style so important to him then.[51] In the early 1970s he was the commencement speaker at Dallas Theological Seminary. He spoke on the apologetics of the resurrection of Jesus, "part of that hard rational, postfundamentalist mindset."[52] Popular for fundamentalists at the time were those few personalities who had not strayed from the fundamentals, but had fresh things to say as creative postfundamentalists with respectable academic credentials. Pinnock was a shining and much-appreciated example.

In just a few years Pinnock would look back and identify his central ministry concerns this way: "To blend my writing, speaking, teaching, witnessing, relating into an effective and relevant witness to Jesus Christ. To respond to those points where the witness is under a threat, and to give some helpful direction beyond current impasses."[53] He had a passion for timely biblical interpretation mixed with a determination similar to the goal that Bernard Ramm had for his academic life. Reports Pinnock: "Bernard Ramm is a quintessential postfundamentalist (evangelical) theologian of the postwar [WW II] period in America.... He wanted to make the conservative Protestant faith theologically profound and intellectually respectable.... [His goal was] to defend classical theology in a nonobscurantist manner using the best tools of

---

[50]Anthony Campolo, a longtime and appreciative friend, recalls Pinnock's New Orleans days. He pictures the young Professor Pinnock as a very gifted and rather confrontational fundamentalist being followed around by admiring seminary students (interview with Barry Callen, April 18, 1998).

[51]Clark Pinnock, in his interview with Barry Callen, November 21, 1998.

[52]Ibid.

[53]Quoted by Darcy Taplin, "Clark H. Pinnock: Growing Out of the Weaknesses of a Fundamentalist Past" (unpublished, based on a Pinnock letter to Taplin), Southern Baptist Theological Seminary (December 1980), 17.

modern scholarship."[54] In speaking of Ramm, Pinnock was also reflecting much of himself, especially in his earlier years.

The formative contexts described above had laid a good foundation for Pinnock to pursue the twin tasks of Christian evangelism and apologetics. His commitment provided the ministry direction, his courage the necessary drive, and his excellent credentials many open doors. He would respond where the faith was threatened and later offer fresh advice beyond the impasses that are capable of dividing and paralyzing the evangelical Christian community. His response to perceived threat was almost immediate, beginning among the Southern Baptists in the United States, specifically the Southern Baptist Convention, the largest Protestant denomination in America. Pinnock had been a Canadian abroad; now the European environment would continue, shifting from England and Switzerland to the French-enriched culture of New Orleans. Choosing to establish residence on Bourbon Street in the Slave Quarters, it was time for a well-educated and highly motivated Christian apologist to launch a formal career of teaching, preaching, lecturing, and writing. He would commute to the seminary, located in the Garden District of New Orleans, and communicate fear-lessly his strong and well-informed Christian convictions.

Pinnock's earliest formative contexts had largely been in the vigorous and even reactionary stream of mid-century Christian fundamentalism. Other influences had also at least touched him early and certainly would impact him increasingly in later years, so that eventually he could hardly be classed as a fundamentalist in the usual sense. Even so, there always would persist in his mind and heart a sincere sympathy for key aspects of fundamentalism. In particular, he would write decades later:

> In my opinion, fundamentalism is orthodoxy in a desperate struggle with secular modernity. It is a unique kind of orthodoxy, shaped by this conflict which it feels so keenly.... I appreciate fundamentalism for its tenacious faith, for its courage to stand up for historic Christian beliefs when they have come

---

[54]Clark Pinnock, in *Perspectives on Theology in the Contemporary World*, ed. Stanley Grenz (Macon, Georgia: Mercer University Press, 1990), 25.

under attack, and for taking a number of important moral stands in contemporary North American society.[55]

Of central concern for fundamentalists who were "holding the line," and clearly for the young teacher-scholar Clark Pinnock, was the unique revelational character of the Bible.

The quote of Jürgen Moltmann at the head of this chapter is one with which Clark Pinnock identifies personally. From the beginning of their Christian lives both men have been active learners, adventurers on journeys of discovery, ever curious and always committed. Pinnock's journey, like Moltmann's, certainly would come to have its surprises and disappointments, its twists and turns. At first, however, the goal was relatively simple and straightforward. It was one of blowing a clear trumpet and enhancing Christian certainty in the midst of the volatile 1960s. Pinnock was sure that God had spoken and that the Bible was a fully dependable record of that speaking—and thus to be believed in its entirety. "Liberals" had to be answered effectively. Unbelievers needed good reason to come to Christian faith. Those preparing for Christian ministry deserved a solid preparation. Young Pinnock had the passion and education to support vigorously what was seen by him as basic to Christian belief, life, and mission. So he emerged on the English and then North American scenes as teacher, lecturer, preacher, and writer, a man of sturdy belief ready to support the belief of others.

---

[55]Clark Pinnock, "Defining American Fundamentalism," in *The Fundamentalist Phenomenon*, ed. Norman Cohen (Grand Rapids: Eerdmans, 1990), 42, 40.

3

The Certainty
of Revealed Truth

A Gospel modulated to the pitch of twentieth century thought will not in the end ease the problem of communication. It will only mute the sound of revelation itself and end up in total silence.[1]

For historical reasons, inerrancy has come to symbolize in our day that full confidence that Christians have always had in the Scriptures. The wisest course to take would be to get on with defining inerrancy in relation to the purpose of the Bible and the phenomena it displays.[2]

For most Christians, especially conservatives, the Bible is an authoritative starting point for identifying the substance of their faith. For Clark Pinnock, his early teaching and writing career focused major attention in this significant area of biblical authority. Over the years he would move from being a fierce defender of a Reformed fundamentalistic view of biblical inspiration and authority to a gentler and nuanced, although still revelationally rooted, view of the Bible. On occasion he would push some aspects of the authority question beyond the comfort level of traditionally staunch conservatives, although always he would think of himself as a committed and loyal "evangelical." Pinnock finally

---

[1]Clark Pinnock, *A Defense of Biblical Infallibility* (Philadelphia: Presbyterian and Reformed Publishing Company, 1967), 31-32.

[2]Clark Pinnock, *The Scripture Principle* (San Francisco: Harper & Row, 1984), 225.

would emerge as a self-styled peacemaker on the controversial issue of the nature of biblical authority.[3] By 1978, for instance, he was seeking to interpret the "inerrancy" debate for a wider audience, appealing to non-evangelical Christians to at least make an effort to understand where evangelicals were coming from on inerrancy and try to sympathize with evangelical concerns. Their central concern, he said, was fear of the negative results sure to arise from the inroads being made by those challenging "the cognitive authority of the canonical scriptures." Here was a perceived threat from fellow Christians that could cause the church to lose its identity and mission as it struggled with the challenge of modernity.

Of particular concern to Pinnock has been "the skeptical attitude toward the unique authority and relevance of Holy Scripture."[4] Into this concern area he boldly stepped, first ready to defend the revelational integrity of the Bible and then later also ready to review critically some aspects of the nature of his own defense. The influential periodical *Christianity Today* helped to make inerrancy the badge of evangelical authenticity, even as Francis Schaeffer insisted that it was the watershed of evangelical fidelity. This periodical once lauded Pinnock's stalwart fidelity, saying that his "bareknuckles challenge of current leading theological ideas will be cheered by people who possess but cannot adequately articulate a disdain for the irrational abstractions sweeping through the ecclesiastical intelligentsia."[5] Later this magazine would take a much more cautious approach to the value of Pinnock's contributions, seeming to judge the "revised" Pinnock in a way similar to the 1986 conclusion of Henry Holloman. In the *Journal of the Evangelical Theological Society,* Holloman would commend Pinnock for capably criticizing the "liberal theological revision" with its "flat

---

[3]Trent Butler, for instance, in reviewing Pinnock's 1984 *The Scripture Principle* for the *Journal of Biblical Literature* (December 1986), highlights Pinnock's obvious awareness of excess on all sides of the debate and Pinnock's expressed hope of supplying a model that might help to transcend the impasse.

[4]Clark Pinnock, "Evangelicals and Inerrancy: The Current Debate," *Theology Today* (April 1978), 65-66.

[5]*Christianity Today*, endorsement on the cover of Clark Pinnock's book *Set Forth Your Case* (1967).

denial of the Scripture principle in the classical sense," and yet insist that "unfortunately Pinnock's proposed Scripture principle with its very lenient view of inerrancy does not offer evangelicals a Biblically sound and logically consistent position to stabilize Christian faith and to withstand the onslaughts of destructive Biblical criticism."[6]

Obviously, between his books *A Defense of Biblical Infallibility* in 1967 and *The Scripture Principle* in 1984, Clark Pinnock had been on a journey in regard to the nature of the certainty of revealed truth. Both early and later on this journey he would care deeply and speak convictionally about the reality of revelation as a central principle on which the Christian faith rests. He would, however, make significant adjustments to his own thought along the way, adjustments he found warranted and important, and ones that some of his conservative colleagues judged unacceptable. His journey toward renewal in the evangelical understanding of biblical authority would lead him, to use his own terms, from a "philosophical biblicism" to a "simple biblicism."

For Pinnock, this postmodern, philosophical-to-simple shift had begun with an early preoccupation with verifiable revelational data that could speak with certainty to the world. He championed the assumption of divinely-given propositional truths that could save humankind from relativism. The journey later moved him to a focus that he always had in an incipient way, but now became dominant, minus the heavy foundationalist overlay. By the resulting "simple biblicism" he means:

> ...the delight evangelicals experience from meditating on Scripture and submitting to it. They feel immense gratitude for this means of grace that the Spirit has bestowed on the church to equip it. Scripture is a gift of the Spirit, and evangelicals want to be open to all that God says in this text. Scripture for them is the tangible sacrament of the Word of God nourishing them like milk and honey. Not a theory about the Bible, simple biblicism is the basic instinct that the Bible is supremely profitable and transforming, alive with God's breath. Without being free of every difficulty, the Bible nevertheless bears effective witness to Jesus Christ.... Although committed without reservation to the

---

[6]Henry Holloman, review of Clark Pinnock's 1984 book *The Scripture Principle*, in the *Journal of the Evangelical Theological Society* 29:1 (March 1986), 96-97.

Relate this to McFague and her view of Scripture

Bible, it has an open attitude when it comes to learning what the Bible says, even about itself. Although wanting a reasonable faith, simple biblicism is not overly anxious about erecting rational foundations in the modern sense. It reflects a post-modern lack of anxiety about such foundations and is content with soft rather than hard rational supports.[7]

Early on, Pinnock was primarily a vigilant doorkeeper of "assured biblical truth." Later he would come to the place where most of his energy was being expended in ways other than withstanding "the onslaughts of destructive biblical criticism." He would begin listening to the Bible, learning all he could, not defensively, but openly and expectantly. First, however, came the vigorous and rationalistic defense of biblical infallibility.

No Diluted Christianity

Clark Pinnock was first introduced to Christianity in a fundamentalistic context that initiated the enduring pattern of his resistance to what he has perceived as diluted and destructive forms of Christian belief. Exactly what he judged to be dangerous and unacceptable would be nuanced or in some cases reversed over the decades, but the tendency to resist dilution has endured. Early and often, the target of his criticism has been whatever sought to weaken confidence in the veracity of Christian faith as revealed dependably in the Bible. As he put it in his inaugural lecture at McMaster Divinity College in October 1977:

> Classical Christians have always sought to exalt the truth of divine revelation, embodied in the Incarnation and attested in the Scriptures, far above the thoughts of mankind. They have considered the Bible to contain didactive thought models to guide their theology, models which were infallibly authoritative because they originated in God's witness to himself. For this reason they have shown themselves committed to an undiluted,

---

[7]Clark Pinnock, "New Dimensions in Theological Method," in *New Dimensions in Evangelical Thought*, ed. David Dockery (Downers Grove, Ill.: InterVarsity Press, 1998), 200.

we might say an undemythologized, biblical framework which enjoyed absolute cognitive authority over them.[8]

The apostle Paul showed the way for Pinnock with the Epistle to the Galatians. False teachers were reported to be operating among those ancient congregations, unsettling them and subverting gospel truth (Gal. 1:7; 5:10). Pinnock shared Paul's strongly worded warning and, as a well-trained biblical scholar, was in no mood to leave unchallenged a provocative article like the one appearing in a leading British newspaper in 1963 that denied the authenticity of many of the letters traditionally attributed to the authorship of Paul.[9] The basis for this denial? A statistical study of vocabulary done with a computer, then a rather new machine admired by many for its amazing capabilities. This use of the supposed objectivity of mechanized science brought from Pinnock nothing short of disdain.[10] He saw false statements of claimed fact and a man who was a "convinced advocate of the radical revision of Christianity long before computers were developed." The bottom line for Pinnock was that such unbelief and irresponsible implications, bolstered artificially and arrogantly by "science," must be countered by committed and properly equipped Christians.

The situation of the 1960s in Western cultures was thought to call urgently for a vigorous defense of the gospel as traditionally understood and proclaimed. Far more was happening than the new uses of computers. Pinnock saw the church facing its greatest crisis ever. Rather than occasional false teachers doing their usual attacking of one doctrine or another, many now were seeking to undermine Christianity's claim to authentic and historically concrete divine revelation on which all doctrine rests. This challenge raised the potential of all Christian truth claims being questioned at once. Such teachers, he judged, certainly

---

[8]This inaugural lecture at McMaster was first published in *Christianity Today* (Jan. 5, 1979, 23-29) as "Evangelical Theology: Conservative and Contemporary." It then was reprinted in *The Untapped Power of Sheer Christianity* (Burlington, Ontario: Welch Publishing Company, 1985, 85-100), which became *Three Keys for Spiritual Renewal* (Minneapolis: Bethany Fellowship, 1985).

[9]A. Q. Morton, in *The Observer* (Sunday, November 2, 1963).

[10]Clark Pinnock, "Honest to Computers?" in *InterVarsity Magazine* (UK), Spring, 1964, 16-17.

were speaking from themselves and not from the mouth of God (Jer. 23:16). Evangelicalism, Pinnock insisted, "is called to maintain a pure testimony.... A Gospel modulated to the pitch of twentieth century thought will not in the end ease the problem of communication. It will only mute the sound of revelation itself and end up in total silence."[11]

By the 1960s Southern Baptists in the United States were moving out of their historic enclaves, both geographical and intellectual, toward a fuller involvement with the religious and intellectual life of the surrounding church and secular cultures. As Mark Noll has noted: "With this expansion has come new influence and prestige, but also fresh impetus to reexamine traditional beliefs and practices. The challenge is felt especially for the historic Southern Baptist confidence in the Bible."[12] In 1968 Pinnock was reminding Southern Baptists of the danger of theological drift from sure foundations. This was especially true about the identity of Jesus Christ, the very center of Christian theology and apologetics.[13] He noted the common liberal blind alleys that reduce understandings of Jesus to the model of religious sensitivity (Schleiermacher), ethical insight (Ritschl), existentialist spirit (Bultmann), or symbol of Being (Tillich).[14] Pinnock announced a bold "no!" to all of this diluting and dehistoricizing. By contrast, the only Jesus known to New Testament writers is both truly man and truly God. Further, "the beauty of the gospel is that it is historically true! Ours is no 'faith in faith'

---

[11]Pinnock, A Defense..., 31-32.

[12]Mark A. Noll, foreword to The Unfettered Word: Southern Baptists Confront the Authority-Inerrancy Question, ed. Robison B. James (Waco, TX: Word Books, 1987), 6.

[13]Note Pinnock's later article in Christianity Today (March 19, 1982) titled "The Many Christs of Current Theology."

[14]In his Foreword to the 1982 reprint of Clark Pinnock's 1971 book Biblical Revelation, J. I. Packer refers to Pinnock as "a brilliant man" and the book as "a triumph—in my view, the major triumph—of Pinnock's first period." Packer continues: "In a flurry of taut formulae Pinnock states and vindicates the historic Protestant view of Scripture as the given Word, true and trustworthy, of the self-announcing God, against the non-cognitive, relativist, existentialist, and ultimately nihilist idea of revelation which in a thousand forms has flooded our mainline churches" (p. 5).

gospel.... It is grounded in factuality, in the flesh and bone of history....
Our task is not to editorialize, but to evangelize."[15]

Given the assumed significance of Christian evangelism, the chief
enemies of the faith were seen by Pinnock as relativism and skepticism.
In his 1969 book, *Evangelism and Truth*, there appears this clear
statement of his early assessment and personal agenda:

> Evangelism is the declaration of a specific message. It is not
> holding meetings, or getting results. It is communication of the
> good news. Therefore, *evangelism and truth are inseparable.*
> Biblical evangelism requires divine truth; divine truth requires
> revelation in language; revelation in language requires the
> deposit of infallible Scripture. As soon as confidence is weakened
> in the integrity of our source material, evangelism is weakened
> to a corresponding degree.[16]

Accordingly, his earliest writings might be called "pre-evangelism
apologetics," a necessary intellectual step that could help to clear away
unnecessary obstacles to evangelism. Assumed throughout is the thesis
that naturalistic mindsets like humanism and scientism were trying to
squeeze God out of the modern worldview. Such squeezing, while much
more subtle, was even going on inside the churches. The 1960s already
had seen far too many churches subjected weekly to "Sunday morning
editorials of pastors-turned-politicians" while their publishing houses
were producing "works of theological faddists."[17]

Only the Christian gospel can supply an adequate basis for needed
meaning and values. With this emphasis, Pinnock was reflecting much
of the burden of Francis Schaeffer, one of his early mentors. In addition,
reflecting a style of defending the Christian gospel typical of his later
colleague at Trinity Evangelical Divinity School, John Warwick
Montgomery, Pinnock also announced that "the beauty of the gospel in

---

[15]Clark Pinnock, "A New Reformation" (booklet, Tigerville, S.C.: Jewel Books,
1968), 14. He insisted in *Christianity Today* (April 12, 1968) that Christians should
"establish our apologetic where the apostles did, on the reality of the incarnation (Jn.
1:14; 1 Jn. 1:1-3) and particularly the resurrection (1 Pet. 1:4).... The beauty of the
Christian message is its open-to-investigation form.... Easter faith requires sound
historical underpinnings, and believers rejoice to know that these are solid" (7).

[16]Clark Pinnock, *Evangelism and Truth* (Tigerville, S.C.: Jewel Books, 1969), 18-19.

[17]Pinnock, "A New Reformation," 4.

the avalanche of competing religious claims is precisely the possibility we have of checking it out historically and factually."[18] The acts of God are not visible only to the eyes of faith, an insistence which Pinnock judges the bane of modern theology. The resurrection of Jesus, for example, is to be explained in light of the available information as being much more probable than the alternative theories of what happened after the crucifixion. It thus should be accepted as the only reasonable explanation for the rise of Christianity—even apart from active religious faith. If Jesus rose, so the logic leads, he is who he said he was. Further, a divine Christ must be believed when he authenticates a high view of the dependability of the biblical record itself. When one combines an historically trustworthy Bible, including its reporting of the real Christ and the actual bodily resurrection of Jesus, with rationally compelling proofs of God's existence, there is reason to be certain and enthusiastic about Christian faith.[19]

In 1965 Pinnock began teaching New Testament as an Assistant Professor at New Orleans Baptist Theological Seminary in Louisiana. He arrived burdened with the fear "that the Christian witness even among Baptists could be jeopardized by the influx of liberal theology seeping into the ranks of the educated elites of the [Southern Baptist] Convention slowly but surely."[20] He was prepared to blow the whistle of alarm. The New Orleans seminary had on its faculty with young Pinnock some conservatives like Samuel Mikolaski, who spoke at the World Congress on Evangelism. In 1966 the congress brought together in Berlin, Germany, evangelicals from one hundred nations. They gathered in a spectacular display of evangelical unity on the basis of biblical theology and a shared burden for the evangelization of all people during the remaining third of the twentieth century. Mikolaski stressed on that large world stage that the vain attempts of modern people "to show what he

---

[18]Clark Pinnock, *Set Forth Your Case: Studies in Christian Apologetics* (Nutley, N.J.: Craig Press, 1967, reprinted Chicago: Moody, 1971), 67.

[19]See his *Set Forth Your Case* (Craig Press, 1967). Pinnock's 1980 *Reason Enough: A Case for the Christian Faith* (InterVarsity Press) would be less dogmatic in tone.

[20]Clark Pinnock, "What Is Biblical Inerrancy?," in *The Proceedings of the Conference on Biblical Inerrancy, 1987* (Nashville: Broadman Press, 1987), 73.

can accomplish without any belief in God at all" were merely reflections of a "scientism" and its skeptical outlook on ethical and religious values.[21]

But the New Orleans seminary also had its "liberals." One professor was deeply and appreciatively immersed in the theological work of Paul Tillich. Here in New Orleans and in many other evangelical seminaries the influence of neo-orthodoxy could be seen—for example, the increased hesitancy to affirm that God's revelation is intelligibly given in the form of informational statements about the divine nature and will. Pinnock understood that at least one reason he had been brought to this Baptist seminary was to help stabilize it theologically. After two years he was appointed an Associate Professor of Theology. Why the change from New Testament to theology? There was a need in that academic department, he had a growing desire to work in both theology and apologetics, and the seminary president thought that Pinnock's potential threat to the liberalizing trends would be increased if he functioned primarily in the theological field. Pinnock believed that theology "is where faith encounters today's world"[22]—and that is where he wanted to be. He now was lecturing at numerous large gatherings of Baptist ministers and on many campuses, often through the auspices of InterVarsity Christian Fellowship. His central thesis echoed a keynote of the consensus statement of those many delegates at that 1966 World Conference in Berlin:

> We are persuaded that today, as in the Reformation, God's people are again being called upon to set God's Word above man's word. We rejoice that the truth of the Bible stands unshaken by human speculation, and that it remains the eternal revelation of God's nature and will for mankind. We reject all theology and criticism that refuses to bring itself under the divine authority of Holy Scripture, and all traditionalism which weakens that authority by adding to the Word of God.[23]

During his four years in New Orleans, Clark Pinnock began for the first time to be noticed widely as a potential shaper of theological

---

[21]As quoted by Carl F. H. Henry, *Evangelicals at the Brink of Crisis* (Waco, TX: Word Books, 1967), 15.

[22]Clark Pinnock, Interview with Barry Callen, April 18, 1998.

[23]As quoted in Carl Henry, *Evangelicals at the Brink of Crisis*, 4-5.

thought among contemporary evangelicals. He was chosen by *Christianity Today* magazine to present its case against form criticism,[24] delivered the Christian Contemporary Thought Lectures at Harvard University in 1966 ("intellectual evangelism in my Schaefferian mode,"[25] he now recalls), and published his first major theological writing in 1967, titled *A Defense of Biblical Infallibility*,[26] followed the same year by the book *Set Forth Your Case*.[27] These two books, along with his much appreciated *Biblical Revelation* in 1971, became the foundation for the early phase of Pinnock's career and quickly established his reputation as a vigorous and sophisticated defender of biblical inerrancy and Christian spiritual vitality and faithfulness in a rapidly secularizing setting.

He insisted that "inductive difficulties encountered in the text cannot change the fact that the Bible claims not to err."[28] Such an exalted view of Scripture, often called plenary and verbal inspiration, was claimed to be the historic doctrine of the church until the modern defection. Recognizing that modern historiography was unknown to biblical writers and that they sometimes used specialized language forms, inerrancy as a view of biblical inspiration is necessarily restricted to the intended assertions of Scripture. To accept inerrancy of the biblical text is certainly not to abandon an adequate hermeneutic. With an adequacy of responsible interpretation in mind, then, many of the purported errors in the Bible were said by Pinnock to dissolve away. He later admitted that in these years he was bitten with the bug of "preoccupation with apologetic certainty."[29] Primarily at stake for him were the clarity

---

[24]Clark Pinnock, "The Case Against Form Criticism," *Christianity Today* (July 16, 1965), 12-13.

[25]Clark Pinnock, Interview with Barry Callen, April 18, 1998.

[26]This book was a revision of Pinnock's Tyndale Lecture in Biblical Theology delivered at Cambridge, July 12, 1966. He and his wife Dorothy had returned to England and Switzerland (Schaeffer's L'Abri community) that summer.

[27]Clark Pinnock, *Set Forth Your Case: An Examination of Christianity's Credentials* (Craig Press, 1967; the 1971 reprint by Moody Press).

[28]Clark Pinnock, *A Defense of Biblical Infallibility* (Philadelphia: Presbyterian and Reformed, 1967), 18.

[29]Clark Pinnock, "A Response to Rex Koivisto," *Journal of the Evangelical Theological Society* (June 1981), 154. Koivisto of Multnomah School of the Bible was critical of Pinnock's "sellout" on the inerrancy issue.

and effectiveness of gospel proclamation. "I may have behaved crudely during the New Orleans years," he would confess,[30] but the vigorous behavior had been motivated by love for a church that he saw being infected by the virus of "liberalism." He was a militant Christian rationalist. "I was caught up in something exciting," he later reflected. "For me it was a righteous crusade."[31] As he put it in 1970:

> Because God has entered into the historical drama in Jesus Christ, materialism and positivism have been *factually* refuted. Meaningfulness has been won for the Christian truth-claim. Because God has published his Word in the words of Scripture, the crisis of *content* has been surmounted. God has disclosed himself in a public and verifiable manner, and communicated his purposes in the modality of human language. At this time when post-liberal theology is breaking up because of its internal weaknesses, it is imperative for evangelicals to speak forth their convictions with cogency and vigor. Theological leadership is up for grabs. The opportunity may not come again soon.[32]

Rational apologetics, however, was never thought by Pinnock to be enough. The need went beyond stabilizing theological foundations to the issue of a spiritual revival based on the substance of real divine revelation. Reflecting the perspective of his 1963 doctoral dissertation, Pinnock insisted in 1968:

> We do not need superficial emotionalism. We do not battle for words and slogans. We need only the power of the Holy Spirit by which all spiritual victory comes (Zech. 4:6). If we would give God his place, Christ his glory, and Scripture its recognition, the Southern Baptist Convention [and other Christians] could arise and evangelize the world.[33]

The influence of young Professor Clark Pinnock on the Baptist campus in New Orleans and in many other places from that base was part of what would evolve into the major conservative "takeover" of the

---

30 *The Proceedings of the Conference on Biblical Inerrancy, 1987* (Nashville: Broadman Press, 1987), 73.

31 Clark Pinnock, Interview with Barry Callen, April 18, 1998.

32 Clark Pinnock, "The Harrowing of Heaven," *Christianity Today* (June 19, 1970), 8.

33 Clark Pinnock, "A New Reformation," 1968, 5.

Southern Baptist Convention. Some of the new generation of vigorous leaders of Baptist conservatism were first Pinnock's students in New Orleans (Paige Patterson, Adrian Rogers, and others).[34] They admired his credentials, public speaking ability, and outspoken biblical and evangelical heritage. Others also were coming to admire him. Previously Pinnock had thought little about the whole subject of millennialism, although he had read George Eldon Ladd's *The Blessed Hope* (1956). But while in New Orleans he met some Dallas Seminary people and read with appreciation Charles Ryrie's *Dispensationalism Today* (1965). He now "warmed to all this wonderful philosophy of history that the Bible appeared to teach." Apparently officials at the Dallas seminary were looking for leaders outside their immediate circle who were appreciative of their general emphases on biblical authority and prophetic dispensationalism. Pinnock obviously had become such a person in their eyes. He was the commencement speaker at Dallas Theological Seminary in 1971.

This was but the beginning of Pinnock's significant involvement with and impact on numerous traditions within contemporary Christianity. The controversy in the 1970s over the issue of biblical inerrancy raged in numerous Protestant groups. Select scholars came to be considered the dependable guides through the conflicts. In the Lutheran Church, Missouri Synod, for instance, scholars like Edward Young, Carl Henry, Harold Lindsell, Gleason Archer, Robert Gundry, and Kenneth Kantzer were judged to be "luminaries in the Evangelical galaxy," according to David Scaer in 1982. Among this "stellar collection,"

---

[34]In 1987 when "inerrancy" was a heated issue in the Southern Baptist Convention, Patterson and Rogers both took vigorous public exception to Pinnock's attempt at a mediating position. Even in this contentious atmosphere, Patterson referred to Pinnock as "my beloved mentor" and "my distinguished and greatly loved professor" (*The Proceedings of the Conference on Biblical Inerrancy, 1987*, 86, 93). Said Rogers on the same occasion: "Who can forget the brilliant young New Orleans Seminary professor who so ably and eloquently defended the cause of Christian orthodoxy and Biblical inerrancy in the Southern Baptist Convention?" (101). In the late 1970s Rogers was elected president of the SBC, initiating formally its conservative swing. In 1998 the SBC elected Patterson as its president. At the time he was president of Southeastern Baptist Theological Seminary in North Carolina and was considered one of the primary architects of the major "fundamentalist takeover" of the SBC.

Clark Pinnock was seen as "a luminary of the highest magnitude for his past defense of inerrancy." Scaer reported that Pinnock was the "class valedictorian."[35] He also reported on Pinnock's "rise and fall." Pinnock may have been at the front of the inerrancy class, but he was hardly standing still. Movement inevitably meant tension.

Affirming and Revising Inerrancy

Evangelical Christianity was not the community of believers that would be the first to lose the Christian gospel in an acid bath of modern relativism, at least if young Professor Pinnock could help it. It was, however, the section of the church that he judged could easily endanger the saving message of Christ by letting down an essential barrier to confusion, the sturdy barrier provided by biblical inerrancy. In his *A Defense of Biblical Infallibility* (1967) Pinnock identified epistemology as the central problem of twentieth century theology. The real issue, he said, is the *truth-claim* implicit in the traditional doctrine of biblical inspiration. The effect of modern biblical criticism "has not been the liberation of divine truth in Scripture but rather the questioning of any normative significance for the Bible at all." The response of Christian theologians in general? They have "retreated from the plain sense of the text into the subjective waters of speculation."[36] Pinnock proceeds to defend the divine inspiration and authority of the Bible, including the necessity of assuming that inspiration insures the text's inerrancy. Specifically:

> The Bible in its entirety is God's written Word to man, free of error in its original autographs, wholly reliable in history and doctrine. Its divine inspiration has rendered the Book "infallible" (incapable of teaching deception) and "inerrant" (not liable to prove false or mistaken). Its inspiration is "plenary" (extending to all parts alike), "verbal" (including the actual language form), and "confluent" (product of two free agents, human and divine). *Inspiration* involves *infallibility* as an essential property, and

---

[35]David Scaer, "The Rise and Fall of Clark H. Pinnock," *Concordia Theological Quarterly* (January 1982), 40.

[36]Pinnock, *A Defense of Biblical Infallibility*, 5.

infallibility in turn implies *inerrancy*. This threefold designation
of Scripture is implicit in the basic thesis of biblical authority.[37]

He does allow that infallibility is restricted to intended assertions of
Scripture. Certain pre-scientific references are incidental to the teachings
intended.

Then in 1968, in his *A New Reformation: A Challenge to Southern
Baptists*, Pinnock warns Southern Baptists to maintain belief in the
evangelical truths of an inerrant Bible, even to dismiss professors in
Baptist institutions of higher education who have abandoned a high
view of Scripture. In 1971 two more books appeared that together
sought to hold the line on biblical authority while moving toward a
constructive proposal for the future of an evangelical theology that,
while being faithful to biblical authority, nonetheless is prepared to
listen carefully to its Christian partners in theological dialogue.

The first 1971 book, *Biblical Revelation*, was hailed by a reviewer as
"the most vigorous scholarly statement of verbal, plenary inspiration
since Warfield."[38] Pinnock later explained that this book was an
expression of the theology of B. B. Warfield, a viewpoint Pinnock had
acquired from J. I. Packer in the 1950s and then had found reinforced in
the 1960s by his association with Francis Schaeffer, although it was
softened somewhat by F. F. Bruce, his doctoral advisor at Manchester
University in England. This viewpoint sought to prove that there is a
perfect Bible which can serve as the first principle for a rational system
of Christian theology.[39] Given the presumption that there is a controlling
divine sovereignty and that the Bible partakes of the divine nature and
thus is the non-negotiable basis of Christian certitude, other views can
hardly be entertained as worthy of serious consideration.[40]

---

[37]Ibid., 1.

[38]Gordon Lewis, in *Eternity* (Jan. 1972), 50. Moody Press was aware of and
appreciated Pinnock's earlier book, *A Defense of Biblical Infallibility* (1967), and had
asked him to write this work.

[39]Pinnock wrote: "Theology is the art of articulating the cognitive substance of
divine revelation of which Scripture is the medium" (*Biblical Revelation*, 107).

[40]Clark Pinnock, foreword to *Clark Pinnock on Biblical Authority* by Ray
Roennfeldt (Andrews University Press, 1990), xviii.

The second 1971 book, *Toward a Theology for the Future*, sought to identify where the contemporary action was and where it should be in the various fields of theological study. Its intent was to exhibit "the determination of Evangelicals to repudiate any trace of a ghetto mentality and to confront the central issues of the day head on." Because of the massive influence of positivistic science, "the question of questions for our time is the very possibility of any theology at all. The time had come for evangelical thinkers to "forsake the unimaginative mimicry of 'textbook' theology and forge an expression of biblical faith which will have the power to grip our generation." Too many theological constructs already had collapsed in the twentieth century. It was time for evangelical scholarship to regain leadership by offering "a convincing and credible way out."[41] To be convincing, it is argued, Christian theology must have both authority and stability in the midst of a relativistic and fluid culture. When absolutes are commonly assumed to have been swallowed up by the sea of historical consciousness, how can Christian theology avoid being "sucked into the full ambiguity of the human predicament"? Pinnock answers by insisting that traditional Christianity has the resources to solve this modern hermeneutical problem. "Resting as it does upon the verified Word received from beyond the human situation," he concluded, "Christian faith is able to keep its poise even in the midst of flux and change."[42]

A vigorous and very public preoccupation with the issues of biblical authority and proclamation helped lead to a professional move for Pinnock. His growing reputation reached the expanding Trinity Evangelical Divinity School in 1969, leading to satisfying and eventful years as a faculty member on this key Illinois campus.[43] During his five growing and productive years at Trinity (1969-1974) his theological style grew more irenic. He reported that he had become "less threatened as an evangelical thinker in a predominantly non-evangelical world of

---

[41]Clark Pinnock and David F. Wells, eds., *Toward a Theology of the Future* (Carol Stream, Ill.: Creation House, 1971), 7, 93-94, 96.

[42]Ibid., 117.

[43]See chapter four for extensive discussion of the theological and political pilgrimages made by Pinnock during his five years at Trinity.

scholarship and more open to viewpoints other than my own."[44] Pinnock was beginning to become a listener as well as a defender, a man who sought to bring fresh strength and unity into the evangelical community, although always with a non-negotiable zeal for effective Christian witness and faithful Christian living based on substantive divine revelation. In 1972, for example, he published two more books, *Live Now, Brother* and *Truth On Fire: The Message of Galatians.* In the exposition on Galatians one can see Pinnock shaping his own agenda by that of St. Paul's. What lay behind Paul's writing of this epistle? Says Pinnock: "Primarily he was concerned that the Galatian believers not lose their grip on the true gospel and forsake it (Gal. 1:6; 5:2). False teachers were operating among the congregations, unsettling them and subverting gospel truth (Gal. 1:7; 5:10). The situation urgently called for a vigorous defense of the gospel."[45] Even so, there was to be gentleness, humility, and grace. Pinnock ends this book by noting how Paul closes the epistle. He invokes the grace of God to be with them all. This, after all, was the point of the whole letter, the central principle that was being seriously threatened. So, concludes Pinnock, Paul's "final prayer is that divine grace may come again to dominate the thinking of his Galatian converts. 'Amen'—so be it!"[46]

Regardless of his sturdy commitment to received truth, which Pinnock tied directly to biblical authority and still defined intentionally by use of the word "inerrancy," he remained in creative motion on the subject. By the early 1970s he had become better able to keep his own poise, to reign in his enthusiastic crusading and make needed confrontation increasingly constructive. Then came Pinnock's three years of teaching at Regent College in Vancouver, Canada (1974-1977), where he experienced more freedom to quest and be creative. In this more open context he was impacted significantly by Stephen Davis' book *Debate About the Bible: Inerrancy Versus Infallibility*[47] which openly challenged

---

[44]Clark Pinnock, in *The Scribe,* publication of Trinity Evangelical Divinity School, 1974, 3.

[45]Clark Pinnock, preface to *Truth On Fire: The Message of Galatians* (Grand Rapids: Baker Book House, 1972).

[46]Ibid., 90.

[47]Davis (The Westminster Press, 1977).

certain assumptions about biblical inerrancy then held by Pinnock. So Pinnock began to review carefully and revise cautiously his inerrancy views.[48] Increasingly he was openly questioning certain traditional defenses and expressions of inerrancy treasured by many conservatives.[49] In his early period of fundamentalism he had leaned on 2 Timothy 3:16-17, the only place in Scripture where the term *inspired* (*theopneustos*) occurs. But now, as a neo-evangelical, he was looking beyond the inspiration issue to appreciate also Paul's emphasis on practical spirituality—what is inspired is "useful for teaching, for reproof, for correction, and for training in righteousness, so that everyone who belongs to God may be proficient, equipped for every good work." That is, God's Spirit breathes through the text to transform believers into maturing and obedient disciples. The focus should be less on textual technicalities of the past (the original text no longer available) and more on faithful and transformative relevance in the present.

It was immediately obvious that reforming a cherished element of fundamentalism like biblical inerrancy would be slow and painful. Pinnock quickly found himself being sharply criticized by some traditionalists, including Harold Lindsell, who earlier had counted Pinnock a valuable ally in the "battle for the Bible." He was beginning what would become his common experience—walking a tightrope, explaining to the liberals why so few revisions were being made and to the fundamentalists why there were so many.[50] Recalling his two early mentors, F. F. Bruce and Francis Schaeffer, Pinnock would characterize

---

[48]See his "Three Views of the Bible in Contemporary Theology" (in *Biblical Authority*, ed. Jack Rogers, 1977), 45-73, and "Evangelicals and Inerrancy: The Current Debate" (*Theology Today*, April 1978), 65-69.

[49]Later Pinnock would see the degree to which the foundationalism of modernity had been reflected in his own early work. "It did so in a covert way," he reported, "since I was not tuned in to these subtleties. Because religion appeals to the need for security in life, it is easy to fall into foundationalism as a way of attaining it. It has a particularly seductive appeal for fundamentalists with their passion for certainty" (as in the unpublished paper of Pinnock delivered in 1997 to the evangelical-process dialogue convened at Claremont School of Theology).

[50]For example, Pinnock's eventual book *The Scripture Principle* (1984) was reviewed critically by James Barr (judged unacceptable from the left—did not go far enough) and Roger Nicole in *Christianity Today* (judged unacceptable from the right—went too far).

his shifting in the 1970s as a move from Schaeffer's militant rationalism to Bruce's more bottom-up irenic scholarship.[51] His move was also toward another key figure in his eyes, C. S. Lewis. This Englishman represented for him a reasonable, commonsense approach to Christian belief that was enriched with wonderful visions and the ability to live with ambiguity.

In 1976 Harold Lindsell published his book *The Battle for the Bible*. Here he vigorously reaffirmed biblical inerrancy and challenged those who claimed to have found biblical errors in its reporting of history and chronology. His thesis was that "when inerrancy goes, it opens a small hole in the dike, and if that hole is not closed, the levee will collapse and the whole land will be overrun with the waters of unbelief not unlike that exhibited by Bultmann and theological liberalism."[52] Of particular concern to Lindsell was the work titled *Scripture, Tradition, and Infallibility* by Dewey N. Beegle (1973). Lindsell saw this work reflecting that author's passion for demonstrating the fallibility of the Bible even though, in terms of logic and espistemology, such wayward thought did not have "a leg to stand on."[53] Lindsell was disappointed that the prominent F. F. Bruce of England had commended Beegle's book by saying: "I endorse as emphatically as I can his [Beegle's] deprecating of a Maginot-line mentality where the doctrine of Scripture is concerned." That is, to claim the domino effect of all truth coming into question if the front of inerrancy is lost was seen by Bruce as a false mentality. Lindsell's own book was a Maginot-line manifesto, engaging in a "battle for the Bible" in the face of Beegle, F. F. Bruce, and those like them.

It is here that Clark Pinnock is brought into the picture by Lindsell. Beegle had criticized Pinnock for stating in *Biblical Revelation* (1971)[54] that the supposedly incontrovertible evidence for biblical errors is, on careful scrutiny, not that at all. Without wishing to minimize the difficulty of interpretation imposed by some of these supposed errors,

---

[51]Clark Pinnock in his interview with Barry Callen, November 21, 1998.

[52]Harold Lindsell, *The Battle for the Bible* (Grand Rapids: Zondervan, 1976), 159-160.

[53]Ibid., 171.

[54]In 1998 this 1971 book of Pinnock's was identified as "one of the best books on biblical inerrancy within this century" (*Christianity Today*, February 9, 1998).

Pinnock nonetheless regarded none of them as insuperable problems. To Beegle, this was Pinnock trying to avoid serious consideration of the actual evidence because of his prior commitment to a "high" and unyielding theory of biblical inspiration. To Lindsell, Pinnock's words were the proper and courageous stance of a man who had earlier proven himself to be "like a tiger stalking his prey"[55] when it came to identifying and confronting false teachings. Lindsell quotes passages from Pinnock's 1968 booklet *A New Reformation: A Challenge To Southern Baptists*, including this: "…today students report that in many places of Baptist higher education the doctrine of Biblical infallibility is either completely ignored or openly held up to scorn.… In the past a professor trembled to contradict God's Word; now he trembles to go against the current liberal consensus."[56]

Pinnock soon elaborated on this pattern of Baptist defection by reference to what he called "the Scriptural principle." This principle, he said, is that truth is not "discerned by human genius, but delivered to us by God through the instrumentality of his apostles and prophets and deposited in the Scriptures." The heart of the defection was identified as the refusal to accept the belief of Christians for eighteen hundred years, namely that God's Word is to be identified with the written text of the Bible.[57] Having said this, however, Pinnock offered this caution to evangelicals about any quick and simplistic equating of the biblical text and the revealed Word of God:

> …we should express some sympathy with the reasons which led men to this conclusion [defection from the Scriptural principle]. For we would be sadly deluded if we concluded that the factors causing these Baptists to change their doctrine of inspiration were insubstantial and of their own making. Conservative Christians have a definitive tendency to minimize the force of biblical difficulties, just as liberal Christians tend to exaggerate them. Often the orthodox stalwarts simply do not seriously

---

[55]Harold Lindsell, *The Bible in the Balance* (Grand Rapids: Zondervan, 1979), 36.

[56]Clark Pinnock, *A New Reformation: A Challenge to Southern Baptists* (Tigerville, S.C.: Jewell Books, 1968), 6-10.

[57]Clark Pinnock, "Baptists and Biblical Authority," *The Journal of the Evangelical Theological Society* 17 (1974), 198.

confront well formulated critical issues. This cannot be excused.
These difficulties cannot be swept aside in a flood of rhetoric.[58]

Without question, Pinnock remained firmly committed to whatever
the Bible claims for itself. By 1979, however, he had reassessed what is
included in this claim. Consequently, Lindsell was then viewing Pinnock
very differently. Now Pinnock was said to have moved from the halls of
Regent College in Vancouver to "the liberal corridors" of McMaster
Divinity College in Hamilton, Ontario. He also had ventured on an
"inexplicable" pilgrimage on the subject of biblical inerrancy, "a
noticeable shift from right to left." Lindsell lamented: "Many of us who
are committed to biblical inerrancy had counted on Dr. Pinnock to
play an important role in the present discussion by reinforcing what we
have to say. Alas, this is not to be."[59]

What intervened to alter Pinnock's view? His own explanation is that
he realized that he had "inflated the biblical claims for inspiration in the
interests of a rationalist paradigm.... I had been engaged in making the
Bible say more than it wanted to in the interests of my system."[60] In fact,
for him the rationalism of a scholastic theological system was slowly
crumbling in light of an enhanced appreciation for the dynamic work
of the Spirit in relation to the biblical authors/editors and his thought
and life (and potentially the thought and lives of all contemporary Bible
readers). Such divine work came to have a substantive impact on
Pinnock's view of biblical revelation and interpretation. He now affirmed
a progressiveness of revelation and thus the need for the interpreter to
give heed to the letter, spirit, and direction of the principles of a text.
With the Spirit's help, one "may need to go beyond Scripture in carrying
out its intentions."[61] Pinnock had come to recognize that Jesus and the
apostles, while holding a high view of biblical inspiration and authority,
used the text in more practical and flexible ways than inerrantists

---

[58]Ibid., 200.

[59]Lindsell, 1979, 36, 43.

[60]Pinnock, in Roennfeldt, xix. He attributed much of his new viewpoint to the
writings of I. Howard Marshall, F. F. Bruce, James D. G. Dunn, and James Barr.

[61]Clark Pinnock, "An Evangelical Theology of Human Liberation," *Sojourners*
(February 1976), 30. This article was originally a 1975 address to a workshop sponsored
by the Evangelicals For Social Action.

typically allowed. He now was open to a more inductive approach to the text that avoided the tendency toward strained exegesis forced by a pre-held theory. He had been helped by scholars like Edward Farley and James Barr to realize without embarrassment that God in fact has given the Scriptures in human forms and languages.

The Bible, so it increasingly appeared to Pinnock, should be allowed to teach God's will and way out of its distinctive diversity rather than out of a forced uniformity. Robert Johnston reflects as follows on the reasons for Pinnock's broadening use of the term "inerrancy": "The perfect errorlessness of non-extant autographs was an abstraction that, for Pinnock, died the death of a thousand qualifications. More importantly, it failed to prove the dynamic authority of the present text."[62] After all, it is the Spirit who causes the reader to be receptive to a text's "surplus of meaning" and, observes Pinnock, "whatever, the reason, stress on the Spirit is noticeably lacking in the literature of inerrancy."[63]

The force that can liberate the message of Jesus for the needs of life today is the Bible read in the wisdom and power of the Spirit. Focusing inordinately on the necessary accuracy of all textual detail, however marginal, can easily become dysfunctional. There was a growing realization that for many believers, strict adherence to the inerrancy doctrine endangers rather than protects evangelical faith.[64] Accordingly, Pinnock commended the 1977 anti-inerrancy polemic of Stephen Davis for its "pastoral service" to those who are troubled with marginal difficulties in the Bible but nonetheless are deeply committed to a biblically-based evangelical faith. The theory of errorlessness sometimes leaves such persons stranded "if a single point however minute stands in

---

[62]Robert Johnston, "Clark H. Pinnock," in *Handbook of Evangelical Theologians*, ed. Walter Elwell (Grand Rapids: Baker Books, 1993), 434.

[63]Clark Pinnock, *The Scripture Principle* (San Francisco: Harper & Row, 1984), 154.

[64]This judgment, of course, was hardly universal in the world of evangelical theologians. Roger Nicole, e.g., reacted in *Christianity Today* (Feb. 1, 1985, 68-71) to Pinnock's 1984 book *The Scripture Principle* under the provocatively critical title "Clark Pinnock's Precarious Balance Between Openmindedness and Doctrinal Instability." Nicole's inference was that there is an establishment evangelical theology that should not be threatened by a methodology that is dynamic enough to be open to any significant theological alterations. Obviously Pinnock had come to disagree.

any doubt."[65] The intent of divine revelation surely is human transformation. People are to be changed, not stranded by their rational
engagement with the biblical text.

Claiming Middle Ground

Clark Pinnock eventually would leave Trinity Evangelical Divinity
School, but for no negative reason. It was just that in 1974 a call came
inviting him to return to Canada. Rather than his home province of
Ontario, the call was from Vancouver, British Columbia, where Regent
College was a new reality in evangelical theological education. Regent
was associated with the North American wing of the same Brethren
denomination with which Professor F. F. Bruce, Pinnock's doctoral
mentor, was long associated in England.[66] These Christian Brethren
rejected the usual distinction between clergy and laity and thus
envisioned for Western Canada a new Brethren seminary for lay people.
It began functioning with a summer school in 1968 and soon was
affiliated with the Vancouver School of Theology and University of
British Columbia. The new school quickly evolved to be trans-
denominational, international, and evangelical in character. The
principal, James Houston, worked to build a quality theological faculty,
including the early appointments of Carl Armerding in Old Testament
and Ward Gasque, who like Pinnock had completed doctoral studies in
New Testament under Professor Bruce at the University of Manchester.[67]

By 1974 the student body of Regent had grown to the point that it
was possible for the school to make its first full-time faculty appointment
in theology. The choice would be Clark Pinnock. He was thought an
excellent choice since he was a Canadian who had studied under F. F.
Bruce, had quickly developed an international reputation, brought
seminary teaching experience in New Testament and theology at New

---

[65]Clark Pinnock, foreword to *The Debate About the Bible*, by Stephen Davis
(Philadelphia: Westminster Press, 1977), 12.

[66]At an early stage in the planning for the new school, some of the founders
hoped that F. F. Bruce would accept leadership in the launching of Regent College.
Instead, James Houston came to play this key role.

[67]For detail on Regent College, see John G. Stackhouse, Jr., *Canadian
Evangelicalism in the Twentieth Century* (Toronto: University of Toronto Press, 1993),
154-164.

Orleans Baptist and Trinity Evangelical seminaries, and could add to the young campus his reputation as one of the more promising of the younger evangelical theologians. Already he had authored four books in the area of biblical authority and Christian apologetics. Pinnock accepted the new post, agreeing to leave Trinity, a large and strong seminary where he had been very happy. "Regent then was a fledging place," he later recalled, "but again I was caught up in the enthusiasm of a vision."[68] As the school had expected, soon his presence on the Vancouver campus proved a plus for academic rigor and student recruitment.

As early as 1976, however, Pinnock was indicating his intention of leaving the Regent faculty. In 1977 he accepted a post in theology on the other end of the continent at McMaster Divinity College in Ontario. He was replaced at Regent by J. I. Packer who relocated from England.[69] Why leave Regent? Again, the issue was not dissatisfaction, but a call and a challenge that he was prepared to embrace. Pinnock loved the British Columbia setting geographically, and he heartily endorsed the young school's vision for lay theological education and the pietism resident in the Brethren tradition. Although deciding to leave, he would return in years to come to teach summer school classes. But for now another vision had invaded his heart. McMaster Divinity College back east in Ontario had extended an invitation that he could not resist. It came from his home area of Toronto where his father still lived (his mother had died in 1974). He was loyal to his Baptist roots and inspired by the opportunity to become a new evangelical influence in a key Canadian Baptist institution located in an exciting university setting in Hamilton, Ontario. There would be theological struggles in the new setting. He admits to going with something of a "messiah" complex, telling the search committee that he could help the school serve better the many evangelical churches in Ontario and Quebec. He had prayed for an evangelical revival at McMaster; now he had a chance to help his own

---

[68]Clark Pinnock, Interview with Barry Callen, April 19, 1998.
[69]The story of Regent's beginnings and Packer's coming to replace Pinnock is told in Alister McGrath, *J. I. Packer: A Biography* (Grand Rapids: Baker Books, 1997), 231-237.

prayers become reality. The school was "mainline" in mentality and probably thought that Pinnock was a conservative it could receive and absorb with relative comfort. He did have good credentials and was a loyal Canadian and Baptist. The decision was made and would turn out to be a wise and long term one for Pinnock and the school alike.

From his new academic post at McMaster Divinity College, Pinnock began in 1977 to reflect his maturing thought to ever-widening Christian publics and to an increasing range of possible implications. Regarding biblical inspiration and authority in the modern world, he now was identifying three general positions within evangelicalism. The first, his own personal heritage, centered in a militant advocacy of a virtually unqualified biblical inerrancy, an errorless Bible presumed to be the essential anchor of true Christianity. The second position actively opposed such strict inerrancy. Although a minority of evangelicals, there were prominent names here, including Pinnock's own revered teacher F. F. Bruce of the University of Manchester in England. These thinkers questioned the assumption of scientific precision and accuracy usually connoted by inerrancy, arguing that such an inerrancy mentality is a modernistic approach not appropriate to the biblical text and not even evidenced in how the Bible treats its own material or in what it claims for itself. They saw inspiration as "a much less formal and more practical affair," a divine action on behalf of the sufficiency of Scripture meant to "nourish and instruct the church for its faith and life, and not to [guarantee] an abstract perfection" in regard to the technicalities of its text or its incidental references to matters outside its central concern.[70]

The third position, which by 1978 had become Pinnock's own, involved a preference to retain the term inerrancy, but only after modifying its definition so as to take into account certain biblical phenomena not compatible with any absolute view of an errorless text (like the presence of a Semitic cosmology, variants of parallel material appearing in the Synoptic Gospels, etc.). Pinnock's own book *Biblical Revelation* (1971) was representative here, as soon would be his "softer" *Reason*

---

[70]Clark Pinnock, "Evangelicals and Inerrancy: The Current Debate," *Theology Today* (April 1978), 67.

Enough (1980) and then his major work *The Scripture Principle* (1984).[71] In the 1984 work he rethought biblical authority in light of its witness to itself, including both its divine and human character and its spiritual dynamic. His style of argument is less rationalistic than his earlier apologetical works, and his stance is a less strict and more nuanced form of "inerrancy." On the one hand, he was acknowledging the need to deal with the biblical text as it is, not with the abstraction of an ideal text (the "autographs") that God did not choose to give the church across the centuries. Reverently pursued critical scholarship has its place, he judged, as does a Spirit-led dynamic reading of the biblical text. On the other hand, such scholarship and hermeneutical focus do not lessen the fact that Scripture is genuinely authoritative in what it intends to teach. There is an objective content to biblical revelation that should caution both against skeptical and subjective biblical criticism and any Spirit focus that disassociates itself from the revealed biblical text. The word "inerrancy" can be retained legitimately, Pinnock concluded, when defined as "a metaphor for the determination to trust God's Word completely."[72]

Pinnock now was championing a potentially awkward and certainly controversial middle position criticized by advocates of both the other positions. He assesses the awkwardness this way: "The militant advocates suspect them [and me] of watering down the inerrancy conviction close to meaninglessness, and left wing Protestants like James Barr

---

[71]A portion of the material in this 1984 book was first presented at Fuller Theological Seminary as the 1982 Payton Lectures. The title of Pinnock's lectures was "Holy Scripture: Divine Treasure in Earthen Vessels."

[72]Clark Pinnock, *The Scripture Principle* (San Francisco: Harper & Row, 1984), 225. The review of Pinnock's *The Scripture Principle* by Randy Maddox affirms the book as "the most nuanced and critically aware exposition of biblical inerrancy available." Even so, Maddox was perplexed by Pinnock's argument for retaining the term "inerrancy" after defining it basically as the belief that Scripture never leads one astray in regard to what it intentionally teaches. Retaining it when thus defined appears essentially to be a political move, "using the approved password to placate a constituency," a move that will not be accepted by others who use the term and retain its traditional meaning (Maddox, in the *Wesleyan Theological Journal*, Spring/Fall 1986, 206). For evidence that Maddox was correct, see Roger Nicole, *Christianity Today*, Feb. 1, 1985, 68-71. Nicole quotes Carl F. H. Henry (68): Pinnock "retains inerrancy as a concept, but seems to thin it out almost to the breaking point."

ridicule the effort to be critically honest and still retain biblical inerrancy in any form."[73] Regardless of criticisms from representatives of both alternatives and his increasing willingness to carefully qualify the exact meaning of his own inerrancy stance, Pinnock continued to maintain at least this:

> The Bible, not modernity, is normative, and our thoughts are to be shaped by its teaching, not the reverse. Only by acknowledging this can we prevent revelation from being buried under the debris of human culture and opinion and from disappearing as a liberating Word from outside the human situation.[74]

By 1984 he was speaking in terms of "the Scriptural principle," by which he meant that the Bible is to be viewed as God's own written Word. God "has communicated authoritatively to us on those subjects about which Scripture teaches...and we believers willingly subject ourselves to this rule of faith." The Bible is "a contentful language deposit" that addresses us with God's authority, a deposit that should not be reduced to a mere expression of human experience and tradition."[75]

Delwin Brown rightly observes that Pinnock's *The Scripture Principle* (1984) "is as much an internal self-criticism of conservatism as it is an external critique of liberalism."[76] For Pinnock, inerrancy had come to mean that the Bible can be trusted in what it teaches and intentionally affirms. A key passage like 2 Timothy 3:15-16 authorizes sturdy belief in the instructional significance of the Bible in matters relating to human salvation, but not necessarily in marginal matters unrelated to the need for, basis of, and practice of new life in Jesus Christ. All Scripture is to be regarded as authoritative, but the character of the authority is relative to the actual content and form of any given text. Those portions of the Bible which plainly intend to teach the will of God constitute the core of authoritative Scripture. The Christian should accept the Bible as teacher in a way consistent with the diversity that the Bible contains. For instance, the way the New Testament uses the Hebrew Scriptures ("Old"

---

[73]Clark Pinnock, "Evangelicals and Inerrancy: The Current Debate," 66-67.

[74]Clark Pinnock, *The Scripture Principle*, 213.

[75]Ibid., 62.

[76]Delwin Brown, "Rethinking Authority from the Right," *Christian Scholar's Review* 19:1 (1989-90), 67.

1984 - "Scriptural principle"
1987 - "Scripture principle"

Testament) makes plain that a text can possess "a surplus of meaning potential that transcends the meaning it originally had." The original meaning is to be the anchor of our interpretation, but under the guidance of the Holy Spirit "the significance of the text for us needs to be searched out.... The picture is that of a canon in which the truth unfolds gradually and dialectically."[77] The Bible remains the norm of belief and must rule in opposition to the liberal reformers who "are in rebellion against the content of the Bible and are determined to adapt it to the 'itching ears' of the present."[78] Innovative and on a journey Pinnock *was*; rebellious and anti-biblical he *was not*.

Pinnock announced this to the 1987 Conference on Biblical Inerrancy of the Southern Baptists: "The reason I defended the strict view of inerrancy in my earlier years was because I desperately wanted it to be true. I wanted it to be true so badly that I passed over the obvious problems."[79] He now had come to speak of the "Scripture principle" and explain it this way:

> It means that there is a locus of the Word of God in a humanly accessible form available to us. It means that the Bible is regarded as a creaturely text that is at the same time God's own written Word, and that we can consult his Word, which reveals his mind, and seek to know his will in it. It means that God has communicated authoritatively to us on those subjects about which Scripture teaches, whether doctrinal, ethical, or spiritual, and that we believers willingly subject ourselves to this rule of faith. More than merely human tradition and merely existential address, the Bible is the informative Word of God to the church.[80]

---

[77]Clark Pinnock, *The Scripture Principle*, 45, 186. He says further: "The Bible in the form it comes to us is the kind of teacher that draws us into the process of learning and helps us learn to think theologically and ethically ourselves in new situations" (194).

[78]Ibid., 208, 211. Some conservatives, of course, now insist that Pinnock himself is a liberal reformer still trying to wear inerrancy clothes. Norman Geisler, for instance, judges: "Strangely, some neotheists such as Clark Pinnock claim to believe in the infallibility and inerrancy of the Bible. However, this is clearly inconsistent" (*Creating God in the Image of Man?*, Minneapolis: Bethany, 1997, 131).

[79]Clark Pinnock, "Parameters of Biblical Inerrancy," in *Proceedings of the Conference on Biblical Inerrancy, 1987* (Nashville: Broadman Press, 1987), 96.

[80]Clark Pinnock, *The Scripture Principle*, 62.

It had become crucial for Pinnock that one both affirm biblical authority in principle and define it with care. He was seeking to claim middle ground in a crucial and complex issue.

It remained the firm assumption of Pinnock that true Christianity depends on a truth deposit once delivered to the saints, a deposit which must be maintained and accepted by faith. This is why he holds staunchly to the "text horizon" of the faith in the face of the obvious role always played by the "reader horizon." The problem he now saw, however, was that evangelicals, for whom the Word of God is of utmost importance, "have spent a great deal of energy defending the authority or inerrancy of the Bible and [have] given little attention to the equally important matter of its interpretation." They have, in fact, often evidenced a "naivete in hermeneutics" that threatens "to drag the meaning of the text into the range of what we want it to say." The text is not there to do human bidding, and it does not mean whatever readers want it to mean. But interpretation is no easy process, in part because "the Bible is not a flat text but a symphony of voices and emphases."[81] Pinnock thus places himself today in an "inerrancy of purpose" category that allows room both to significantly nuance the specific textual meanings of inerrancy[82] and continue to sign the statement of the Evangelical Theological Society which affirms that "the Bible alone, and the Bible in its entirety, is the Word of God written, and is therefore inerrant in the autographs." He actually prefers the wording of the

---

[81]Clark Pinnock, "Catholic, Protestant, and Anabaptist: Principles of Biblical Interpretation in Selected Communities," *Brethren In Christ History and Life* (December 1986), 268, 275.

[82]Note, for instance, Pinnock's "Climbing Out of a Swamp: The Evangelical Struggle to Understand the Creation Texts," *Interpretation: A Journal of Bible and Theology* (April 1989), 143-155. He is concerned that evangelicals be true to their own premise of "letting Scripture speak definitively above the noise of human opinions" (153). He also is concerned, however, that near the surface of evangelical interpretation is a "docetic" tendency, "an unconscious wish not to have God's Word enter into the creaturely realm" (153). He concludes: "Evangelicals are understandably nervous about existential hermeneutics, but that is no reason to overreact and make the Bible a victim" (154). Modern scientific perspectives and calls for "factual" information may be quite other than the biblical intent in the Genesis texts (and elsewhere). To honor biblical authority is to affirm claims to assured truth only within the context of the intent of biblical teaching (which relates to salvation and not science, for instance).

Lausanne Covenant that says the Bible is "inerrant in all it affirms" or that of the Chicago Statement of Biblical Inerrancy that says: "We deny that it is proper to evaluate Scripture according to standards of truth and error that are alien to its usage or purpose." In other words, the Bible may *contain* errors of incidental kinds, but it *teaches* none.[83]

Clearly, by the 1980s Pinnock had opened himself to modern biblical scholarship to a degree he had previously rejected. In 1968 he had warned Southern Baptists about new teachers then in their ranks who "had found it expedient to jettison the historic high view of Scripture and accept a scaled down version.... Scholarship is the gift of God. But scholars have erred time and time again, while Scripture has never erred!"[84] The next year he had joined the faculty of Trinity Evangelical Divinity School and affirmed its statement of belief, point one of which was: "We believe...the Scriptures, both Old and New Testaments, to be the inspired Word of God, without error in the original writings, the complete revelation of His will for the salvation of men, and the Divine and final authority for all Christian faith and life." But by the 1980s he had qualified the precise meaning of appropriately affirming an inerrant Bible, insisting that "qualify" and "scale down" differ in meaning. For him the Bible's authority and reliability had not thereby been diminished.

The Bible is believed by Pinnock, early and late in his journey, to be "inerrant" in all that it intentionally affirms. What changed somewhat in his view is the identification of exactly what the Bible actually affirms. Doing such careful identifying is a central and ongoing challenge for contemporary Christians. The task of interpretation would be much easier, of course, if the actual words of the Bible were identical with

---

[83]Note this from Donald Bloesch (*Holy Scripture*, 1994, 116): "I affirm that the message of Scripture is infallible and that the Spirit infallibly interprets this message to people of faith. But the perfect accuracy of the letter or text of Scripture is not an integral part of Christian faith. Because the term *inerrancy* is so often associated with the latter position, I agree with Clark Pinnock that it is not the preferable word to use in theological discussion today, even though it should not be abandoned, for it preserves the nuance of truthfulness that is necessary for a high view of Holy Scripture." He refers to this statement of Pinnock (*The Scripture Principle*, 225): I wish to retain the word inerrancy because it "has come to symbolize in our day that full confidence that Christians have always had in the Scriptures."

[84]Clark Pinnock, "A New Reformation," 7, 10.

divine revelation. But it may be said that human words are to divine revelation what form is to content. Therefore, there is danger in any rote application of Augustine's classic statement: "What the Bible says, God says." When such a statement is applied mechanically to the biblical text, there is the tendency "to dehistoricize the vehicle of revelation and to make each text an immutable and inherent proposition." In fact, tradition, experience, and reason (key elements of the Wesleyan "Quadrilateral") all are needed to assist a person of faith in understanding and applying the Word of God. "Sola scriptura" may have been a distinguishing slogan of the Protestant Reformation, but it was never literally true. Probing the sacred text is always done within some reading tradition that relies at least in part on a given pattern of logic and experience. Even so, it remains the case for Pinnock that the Bible—with all its humanness—extends beyond being merely a crucial cultural heritage for believers to being the normative rule of faith that should define belief itself.

This revised inerrancy position came to be judged by Pinnock to be both justified by all the facts, textual and contextual, historical and hermeneutical, and able to provide a viable position to mediate the authority struggle in the evangelical community.[85] In 1965 he had seen the Southern Baptist Convention, into which he then was entering as a new professor, in danger of serious infiltration by a Bible-evading and doctrine-eroding liberalism. This he fought. For instance, he provided interpretation for the dramatic action of the 1970 Denver gathering of the SBC which had directed that a volume of the new *Broadman Bible Commentary* be rewritten, this time "with due consideration of the conservative viewpoint." Before this Convention, Pinnock said the following about the introductory Old Testament book in question:

---

[85]Carl F. H. Henry was a stalwart evangelical defender of the distinctiveness and even propositional nature of divine revelation, the one thing, he argued, on which evangelicals can confidently construct a substantial, coherent, and trustworthy theological system. Clark Pinnock, however, countered that it is impossible to set forth an infallible Scripture as the foundational axiom of Christian theology. Argues Pinnock: "The problem in a nutshell: If reason is given its head, will it reliably lead to orthodox conclusions? Progressives certainly do not believe that it will" (*Tracking the Maze*, Harper & Row, 1990, 46-47).

Unfortunately, from the viewpoint of the evangelical reader, the Old Testament volume reflects the *negative* critical theories of the current Old Testament scholarly consensus, and lacks the moderate conservatism of the New Testament volume.... Professor Davies holds that God has given us *two* sources of revelation, the Bible and nature, and that we should assess the truthfulness of Genesis in matters of fact in accordance with the findings of science.... This dodge...robs the plain assertions of Scripture of normative significance and makes faith meaningless. To allow that the Bible is mistaken in the testable (scientific) parts is to make the claim wholly unconvincing that it is truthful in the untestable (theological) parts.... Editor Allen rejects verbal and plenary inspiration in favor of an imprecise "dynamic" theory.[86]

After the Convention's action, he rejected the claim by "liberals" in the Convention that the action to force a rewrite was an unfortunate act of anti-intellectualism. Pinnock declared that the documentary hypothesis is "an imaginary invention, developed largely in isolation from truly objective archeological and linguistic findings, and amounts to little more than a badge of academic respectability." The time had come for an elevation of the right kind of scholarship, an "evangelical scholarship of the highest order." Admittedly, this would be difficult since it both resisted the conventional wisdom of so much liberal scholarship and had to face the widespread Baptist mentality of revivalism which, he judged, "tends to reduce the glorious riches of Christian truth to a dramatic experience, which likes its preaching loud [and] low in content," meaning that "Southern Baptist conservatism has neglected her intellectual defenses and become easy prey to liberalism, which after all is also a religion of experience."[87]

By 1987, however, Pinnock saw the primary danger to the SBC having shifted from the external assault of liberalism to a dangerous division within the Convention itself, nearly a holy war among the parties of its non-liberals (moderates to fundamentalists). A primary

---

[86]Clark Pinnock, in *Christianity Today* (December 5, 1969), 17.

[87]Clark Pinnock, "Correct Action Awaits Vindication," *Mississippi Baptist and Record* (October 22, 1970).

dividing line was between competing theories of biblical inspiration. The truly frightening prospect, as judged by Pinnock, was that in a time of unprecedented worldwide mission potential "the possible fragmentation of believers could have disastrous consequences for world evangelization," even causing Baptists to "snatch defeat from the jaws of victory."[88] He announced to a large gathering of Baptist scholars that there was the option of peace without compromise. He insisted that "the key issue is to maintain the right amount of form and freedom" and he supported this insistence with his own experience:

> I did not see my colleague at L'Abri, the strict inerrantist Francis Schaeffer, spending his time seeking to drive out my doctoral mentor, the moderate F. F. Bruce, from the evangelical coalition just because of a difference of opinion over a theological theory and not the gospel.[89]

Pinnock was speaking to a large body of mostly Southern Baptist scholars gathered for the Conference on Biblical Inerrancy at Ridgecrest, North Carolina, in May 1987. In the midst of presentations by persons ranging from strict inerrantists to significant revisionists, Pinnock's inclination was to be a peacemaker. He supported the 1978 Chicago Statement of the International Council on Biblical Inerrancy which declared in its famous Article 13 that textual phenomena like chronological order, loose quotations, and disagreeing numbers should not be considered "errors." He argued that Bible believers over the centuries have come to no consensus on the precise meaning of "inerrancy," that the Chicago Statement made room for nearly every well-intentioned Baptist, and that "old-fashioned love and understanding" was the real need of the hour. On the one hand, there should be correction of any "unbalanced over-belief which overlooks the human and historical dimension of the Bible," but he warned on the other hand, "Let us never fail to express our unsurpassed confidence in the divine treasure which the Bible surely is."

---

[88]Clark Pinnock, *The Proceedings of the Conference on Biblical Inerrancy, 1987* (Nashville: Broadman Press, 1987), 73.

[89]Ibid., 74.

The bottom line? It should be mission, said Pinnock, not fruitless and debilitating internal combat over technicalities largely of human devising. What he saw happening was that the liberals already had lost the day, while conservatives, properly but not very gracefully, were now "trying to get the wrinkles out of their sounder view of inspiration."[90] Pinnock's own approach was to adopt "a simpler, more spontaneous biblicism" which trusts the Bible without reservation, but at the same time does not "burden the Bible reader with too much human theory lest he or she miss what God is saying in the text."[91]

This more spontaneous biblicism approach was similar to that of fellow Baptist theologian Bernard Ramm who, according to Pinnock, toward the end of his career "was able to experience freedom from the methodological fixation."[92] Ramm had wearied of evangelicals fighting over inerrancy and, judged Pinnock, "longed for them to be able to rejoice in its [the Bible's] solid testimony to Jesus Christ in the power of the Holy Spirit." Pinnock himself had come to the place to which Ramm also had arrived. He concluded this about Ramm:

> For him inerrancy always meant something quite simple. Because inerrancy is not a restrictive notion, it always leaves one free to interpret scripture as the several texts require. He felt no need either to argue about it or to abandon it. Since he knew what the term meant to evangelical people, because of their recent history, his strategy was to define it in a nuanced way and get on with the task of interpretation. I think Ramm has been consistent throughout his life on this and has chosen the way of wisdom.[93]

---

[90]Clark Pinnock, afterword to *The Unfettered Word: Southern Baptists Confront* the *Authority-Inerrancy Question*, ed. Robinson B. James (Waco, TX: Word Books, 1987), 186-187.

[91]Clark Pinnock, *The Proceedings...*, 75. For an excellent overview of the apparent strengths and weaknesses of this "later" position of Pinnock, see Ray Roennfeldt, *Clark H. Pinnock on Biblical Authority: An Evolving Position* (Berrien Springs, MI: Andrews University Press, 1993), 321-341.

[92]Clark Pinnock, "Bernard Ramm: Postfundamentalist Coming To Terms With Modernity," in *Perspectives on Theology in the Contemporary World: Essays in Honor of Bernard Ramm*, ed. Stanley Grenz (Macon, GA: Mercer University Press, 1990), 26.

[93]Ibid., 24.

Where had Pinnock's journey brought him on the inerrancy debate? The Bible, he had concluded, seldom addresses its "authority" and says nothing about its "inerrancy." The rationalistic (Western) model of biblical authority that Pinnock had learned early from Warfield and others had exaggerated these concepts to fit a system that had been adopted in advance. Pinnock and other evangelicals were now learning "not to force the Bible onto a Procrustean bed of extra-scriptural assumptions about authority and perfection...."[94] Timothy Smith was right:

> Those of us who come from Wesleyan, Lutheran or Calvinist backgrounds draw upon the writings of the Reformers themselves to affirm our conviction that the *meanings*, not the *words*, of biblical passages are authoritative, and that understanding these meanings requires close and critical study of the texts, rather than incantation of supposedly inerrant words.[95]

Gary Dorrien offers good perspective. In mid-career Pinnock had realized that evangelicalism was needlessly struggling and dividing over an assertion of total biblical inerrancy, an assertion that just cannot be sustained by the biblical text itself. So "he redrew the line at infallible-teaching inerrancy and invested the same passion he had earlier shown for strict inerrancy in defending this fallback position against theological relativism."[96] Pinnock now knew that Karl Barth had good reason for rejecting the concept of revelation as primarily "information" (which turns revelation into an object that is available for human control), but he also remained troubled about how this "neo-orthodox rejection had led so much of modern theology to retreat from the belief that revelation yields necessary content, leaving theologians "free to pursue enticing

---

[94]Clark Pinnock, "New Dimensions in Theological Method," in *New Dimensions in Evangelical Thought*, ed. David Dockery (Downers Grove, Ill.: InterVarsity Press, 1998), 204.

[95]Timothy L. Smith, in *The Christian Century* (March 2, 1977), 198. At the time of this writing, Dr. Smith, a Wesleyan, was a member of the Department of History, Johns Hopkins University.

[96]Gary Dorrien, *The Remaking of Evangelical Theology* (Louisville, KY: Westminster John Knox Press, 1998), 140.

doctrines of their own making and preference."[97] There must be forged a middle ground where revelation is real and meaningful without being prejudged and restricted to a human system of thought that is brought to the biblical text more than found in it.

Pinnock had found a relative freedom from an epistemology that is mechanical and rationally restrictive. Biblical texts are not free of the issues of cultural relativism. Biblical revelation is progressive in character, requiring attention to where a text lies in the living organism of Scripture. What something meant originally and what it means authoritatively now may differ, at least at the levels of language and culture. Even so, the "Scripture principle" holds. For Pinnock, the needed nuancing of the inerrancy concept had not violated the heart of what evangelicals had taught all along. Scripture can be trusted to be truthful in all that its teaching affirms. Rather than the "hard rationalist" approach to biblical authority and interpretation, Pinnock had come to appreciate the story and mystery of Scripture, the key role of the Spirit's ministry in original inspiration and current illumination,[98] and the need to listen as well as reason. He now often spoke of "growing as hearers of the Word of God."

Pinnock's conviction had become one of certainty of truth arising more from the work of the Spirit through the biblical text than from a tight rationalism rooted in the supposed human theory of biblical errorlessness. He nonetheless saw a retaining of the "inerrancy" word as the path of wisdom given circumstances in the evangelical community. He also saw the need to carefully nuance the implications of this word given the circumstances of the biblical text itself. He recalled that Paul in 1 Corinthians 2:4 speaks about a certainty which does not result from the wisdom of human words. It is born of the Spirit's witness to human hearts. Finally, then, for adequate biblical interpretation, attention must be given to the key place of authentic piety or Spirit reality in Christian life.

---

[97]Clark Pinnock, *The Scripture Principle*, 26.
[98]For discussion of the coordinate roles of inspiration and illumination as taught by John Wesley, see Barry L. Callen, *God As Loving Grace* (Nappanee, IN: Evangel Publishing House, 1996), 316-323.

The Place of Piety

Clark Pinnock's whole agenda in his early years appears to have been centered in his deep concern to enable conversions to Jesus Christ. As changes came in some of his views, he did not retreat from his central evangelistic concern or rebel and generally reject evangelical Christianity once he had examined it critically. Many others did bolt from their evangelical upbringings and became some of today's liberal theologians. Why not Pinnock? He has suggested that it might have been his temperament, maybe his ability to make changes without throwing out the baby with the bathwater. Perhaps it was "the depth of my conversion which would not be denied, or the fact that I was raised in liberal Christianity and knew how little it has to offer.... Not having been a fundamentalist culturally was a definite advantage."[99] Whatever the reasons, he was on a journey of renewal that later he would characterize as finding his way "from the scholastic to the pietistic approach" to Christian believing and living. In fact, he would see "postmodern" developments in the late twentieth century, with their emphasis on the particular and experiential, as favoring an "evangelical pietism."[100]

Robert Price observes that Pinnock's "whole theological and apologetic structure is built on the foundation of piety.... The right theology is that which is consistent with Evangelical conversion and the bliss of spiritual certainty.... [This] implies that Pinnock's own theology is profoundly, even fundamentally, experience-centered."[101] In fact, this

---

[99]Clark Pinnock in Roennfeldt, xvii.

[100]Clark Pinnock, "Evangelical Theologians Facing the Future: Ancient and Future Paradigms," *Wesleyan Theological Journal* 33:2 (Fall 1998), 11. Note the similar thesis of Pinnock's colleague Stanley Grenz (*Theology for the Community of God*, 1994, x): "I discovered anew the importance of the pietist heritage in which I had been spiritually nurtured. Since 1988, I have been seeking to integrate the rationalistic and pietistic dimensions of the Christian faith.... Thus, while theology may be an intellectual search for truth, this search must always be attached to the foundational, identity producing encounter with God in Christ. And it must issue forth in Christian living."

[101]Robert Price, "Clark H. Pinnock: Conservative and Contemporary," *Evangelical Quarterly* 60:2 (1988), 164. Price notes the logic of grace and prayer and the similarity of Pinnock's theology and that of Schleiermacher, an epistemology "more liberal than he imagines." Pinnock himself resists the correctness of this observation. See further discussion of this in chapter five.

appears to be an overstatement when one considers Pinnock's sturdy defense of a text-oriented revelation, even though he was increasingly coming to value the significance of spiritual experience in relation to biblical interpretation and theological work. True, Pinnock's early publishing was heavy with rational apologetics and extensive defense of a particular understanding of biblical revelation. Already in 1967, however, he was feeling a lack of spiritual reality and evident power in his own life of faith. Maybe he was engaged in too much of a lopsided concentration on the intellectual side of Christian truth. He would not ignore this awkward question, although often it is ignored by professional scholars—including many Christian theologians. What followed for Pinnock was an enlarged spiritual awakening that would significantly shape his future theological concerns and agenda.

It was 1967 in New Orleans when young Professor Pinnock realized that the proper mind-spirit relationship was out of balance for him. He had yielded to a temptation readily available to theologians, exercising primarily the mind at the expense of the heart. Sarah was born to the Pinnocks that year, and Clark suffered a detached retina that left him essentially blind in one eye. The family was living in the French Quarter on Bourbon Street, loving this setting, and so was not particularly a part of the local Baptist seminary culturally. Not required by the seminary to identify with a Baptist congregation, the Pinnocks had chosen to attend Canal Street Presbyterian Church where the pastor was "wonderfully loving" and the congregation "oozed with piety." Here was found an authentic "charismatic" renewal in progress in a mainline church. Pinnock found this congregation "immensely nourishing." He loved to be in a fellowship that seemed "just like New Testament Christianity." While he does not recall the "tongues" phenomenon being a public part of it all, the people certainly were open to God and prayers were regularly answered.[102]

There was much small group life at the Canal Street Church. The Pinnocks were welcomed and often participated. After church one

---

[102]Clark Pinnock, Interview with Barry Callen, April 18, 1998. Despite his rationalism, Pinnock recalls that Francis Schaeffer himself was a genuinely pious man of prayer.

evening, Clark and Dorothy were invited to visit a home fellowship and prayer meeting. The enthusiastic prayers and testimonies of this small group convinced Clark that these were people "alive unto God," as St. Paul says. The result? That evening he asked that hands be laid on him by the group. "I was touched by God that night. I glimpsed the dimension of the Spirit which the New Testament describes but is so often absent in churches today.... Being a Christian became an exciting adventure instead of a drag. I was filled with the Spirit."[103] A close parallel to this experience, in his view, was that of John Wesley in 1738 when his heart was "strangely warmed."

Previously Pinnock had expressed suspicion about any evangelical focus on "charismatic" renewal that was not thoroughly checked by Bible definitions and restrictions. He tended to denigrate subjective religious experiences as indistinguishable from a case of indigestion unless there was an inerrant Bible to separate the true from the false.[104] There was worry that Baptists, mixing non-creedalism with revivalism, tend to locate truth in the saving encounter with Christ—maybe a key reason why many were "ravaged by liberal and later neo-orthodox theology" and thus became vulnerable to theological compromise. This tendency, he judged, "is even more true of the world-wide Pentecostal movement whose emphasis on religious subjectivity is even more complete."[105] During the 1970s, however, Pinnock came to soften his negative critique of pentecostalism, but without granting spiritual experience a position of equal partnership with biblical authority in defining Christian truth. Soon he would freely endorse a more overtly charismatic spirituality. Concludes Robert Rakestraw: "For a Southern Baptist leader in the conservative South in the 1960s this was a remarkable occurrence, indicating in him a thirst for God and His truth wherever that may lead and regardless of whose theological system it

---

[103]Clark Pinnock, *The Untapped Power of Sheer Christianity* (Burlington, Ont.: Welch Publishing Company, 1985), 51. Published in the U. S. as *Three Keys to Spiritual Renewal* (Minneapolis: Bethany House, 1985).

[104]Clark Pinnock, *Set Forth Your Case* (Nutely, N.J.: Craig Press, reprinted by Moody Press, Chicago, 1971), 73.

[105]Clark Pinnock, "Baptists and Biblical Authority," *The Journal of the Evangelical Theological Society* 17 (1974), 203.

may violate."[106] Pinnock later would report a divine healing in his one functioning eye, commenting: "I know from personal experience that one such incident can be worth a bookshelf of academic apologetics for Christianity (including my own books)."[107]

Now he published pace-setting articles in *Christianity Today* with the provocative titles "A Truce Proposal for the Tongues Controversy" (Oct. 8, 1971), "The New Pentecostalism: Reflections by a Well-Wisher" (Sept. 14, 1973), and "Opening the Church to the Charismatic Dimension" (June 12, 1981). He argued that Bible-believing evangelicals would have to find a way to get over their rigid rationalism and inordinate fear of emotional excess in order to avoid a quenching of the Spirit. Pinnock had no personal case to make for any divisive spiritual elitism or for anyone's insistence that a divine gift like "speaking in tongues" is for every believer as a necessary sign of the reception of the Spirit. It was just that he appreciated charismatics as "those evangelicals with a little more spiritual voltage." He was one with them, at least in their claims for the "heart dimension" of the faith—what to him was like returning to the best of the older and less scholastically bound evangelicalism. Later he would observe the following to Southern Baptist scholars in the midst of their scholastic-like resurgence of insistence on the "inerrancy" theory of biblical inspiration:

> Let us not forget that the Jehovahs Witnesses combine strict inerrancy with heretical doctrine, and the Orthodox Lutheran churches of Germany after the Reformation combined strict inerrancy with vehement resistance to the fires of evangelical revivals which were breaking out among the Moravians and Pietists. Strict inerrancy guarantees neither orthodoxy or spiritual life and power.[108]

---

[106]Robert Rakestraw, "Clark Pinnock," in *Baptist Theologians,* eds. Timothy George and David Dockery (Nashville: Broadman Press, 1990), 662. See Appendix A, especially Pinnock's 1999 postscript where he reports: "My own roots spiritually were warmly pietistic and my sympathies charismatic."

[107]Clark Pinnock, "A Revolutionary Promise," review of *Power Evangelism* by John Wimber and Kevin Springer, *Christianity Today* (Aug. 8, 1986), 19.

[108]*Proceedings of the Conference on Biblical Inerrancy, 1987* (Nashville: Broadman Press, 1987), 79-80.

In a sense, Pinnock's doctoral dissertation in 1963 was a sophisticated reflection on his own emerging pietism. Even in his most "ideological" writings in the 1960s, he reports, "I was always pietistic also, but then a pietist anxious to build a rationalistic framework to explain and defend such deep Christian experience."[109] Later this anxiety would lessen, so that he could say: "I love the experiential, the power, the practicality, the mission of the charismatics, not their excesses and peculiarities."[110] He also would write convincingly and movingly about the coordinate roles of mind and heart (in *Flame of Love*, p. 199, for instance) that Pentecostal scholar Terry Cross would offer this generous judgment in 1998:

> Because of its method and message, *Flame of Love* [Pinnock, 1996] is a vital theological treatise for Pentecostals and charismatics. It is the most needful and yet most provocative book I have read in a decade. It is needful for the church at large since the doctrine of the Spirit is visibly absent and the urge to consider the work of the Spirit in our lives is also missing; it is needful for the renewal movement since we are lacking good systematic theological reflection on the whole.[111]

Regarding biblical inspiration and authority, Pinnock has retained a sturdy grip on the significance of real divine revelation dependably made available in the biblical text for serious seekers. Nonetheless, he has been on a spiritual journey himself, and as Millard Erickson has observed, "it is apparent that his aim is not to propound a Barthian view of revelation but to revitalize the evangelical doctrine of illumination of Scripture by the Holy Spirit."[112] Clearly, Pinnock has come to value *function* as much or even more than *form* in the area of biblical authority and meaning, looking with disfavor at any excessive intellectualism and abstraction that detracts from concrete Christian discipleship and mission. The important question to him had come to be: How can

---

[109]Clark Pinnock, Interview with Barry Callen, April 18, 1998.

[110]Clark Pinnock, Interview with Barry Callen, April 19, 1998.

[111]Terry L. Cross, "A Critical Review of Clark Pinnock's *Flame of Love: A Theology of the Holy Spirit*," in *Journal of Pentecostal Theology* 13 (1998), 4.

[112]Millard Erickson, *The Evangelical Left: Encountering Postconservative Evangelical Theology* (Grand Rapids: Baker Books, 1997), 79.

Scripture be a lamp to our feet and a light to our path, the vital function of Scripture that "has little to do with the perfect errorlessness of non-existent autographs and a great deal to do with the continuing authority of a (slightly) imperfect document"?[113] The Christian agenda should be less a preoccupation with a theory of precise inerrancy and much more with a healthy concern for a spiritual power enabled by the Spirit of God who both speaks through ancient Scripture and illumines the contemporary reader for real life and mission.

Pinnock now would seem to agree with Steven Land's conclusion: "Therefore, to do theology is not to make experience the norm, but it is to recognize the epistemological priority of the Holy Spirit in prayerful receptivity."[114] In Pinnock's view, Robert Alley had tried in 1970 to make spiritual experience the Christian norm in his book *Revolt Against the Faithful*. The published book review by Pinnock bluntly announced "the total vacuity and absurdity of his [Alley's] own position." Christianity is not about a "free encounter" with divine reality "that takes place within personal experience and is entirely contentless and self-authenticating." He called Alley's position "an existential humanism in which man gives revelation to himself and salvation is from within." That surely was nowhere close to what Pinnock believed. He called the Alley position "mere psychological illusion." The fact is that "freedom without form is impossible in art or theology."[115] As early as 1966 he had made clear his view that "experience *confirms* the gospel proclamation which history validated and which philosophy studies, but it does not *create* it."[116]

---

[113]Clark Pinnock, "Evangelicals and Inerrancy: The Current Debate," (1978), 68.

[114]Steven J. Land, *Pentecostal Spirituality: A Passion for the Kingdom* (Sheffield, England: Sheffield Academic Press, 1993), 38.

[115]Robert S. Alley, *Revolt Against the Faithful: A Biblical Case for Inspiration as Encounter* (Lippincott, 1970). Pinnock's review of Alley appeared in *Christianity Today* (November 20, 1970), 35-36.

[116]Quote from an address given by Clark Pinnock before the Collegiate Club of Park Street Church in Boston, February 13, 1966, published in the *Park Street Spire* (May 1966), 13. Millard Erickson, in discussing *Revisioning Evangelical Theology* by Stanley Grenz, comments that Grenz (a respected Canadian colleague of Pinnock) "in some ways [is] more radical than Pinnock" since Grenz defines evangelical Christianity "more in terms of a personal relationship to God…[and] a particular spirituality" (Erickson, *The Evangelical Left*, Baker Books, 1997, 45).

What about Robert Price's judgment that Pinnock's own theology is profoundly experience-centered, even experience-generated, making him more of a "liberal" than he himself recognizes? Without question Pinnock has been on a spiritual journey that he refuses to separate from his theological work. Also without question has been his persistent intent to retain a good balance between revealed and experienced truth. On the one hand, he openly and repeatedly rejects the theism of most "process" theologians, in part because he judges their concept of God to be inadequate in the face of the "evangelical experience" and the religious needs of fallen humans.[117] On the other hand, he also rejects the suggestion of Price that, like Schleiermacher, he (Pinnock) has been extrapolating theology from the consciousness of piety. Responds Pinnock: "Just because a person sees more importance in experience than he used to does not make him/her a liberal!"[118] Regarding Schleiermacher's use of religious experience as a critical criterion for assessing the teachings of Christian faith, Pinnock argues:

> The use of an outside criterion by which to understand the kerygma appears to allow the Gospel itself to come under alien control. Instead of Scripture being the norm, theology is governed by the 19th or 20th century cultural ego instead.... We are often attracted by the novel theology which comes up with a brilliant fusion between the Bible and something contemporary. But this is not what God is after. He desires us to be faithful stewards of his Word, who do not seek glory in this age, and do not value what man thinks above what God has said, but open ourselves to his Spirit, walk by faith and not by sight, and proclaim the Gospel with fearlessness and undiminished power.[119]

What does this say about the theological enterprise of Clark Pinnock? He would report in 1985 that it makes one a prophetic voice

---

[117]See, e.g., Clark Pinnock, "Between Classical and Process Theism," in *Process Theology*, ed. Ronald Nash (Grand Rapids: Baker Books, 1987), 313-325.

[118]Clark Pinnock, Letter to Diane DeSmidt, Bethel Theological Seminary, November 11, 1988. Also see Pinnock's *Tracking the Maze* (Harper & Row, 1990, 99ff) for more on his view of the theological method of Schleiermacher.

[119]Clark Pinnock, *Three Keys To Spiritual Renewal* (Minneapolis: Bethany Fellowship, 1985), 95, 100.

within evangelicalism, a voice that speaks on behalf of a balanced and holistic view of Christian life and mission. Why, he asked, are evangelicals so numerous in North America and yet have so little real impact on the society? Renewal is needed and would come only as evangelicals got "our message straight, and our religion vital, and our obedience worthy of the gospel." Here is the strong note of piety: "It is not enough to be biblically sound if we are not spiritually alive at the same time."[120] Here also is a vigorous and practical call to evangelism and social responsibility.[121] Pinnock was moving toward the view more typical of Eastern Christianity that Christian theology is essentially a *practical* endeavor instead of a *theoretical science.*[122] This view encourages a closeness between theological understanding and spiritual life.

Note Pinnock's approving reference to how theologian Donald Bloesch "captures the spirit" of true evangelicalism, moving beyond any preoccupation with detailed and mandatory "doctrinal consensus" to more of "the style of religious experience":

> An evangelical is one who affirms the centrality and cruciality of Christ's work of reconciliation and redemption as declared in the Scriptures; the necessity to appropriate the fruits of this work in one's own life and experience; and the urgency to bring the good news of this act of unmerited grace to a lost and dying world. It is not enough to believe in the cross and resurrection of Christ. We must be personally crucified and buried with Christ and rise with Christ to new life in the Spirit. Yet even this

---

[120]Ibid., 9-11.

[121]Such a stance was being echoed at the same time by William J. Abraham in his provocative book *The Coming Great Revival: Recovering the Full Evangelical Tradition* (San Francisco: Harper & Row, 1984). Abraham observed that Carl F. H. Henry had rejected Pinnock's insistence on a dynamic dimension to the supposed rigid meaning of biblical "inerrancy" (Henry, *God, Revelation and Authority*, vol. 4, Word, 1979, 178). Abraham joined Pinnock in the face of establishment evangelicalism by "proposing that we make a virtue of our failure to reach agreement on the essentials of evangelicalism" (79).

[122]Randy Maddox says that John Wesley also is to be characterized by a "practical divinity" ("John Wesley and Eastern Orthodoxy," *Asbury Theological Journal*, 45:2, 1990, 33).

is not all that is required of us. We must also be fired by a burning zeal to share this salvation with others.[123]

Pinnock had become (or always was) a "good news evangelical." He was willing to risk fresh thinking that might enhance Christian credibility in the service of the church's world mission. For instance, in wondering about the future possibility of more powerful symbols of Christian unity (even a Baptist-friendly papal office!), in 1998 he would recognize "the need to articulate Christian ideas and practices for the whole world to hear and to limit uncontrolled subjectivity of inter-pretation."[124] Here is the important balance. An authentic piety, absolutely! An unchecked subjectivity, never!

These concerns were enlivened increasingly for Pinnock during the 1970s as he reshaped his view of biblical inspiration. He now was on a broader journey that soon would bring change to much of his theological thinking. The story of his broader theological change is the subject of the following chapters. Its settings would be other than New Orleans.[125] The ecclesiastical temperature rose around the Louisiana Baptist campus after Pinnock had been there for a year or two. Some Baptist leaders at the national level quietly considered him a renegade troublemaker who needed to stop his righteous crusading.[126] President Eddleman felt this heat and urged the Pinnock family to move onto the campus—a symbol of "getting in line," even while he shifted his primary

---

[123]Donald Bloesch, *The Future of Evangelical Christianity*, 17, as quoted by Clark Pinnock, "Evangelical Theology in Progress," in *Introduction to Christian Theology*, ed. Roger Bedham (Louisville: Westminster John Knox Press, 1998), 77. Pinnock adds: "Bloesch came to the [evangelical] movement, not from fundamentalism, but from an older evangelicalism of German pietism in the Protestant mainline. He illustrates the success of neofundamentalism in attracting such eminent scholars" (83).

[124]Clark Pinnock, "Does Christian Unity Require Some Form of Papal Primacy?" *Journal of Ecumenical Studies*, 35:3-4 (Summer-Fall, 1998), 380.

[125]Pinnock continued to experience his ecclesial identity as primarily parachurch or ecumenical (wherever the Spirit was at work). Although a loyal Baptist by heritage, he found the New Orleans seminary scene to be awkward for him since it was so important there for people to be Baptist.

[126]See Appendix A, especially Pinnock's 1999 postscript where he laments his call in the 1960s to "ecclesiastical warfare and schism." In the late 1960s, he now reflects, "I found myself heralded as a conservative voice and I succumbed to the populist adulation."

teaching focus from New Testament to theology where the president and he thought that he could have more conservative influence. Influential he was, but long-term at the Baptist seminary he was not.

By 1968 he had become an active member of the Evangelical Theological Society, had become acquainted with Kenneth Kantzer, then Dean of Trinity Evangelical Divinity School, and was doing some teaching at Trinity by traveling on weekends by air.[127] That seminary was growing and was more northern in location, like the family roots of both Clark in Ontario and his wife Dorothy in Wisconsin. An invitation for a full-time position in systematic theology came, and the Pinnocks decided to leave New Orleans in 1969 to move north. They bought a home in nearby Kenosha, Wisconsin (Dorothy's hometown), and joined the Trinity family. This was a long way from the culture and pace of the deep south.

The Trinity campus was six miles from the shores of Lake Michigan, twenty-five miles north of the famous Chicago "Loop," and only fifteen miles from O'Hare Airport, then the busiest in the world. Clark Pinnock was moving into the middle of a dynamic and influential place. He would flourish and change in several significant ways in the years immediately ahead. Always biblical in orientation and clearly now on a journey of understanding in relation to the nature and authority of the Bible for contemporary Christians, Pinnock's coming change would flow from such an altered understanding of the Bible itself. For Pinnock, theological orientation is to be a reflection of biblical teaching. Soon his understanding of select highlights of such teaching would bring tension and change to the "system" he unconsciously had been bringing to, and laying on, the biblical text.

---

[127]Trinity Evangelical Divinity School was a seminary of The Evangelical Free Church of America. Dr. Kantzer had been Dean since 1963 and was key to the gathering of numerous evangelical scholars to that growing campus. According to the 1970-1971 catalog (p. 32): Outstanding teachers "noted for their staunch defense of orthodox Christianity and committed to earnest piety and evangelical faith…were added to the faculty from many denominations." One was a Baptist, Clark Pinnock.

4

Unraveling Reformed Scholasticism

I thought it would be wonderful to possess absolute truths, based on heavenly oracles, yielding black and white doctrinal and ethical maxims. Once one buys into this framework, it takes time for doubts about its philosophical validity and theological appropriateness to dawn.[1]

...one of the links in the chain of the tight Calvinian logic broke. It had to do with the doctrine of the perseverance of the saints.... What had dawned on me was...that there is a profound mutuality in our dealings with God.[2]

Beginning with his arrival on campus in 1969, Clark Pinnock found Trinity Evangelical Divinity School to be "a great place," a stimulating environment with wonderful students and renowned colleagues like Gleason Archer, Jr., in Old Testament, Gary Collins in pastoral psychology, Kenneth Kantzer in biblical and systematic theology (and Dean), and John W. Montgomery in church history. To Pinnock this campus resembled an InterVarsity setting. It was biblical, evangelistic, interdenominational, and mildly rationalistic. He was right at home.

---

[1]Clark Pinnock, unpublished paper delivered at the evangelical-process dialogue convened at Claremont School of Theology, 1997.

[2]Clark Pinnock, "From Augustine To Arminius: A Pilgrimage in Theology," in *The Grace of God and the Will of Man*, ed. Clark Pinnock, (Zondervan, 1989, rev. ed., Minneapolis: Bethany Publishing House, 1995), 17-18.

This school expected genuine scholarship that was built on a strong biblical base. The place "fit me perfectly, both my Bruce and Schaeffer sides."[3] His love of new insights, his willingness to be creative, his hunger to learn and grow, and his unusually active mind quickly made him a very popular teacher on the Trinity campus. He soon became close to students like Grant Osborne who, while yet a student, had an important impact on Pinnock and later would himself become a long-term faculty member at Trinity.[4]

It now was time for Pinnock to grow, search, and even risk. He soon would call Trinity a "ghetto," that is, a "cognitively defiant institution…[that] stands against a host of modern opinions held to be unquestionable at other schools." Trinity, he reported as a committed faculty member, "exists to supply the well-honed intellectual weapons to stave off the overt and inovert assaults made upon the Christian faith by the armies of secularity." At this time Pinnock viewed non-evangelical options as "wearing pretty thin." Consequently, he understood Trinity to be "the launching pad for an evangelical counterattack on the tottering secular culture and the disintegrating theological playground."[5] His educational experience and personal instincts had prepared him well to help lead such a counterattack.

Organizationally speaking, he now brought to bear one aspect of his earlier experience in England. The Theological Students Fellowship (TSF) originally was a branch of the British InterVarsity Christian Fellowship, designed to help university and seminary students stay evangelical throughout their academic lives. Pinnock had first met J. I. Packer at an English TSF conference and reports that this organization "very much met my needs as a young evangelical in England."[6] Now Professor Pinnock decided that a TSF was needed in North America. So from his base at Trinity he launched such an organization in 1973. It soon developed the *TSF Bulletin*, an innovative periodical in which Pinnock often published articles and book reviews. For the years to

---

[3]Clark Pinnock, Interview with Barry Callen, April 18, 1998.

[4]Source: a January 1999 telephone interview. For more detail, see chapter 6.

[5]Clark Pinnock, "Trinity is a Ghetto," *The Scribe* (student publication of Trinity Evangelical Divinity School), 1:7, n.d., n.p.

[6]Clark Pinnock, Interview with Barry Callen, April 19, 1998.

come, with Pinnock happily moving away from a key administrative role in its organization, the American TSF would gather students at Trinity, Harvard, Yale, and elsewhere to encourage their evangelical commitments and stimulate their scholarly potentials. It was a distinctive and crucial ministry.

Clark Pinnock was increasingly active theologically during his five Trinity years (1969-1974). If seeking continuing confidence in the accuracy and authority of revealed truth was a central preoccupation in the evangelical community of the 1960s and 1970s, the search was not without its considerable ferment. Pinnock placed himself in the center of the action. This was the case on both the fronts of first defending biblical inerrancy and then crossing a hazardous frontier by seeking to unravel the scholasticized, Calvinistic logic which had been the dominant, defining paradigm for much of twentieth-century American conservatism—and the formative paradigm for Pinnock himself. At this stage of Pinnock's journey, he was intending only to engage in modest modifications of what now appeared to be certain unjustified Calvinistic extremes, somewhat like Norman Geisler is now doing with his critique of "extreme Calvinism."[7] Broaching this frontier of modifications would be central for the future decades of Pinnock's work. For him, what at first was a careful nuancing of certain aspects of the Calvinistic tradition eventually would lead him well beyond Geisler's limited agenda to truly significant alterations of the received tradition.

Toward a More Dynamic Theology

During the early 1970s Clark Pinnock thought that he had only entered into a process of making some select theological adjustments to his received theological tradition. This tradition was the scholastic paradigm that supported a deterministic mindset and its strict view that biblical inerrancy is the necessary foundation for a sound pattern of Christian believing and witnessing. He later came to understand that something more extensive was in process in his case. Specifically:

---

[7]Norman Geisler, *Chosen But Free: A Balanced View of Divine Election* (Minneapolis: Bethany House Publishers, 1999).

I was also moving away from the larger framework of Calvinism
itself to more dynamic ways of thinking theologically. I was
being drawn to a new orientation which sees God as love, away
from the view of God as authoritarian and austere judge. I was
giving up the view according to which God is thought to relate
primarily to us as all-determining monarch and law-giver and
shifting to the paradigm in which God relates to us primarily as
parent, lover, and covenant partner.[8]

He was coming to realize that the quest for certainty in faith,
typically evidenced by the insistence on inerrancy of the biblical text, is
but one key reflection of the creed of Reformed scholasticism.[9]
Underlying this creed is the foundational assertion of the supposed
total divine control of this present world, an assertion that Pinnock
was beginning to question. Although at first he was hardly intentional
about pursuing an agenda of "postmodernizing" Christian faith,
Pinnock nonetheless was doing just that in the "soft" sense described and
affirmed by a prominent theological colleague.[10]

---

[8]Clark Pinnock, foreword to *Clark Pinnock on Biblical Authority*, by Ray
Roennfeldt (Berrien Springs, MI: Andrews University Press, 1993), xx-xxi.

[9]It should be noted that Pinnock distinguishes between Reformed theology
generally and the scholastic (fundamentalistic) version of it so common in
contemporary evangelicalism. Once he referred to the "noble tradition" of Calvinism
which, he recognizes, can be pursued in non-fundamentalist ways. He had been
nurtured personally in a five-point Calvinism that valued highly the propositional
nature of a sturdy foundationalism. It was against this rigid five-point framework that
he now was reacting. Notice that even Norman Geisler, a Thomistic-style Calvinist well
known for his extensive writing and debating on the subject, now proposes a more
"moderate Calvinistic view" featuring a fresh evaluation of the Canons of Dort (1619),
which he says are "widely considered to be a modern origin of extreme Calvinism"
(Geisler, *Chosen But Free*, 1999, Appendix 8).

[10]Millard Erickson, *Postmodernizing the Faith: Evangelical Responses to the
Challenge of Postmodernism* (Grand Rapids: Baker Books, 1998), 18-20. Erickson
thinks of the "hard" variety of postmodernizing as the agenda of radical
deconstructionism that rejects almost entirely both objectivity and rationality in favor
of a pluralism of personal truths. He expresses both appreciation for and caution about
the "softer" agenda of Pinnock and his Canadian colleague Stanley Grenz (83-102).
The caution disputes any tendency to characterize North American evangelicalism after
the 1940s as a mindset based heavily on the Enlightenment approach to knowledge and
truth. Speaking specifically of Grenz, Erickson concludes: "But to the degree that in the
desire to make his theology harmonious with postmodernism, it has modified received
evangelicalism, it cannot serve as a valid option for us" (102).

Pinnock's theological journey now was leading away from the rationalistic mindset in which he had been formed originally.[11] He was seeing with increasing clarity that "evangelical" is a word that belongs to the whole church (meaning simply "gospel" people) and must not be restricted to "a conservative, postfundamentalist subculture in the church," even to a "subsect of the subculture."[12] So Pinnock found himself following a contemporary track described by William Abraham as moving from "criterion to canon," reversing a long negative trend from "ecclesial canonicity to epistemic normativity." Pinnock was joining what Abraham further calls "a Protestant underworld of protest" which seeks the fuller canonicity of the early church. Thus:

> Pietism, early Methodism, and Pentecostalism represent a Protestant underworld of protest which has sought to return to a soteriological vision of the Scriptures. Uneasy with a purely cognitive approach to the Christian faith, its inhabitants have searched the Scriptures for salvation....[13]

Pinnock was pietistic, prone to search the Scriptures for fresh insight, and willing to protest when long-standing inadequacies were thought to be found.

The Westminster Confession asserts that "God from all eternity did, by the most wise and holy counsel of his own will, freely and un-

---

[11]As Pinnock was moving away from the Calvinistic mindset to a more open, dynamic, and in many ways Wesleyan stance, J. Kenneth Grider, in discussing the inerrancy issue, was urging the Wesleyan Theological Society in a similar way to not accept readily the "spillover from the right wing of the larger segment of the evangelical camp, Calvinistic evangelicalism" (*Wesleyan Theological Journal*, Fall 1984, 60). By 1984 Pinnock had become a champion of views that would resist vigorously any such "spillover." He was criticized by people like Donald Bloesch who judged compromisingly "avant-garde" any championing of a postmodern theology (Thomas Oden or Clark Pinnock) "because of its avoidance of metaphysical questions, its seeming idealization of the past, and its virtual reduction of the gospel to narrative" (*Holy Scripture*, 1994, 14). Despite the admitted value of such caution, Pinnock nonetheless judged it crucial to proceed with changes that caused some colleagues considerable concern.

[12]Clark Pinnock, "Evangelical Theology in Progress," in *Introduction to Christian Theology*, ed. Roger Badham (Louisville: Westminster John Knox Press, 1998), 75.

[13]William Abraham, *Canon and Criterion in Christian Theology* (Oxford: Clarendon Press, 1998), 474.

changeably ordain *whatsoever* comes to pass." A natural perspective derived from such an all-pervasive divine ordination is the deductive thinking of inerrancy which is rooted in the assumption of total divine control. But it is this very assumption that Pinnock was now starting to question openly, both biblically and theologically. So far as biblical inspiration is concerned, altering this assertion would mean that evangelicals could allow for a real human element in the composition of the Bible, a humanity that stands in a dynamic relation to the strong and coordinate role of the Spirit of God. Pinnock wanted to avoid "both the idea that the Bible is the product of mere human genius and the idea it came about through mechanical dictation. The *via media* lies in the direction of a dynamic personal model that upholds both the divine initiative and the human response."[14]

In 1979 Harold Lindsell had expressed the hope that Pinnock would go no further than limiting inerrancy to matters of Christian faith and practice, but "his uneven track record leaves some of us with an uneasy thought that additional damaging concessions may be on the way."[15] More indeed would come. Characterizing them as "damaging concessions" is, of course, only a matter of judgment. Pinnock would be more inclined to refer to them as fresh biblical insights that join to form a new and liberating theological paradigm. These fresh insights came to Pinnock largely in his years on the faculty of Trinity Evangelical Divinity School (1969-1974), years of great turmoil in the culture and in a seminary setting that stimulated and supported Pinnock's creativity. This creativity focused primarily on breaking the chain of Calvinistic

---

[14]Clark Pinnock, *The Scripture Principle* (San Francisco: Harper & Row, 1984), 103. See Appendix D in this present work, especially Pinnock's 1999 postscript in which he observes: "In addition to rationalism and militancy, Calvinistic theology was part and parcel of fundamentalistic evangelicalism. The original movement was an alliance of the dispensationalists and the old Princeton Presbyterians (among others). Thus it was that, along with other problems, there came theological determinism into the evangelical stream. It would mean (at least for me) that the doctrine of the attributes of God would need rethinking, as well as epistemology and the doctrine of Scripture. My 1989 writing ["From Augustine To Arminius: A Pilgrimage In Theology," in *The Grace of God and the Will of Man*] is part of my testimony about how I got free from hyper-transcendence. Had I been a Wesleyan, I might have had an easier time of it."

[15]Harold Lindsell, *The Bible in the Balance* (Grand Rapids: Zondervan, 1979), 43.

logic, a chain which much of evangelical Christianity insisted cannot be broken without serious doctrinal consequences. Maybe, concluded Pinnock, failing to break it is where the negative theological and doctrinal consequences really lay.

In brief, this chain of theological logic proceeds with its argumentation as follows. The one rock on which Calvinism builds is an assumption of the absolute and wholly unlimited sovereignty of the eternal and self-existent God. Humans are held to be in a radically fallen condition because of sin, and thus are unable to take any dependable initiative in spiritual matters. The moral inability of sinners places God on the throne where only God belongs. Then comes divine initiative as only God chooses. The truth contents of the Bible are revealed by God. Real religion rests on this divine revelation, not on human opinions and reasoning. God's objective revelation in the Bible can be accepted only through the exercise of a God-given faith. Salvation for humans, illumined by biblical revelation, is the outcome of divine election only; it is a matter of unmerited grace and nothing else. According to the Bible, God has graciously elected only some to salvation, with none deserving. This electing grace is irresistible. It regenerates those elect people who were hopelessly depraved. Those who have been predestined for salvation are promised the final perseverance of their election. What God sovereignly begins, God sovereignly will end. Those not elected will receive their terrible and fully warranted eternal punishment.

B. B. Warfield once summarized the central characteristics of a true Calvinistic believer: "The Calvinist is the man who sees God behind all phenomena and, in all that occurs, recognizes the hand of God working out His will; who makes the attitude of the soul to God in prayer its permanent attitude in all its life-activities; and who casts himself on the grace of God alone, excluding every trace of dependence on self from the whole work of his salvation."[16] Ben Warburton makes the common assertion that "there are no broken links in this golden chain of truth."[17] Pinnock was coming to judge that, while this assertion may be right

---

[16]B. B. Warfield, *Calvin as a Theologian and Calvinism Today* (Philadelphia: Presbyterian Board of Publication, 1909), 23-24.

[17]Ben A. Warburton, *Calvinism* (Grand Rapids: Eerdmans, 1955), 171.

within this tight logical framework, Calvinism generally may be wrong about the appropriateness of the chain as a whole. It may be a coherent line of reasoning that, because of faulty assumptions at the beginning of the argument, is seriously flawed in several of its outcomes.

Increasingly Pinnock now was asking and pursuing alternate answers to important theological questions. What about an evangelical community that relies heavily on this Calvinistic chain of truth logic? What about the assumptions behind this reliance? Is the chain as biblical as it is confidently claimed to be? What would be the results if the assumptions were challenged on biblical grounds? Initially he welcomed the foundationalism of the Calvinist system as an effective apologetic tool and an avenue to theological certainty. Later, however, he offered this self-criticism: "I thought it would be wonderful to possess absolute truths, based on heavenly oracles, yielding black and white doctrinal and ethical maxims. Once one buys into this framework, it takes time for doubts about its philosophical validity and theological appropriateness to dawn."[18] For Pinnock, the dawning came during the 1970s. He realized that there was at least one faulty assumption at the very beginning of the Calvinistic chain of logic—a misfocused perception of God. The resulting weakness of the whole chain had led to a series of inadequate conclusions that needed challenging for the sake of contemporary Christian mission.

If contemporary evangelicalism is pictured as a tent, how big is it? Would there be room for Clark Pinnock's challenge of the reigning deterministic scholasticism? Beyond the large numbers of adherents that the tent obviously must accommodate, what range of diversity can it handle and will it tolerate? Pinnock's respected friend Roger Olson has argued for a theological core that both defines an "evangelical" minimum and allows for the presence of both "traditionalists" and "reformists" in the big tent. Both groups, he says, "passionately embrace the basic evangelical paradigm and work out of it." But one group seeks to defend absolute boundaries, judging traditional theological formulations as "first-order language of revelation." The other prefers to

---

[18]Clark Pinnock, unpublished paper delivered at the evangelical-process dialogue convened at Claremont School of Theology, 1997.

keep the boundaries relatively undefined and under examination, judging doctrinal formulations to be more fragile second-order language. Reformist thinkers are said to look to a scholar like Clark Pinnock as pioneering a "cautious, biblically committed evangelical reformism."[19] But will the evangelical big tent tolerate such reformism?[20] Evidence of possible intolerance was made evident when Thomas Oden and Timothy George responded to this Olson analysis.

Oden said that Pinnock is not generally anxiety producing for him as long as he manages to remain "centered in the apostolic testimony and not fixated upon modern accommodation." He proceeded, however, to identify one point in Pinnock's work as "a heresy that must be rejected on scriptural grounds" (a proposed limitation of divine omniscience). Timothy George, expressing appreciation for Pinnock, nonetheless felt the need to recall that he earlier judged one of Pinnock's writings on theism as "a misguided, though well-meant, effort to construct a user-friendly God for a North American elite."[21] What was Olson's reaction to these comments of Oden and George? They seemed to him "somewhat overblown in terms of defensiveness and at times even border on offensiveness.... There is room within the evangelical theological community for *both* staunch defense of the Great Tradition of the church universal *and* ongoing examination of its details in light of God's Word." Olson notes the irony that Oden (a Methodist) and George (a Baptist) represent traditions that "began with very controversial reforming achievements."[22] Accommodation to modern culture is always an easy accusation to make, but not an easy one to lay successfully on Pinnock when Pinnock's work is examined carefully and

---

[19]Roger Olson, "The Future of Evangelical Theology," *Christianity Today* (February 9, 1998), 41-42.

[20]Roger Olson posed this important question again in his *Christianity Today* article titled "Don't Hate Me Because I'm Arminian" (Sept. 6, 1999, 87-94).

[21]The comments of Thomas Oden and Timothy George also appear in the February 9, 1998, issue of *Christianity Today*. George's earlier criticism of Pinnock's theism was in reference to the book *The Openness of God* (by Pinnock and others, InterVarsity Press, 1994).

[22]Roger Olson, published letter to the Editor, *Christianity Today* (April 6, 1998), 7.

holistically.[23] Are Oden and George, admittedly outstanding evangelical scholars and churchmen, committed more than they realize to the history and traditions of evangelicalism itself, even at points at the expense of adequate openness to the fresh voice of the Spirit through Scripture? The answer may not be obvious to all, but it is an important one to ask.

It was becoming the working thesis of Clark Pinnock that a truly valid and fully adequate evangelical theology will run the risk of displeasing both conservatives content to rehearse the doctrinal slogans of the past and liberals so committed to the modernistic agendas of the present that they are prepared to be freed from the constrictions of biblical norms. In running this risk, Pinnock was classed by Millard Erickson at the end of the twentieth century as a leader of the postconservative "evangelical left,"[24] the best-known theologian who by then had produced the most writing over the longest time. These post-conservatives are said to acknowledge the historically conditioned character of all theology. While continuing to affirm the central role of biblical revelation, other sources of influence are affirmed. Pinnock, for example, increasingly would appreciate the breadth and balance of the "Wesleyan Quadrilateral" (Bible, tradition, reason, and experience)[25] and contrast a narrative style of theology with what he had come to judge the less appropriate older style of propositionalism. As Erickson summarizes:

> Propositional theology forms concepts and asks for an intellectual response.... Narrative theology, on the other hand, proclaims the Good News of Christ, and thinks about how to express it and live it; it tells stories that cannot be completely captured in logical systems; rather than spurring debate, it

---

[23]In the book *Theological Crossfire*, for instance, it is Pinnock who is openly critical of the liberalism of Delwin Brown precisely because, in Pinnock's view, it gives excessive weight to modern perspectives against the normative biblical tradition from the past.

[24]Millard Erickson, *The Evangelical Left* (Grand Rapids: Baker Books, 1997), 30-31. Others featured in Erickson's analysis are Bernard Ramm, Stanley Grenz, and James McClendon.

[25]Clark Pinnock, *Tracking the Maze* (San Francisco: Harper and Row, 1990), 171ff. Also see Pinnock and Delwin Brown, *Theological Crossfire* (Grand Rapids: Zondervan, 1990), 40-44.

evokes participation and following of Christ. It integrates knowing and doing better than propositional theology.[26]

The move "leftward" among some evangelical theologians, Clark Pinnock being prominent among them, is motivated in part by reactions to the excessive structures of their earlier conservative orientations. Erickson names Pinnock as "most conspicuous" in this regard. He and the others are said to have less immediate experience with the unfortunate effects of liberalism and thus have focused much on the downsides of "establishment" evangelicalism. Erickson is concerned that the result is a "functional-existential" concept of truth that will have an increasingly negative influence on theology, especially in another generation.[27]

While this concern certainly has not been ignored by Pinnock, he nonetheless has chosen to champion the potential rather than be paralyzed by the possible pitfalls that admittedly exist with an open and dialogical stance to the doing of Christian theology today. He has proceeded with an obvious evangelical reserve, but also with relatively little evidence of either fear or hesitancy. Identifying the major theological division now existing among Christians as the liberal-evangelical gap, he concludes: "Our two modes of interpreting Christian faith in the modern world need to confront one another for the good of the church—for purposes of reconciliation, self-criticism, and mutual enrichment.... This is not to say the dialogue will be easy, only that it is necessary."[28] Moving beyond the mere theory of this affirmation, Pinnock, an evangelical, developed a respectful friendship with Delwin Brown, a liberal, and during the 1980s participated with him in occasional public debates that finally led to the dialogically organized book *Theological Crossfire* (1990) which these two men co-authored. In this book Pinnock affirmed that the common task of the two theological modes, which provides a good basis for a potentially constructive dialogue, is "to correlate the Christian message with human existence,"

---

[26]Ibid., 43-44.

[27]Erickson, *The Evangelical Left*, 12, 137.

[28]Clark Pinnock, in Pinnock and Delwin Brown, *Theological Crossfire: An Evangelical/Liberal Dialogue* (Grand Rapids: Zondervan, 1990), 10.

with evangelicals "relatively more preoccupied with the message pole and liberals relatively more with the pole of human existence." Evangelicals "treasure a truth deposit that we believe we must guard and steward" while liberal theologians "are creative people who are willing to run the risks of being discontinuous with Christian tradition."[29] The difference lies in the balance that each gives to the wisdom of the past versus judgments characteristic of the present time. Conservatives finally rely on the truth believed to be in Christ as biblically reported; liberals certainly are open to the Christian past, but finally tend to live by the best of modern conclusions.

For Pinnock, Christian theology ultimately rests on divine revelation in history, especially in Jesus the Christ. The Bible is central, although the exact nature of biblical revelation requires some reconsideration now that the Bible's own historical character has been opened to our fuller understanding (more than when conservatives saw the Bible rather woodenly as a catalog of pre-formed truths, the source of definitive doctrinal propositions). The dilemma is that the truth lies somewhere between an old fundamentalism that stands on an inflexible body of fixed content as the standard of orthodoxy and a Rudolf Bultmann who sees the New Testament issuing existential challenges to needy modern humans without offering reliable historical information or religious dogmas. For Pinnock, Christianity indeed is a doctrinal faith, with real truth content that informs and inspires rather than merely arising from and addressing contemporary human experience. Even so, evangelical/liberal dialogue is crucial in pursuit of the larger truth. Pinnock and Delwin Brown have engaged in their public debates on theology because of their mutual belief that to do so serves the church well. Here is Brown's evaluation of this process:

> I, the liberal in this discussion, was raised in a small evangelical group. Clark Pinnock, the evangelical or conservative, was raised in mainline Protestantism. We share the fact that we intentionally, and largely for theological reasons, departed from our pasts. But we also share the fact that we left our traditions aware of their gifts, their strengths, as well as their shortcomings. We

---

[29]Ibid., 11, 13.

find it unfortunate that so many of our present allies, Pinnock's conservative colleagues and my liberal ones, are so thoroughly ignorant of the splendid histories and the inner realities of the other side. We are disturbed by the occasional smugness that perpetuates this ignorance. We believe that liberalism and evangelicalism are both inadequate as they are. We think that both would benefit from a dialogue with their counterparts in North American Christianity.[30]

A priority of Clark Pinnock early in his journey had been to support effective Christian evangelism by arguing for the faith's intellectual integrity and fully accurate revelation in the Bible. His early view was that a Calvinistic theological orientation was an essential part of valid Christian believing and evangelizing. So much was this the case that in 1983 the satirical publication *The Wittenberg Door* teased by identifying Pinnock's appropriate academic title and institution and then adding this without qualification: Pinnock "is presently translating Calvin's *Institutes* into Navajo sign language."[31] Any alternative (like Arminianism) was judged unacceptable since presumably it would imply that sinners could somehow aid in their own salvation—which is by *grace alone*.[32] At the same time, he was taking an early first step away from adherence to a strict Calvinism. Sinners *can* do something on behalf of their own salvation, if that something is only to listen and consider the claims of Christ. Surely, where there is a high level of *accountability*, there is granted some level of real *ability* to hear and respond to the overture of divine grace, thus making one truly *responsible*.

In part it was out of his frustration that Clark Pinnock edited the book *Grace Unlimited* in 1975. He wanted to help give "a louder voice to the silent majority of Arminian evangelicals." His perception was that only a few evangelical theologians were prepared "to go to bat for non-Augustinian opinions" even though the believing masses appeared to him to take for granted a belief in human free will, and virtually all evangelists "seem to herald the universal salvific will of God without hedging." Why, then, this frustrating irony? Pinnock judged that it was

---

[30]Ibid., 17.

[31]*The Wittenberg Door* (December 1982—January 1983), 18.

[32]Clark Pinnock, *Evangelism and Truth* (Tigerville, S.C.: Jewel Books, 1969), 28-29.

because Calvinists still maintained substantial control of the teaching of theology in the large evangelical seminaries, the largest publishing houses, and the inerrancy movement.[33] This was true despite the facts that their overall influence had been lessening since the 1950s and that it had become harder to find a Calvinist theologian "willing to defend Reformed theology…in all its rigorous particulars now that Gordon Clark is no longer with us [1902-1986] and John Gerstner is retired."[34]

Pinnock had found himself ready to break free of the prison of some of these "rigorous particulars" and begin a quest for a more adequate Christian theology. Adequacy would necessarily involve doing theology in a more dynamic way as the Spirit of God might lead. Many years later he would characterize his approach this way:

> I often try to break new ground as a theologian. Theology is such an adventure and a rich feast. Surely a Spirit-led orientation in theology will not produce theological tedium or the stuck-in-the-mud kind of work associated with standard evangelical theology. There is so much to be done and the Spirit will make me thirsty to see that it gets done.[35]

The Results of Reciprocity

The significant theological changes in Clark Pinnock's thinking during the 1970s were enabled primarily by having "the insight of reciprocity in hand."[36] Although not at first consciously aware or intentionally motivated by particular Christian traditions that in significant ways are reciprocity oriented, Pinnock soon realized that his emerging biblical insights were deep in various Christian traditions. His insights were both very old and quite fresh.

---

[33]A good source for understanding American evangelicalism since the 1940s is the autobiography of Carl F. H. Henry (*Confessions of a Theologian*, Word Books, 1986). He details his own key roles in the launching of Fuller Theological Seminary and the influential periodical *Christianity Today*.

[34]Clark Pinnock, "From Augustine To Arminius…," 26-27.

[35]Clark Pinnock, from his Azusa Street Lecture, Regent University, Virginia Beach, Virginia, April 20, 1999 (forthcoming in a 2000 issue of *Journal of Pentecostal Theology* as "Divine Relationality: A Pentecostal Contribution to the Doctrine of God").

[36]Clark Pinnock, "From Augustine To Arminius…," 19.

The large and ancient Christian Orthodox tradition of the East, for example, does not assume that the human fall into sin has deprived persons of all divine grace or responsibility for responding to God's offer of restored relationship with Christ. Salvation necessarily involves cooperation in divine-human interrelations. While Western theologians typically have shied from such reciprocity, fearing a works-righteousness heresy, Eastern theologians have insisted that, while never *meriting* God's acceptance because of human action, it nonetheless is the case that God's freely-bestowed grace empowers humans for responsible cooperation. John Wesley affirmed the universal gift of "prevenient grace," probably deriving this view largely from early Greek theology (especially Macarius).[37] Pinnock now joined this long trail of church tradition, freshly championing a divine-human mutuality that would stimulate a wave of theological innovation in evangelical circles ("innovation" meaning a reconsideration of things quite old). If John Wesley had united "pardon" and "participation" motifs, resulting in what some judge his greatest contribution to ecumenical dialogue,[38] Pinnock now was beginning a similar journey that he hoped would make a significant contribution to the renewal of contemporary evangelicalism.

Even though some critics have assigned other motives to his pattern of theological changes in the 1970s, Pinnock claims that they were driven by his own reflections on biblical teaching. With respect to the central issue of the nature of the Bible's inspiration and authority, the differences between the young and mature Pinnock probably are best explained in the larger context of his theological paradigm shift. Ray Roennfeldt explains:

> In the formulation of his early view of Scripture, Pinnock used the presuppositions of Reformed theism, whereas the later Pinnock consciously works from a more Arminian model

---

[37]Randy Maddox, "John Wesley and Eastern Orthodoxy," *Asbury Theological Journal*, 45:2 (1990), 35. Maddox develops Wesley's whole theological vision around the concept of "responsible grace" (*Responsible Grace*, Nashville: Kingswood Books, Abingdon Press, 1994).

[38]See, for example, Albert Outler, "The Place of Wesley in the Christian Tradition," in *The Place of Wesley in the Christian Tradition*, ed. K. A. Rowe (Metuchen, NJ: Scarecrow, 1976), 30.

without rejecting all aspects of Calvinism. He now [1993] considers that Scripture should be understood as the result of both divine initiative and human response. It is his contention that a strict belief in biblical inerrancy is incompatible with anything less than belief in Calvinistic determinism. The Arminian paradigm, which took about ten years to affect Pinnock's doctrine of Scripture, has been gradually filtering down into all of his theological reflections.[39]

It is this process of "filtering down" that brings the pattern of theological change. This pattern may be called the results of reciprocity.

The first link in the Calvinistic chain to break for Pinnock was the doctrine of the perseverance of the saints. At this time he was teaching at Trinity Evangelical Divinity School and giving attention to the book of Hebrews. Why, he wondered, are Christians warned not to fall away from Christ (e.g., Heb. 10:26) and exhorted to persevere (e.g., Heb. 3:12) if they enjoyed the absolute security taught by Calvinism?[40] In fact, human responses to God are taken seriously by God. Is there not a dialectic of divine and human interaction, a relationship of reciprocity? The garment of Calvinism started coming apart with this realization of the essential and extensive truth of reciprocity. A believer's security in God is linked to the faith relationship with God that must be intentionally maintained and never forsaken. In other words, there is a "profound mutuality" between God and believers.[41] God's will can be frustrated by human intransigence. A believer's continuance in the saving grace of God depends, at least in part, on the human partner in the divine-human relationship. Pinnock now was beginning to understand that, once the factors of reciprocity and conditionality are introduced, the landscape of theology is altered significantly. He could begin to regard people "not as a product of a timeless decree but as God's

---

[39]Ray C. W. Roennfeldt, *Clark H. Pinnock on Biblical Authority: An Evolving Position* (Berrien Springs, MI: Andrews University Press, 1993), 364.

[40]It is to be recalled that the teachings of John Calvin himself and what later was formalized as "Calvinism" (e.g., at the Synod of Dort in 1618-19) are not always identical.

[41]Clark Pinnock was influenced by I. Howard Marshall's examination of the security issue (*Kept by the Power of God*, 1969).

covenant partners and real players in the flow and the tapestry of history."[42]

A sure early signal of Clark Pinnock's theological shifting can be seen in his essay contributed to the 1971 festschrift honoring Cornelius Van Til, titled *Jerusalem and Athens*. Pinnock criticized Van Til's dependence on Calvinistic presuppositions and indicated his own increasing tendency to assume a relative autonomy of humans who have been divinely created with a meaningful freedom for choice and responsibility.[43] He began to note that scholars like I. Howard Marshall were reading the Bible differently than did those with a Calvinist mindset, especially in regard to God's relations with the world. Human responses actually do matter to God. Two forces now were at work in Pinnock. First, as an experienced apologist in the Calvinistic tradition, he tended to think logically, seeing a systematic sequence of results naturally emerging from his new premise of reciprocity. Second, and he insists more basic, was biblical teaching itself. When reconsidered in light of God-human mutuality, the Bible presents itself as highly congenial to the fresh insights being inspired by the concept of reciprocity.

Five doctrinal moves occurred for Pinnock during the 1970s, all results of the reciprocity assumption.[44] They may be summarized briefly as follows.

---

[42]Pinnock, "From Augustine To Arminius…," 18. Pinnock's colleague and friend John Sanders was traveling a similar road. The shift in theistic view first came to him through Bible reading, especially in relation to petitionary prayer. Why pray in a petitionary way if God already has determined everything? To the contrary, he observed, there is a divine-human mutuality (see Sanders, *The God Who Risks*, InterVarsity Press, 1998). While Pinnock was supplementing his Bible reading with Wesleyan, Pentecostal, and Process sources and finding there much support for an open free-will theism, Sanders was finding the same support by reading some Dutch Reformed sources, especially Vincent Brümmer.

[43]Clark Pinnock, "The Philosophy of Christian Evidences," in *Jerusalem and Athens: Critical Discussions on the Theology and Apologetics of Cornelius Van Til*, ed. E. R. Gehan (Presbyterian and Reformed, 1971), 420-427.

[44]A critic of Pinnock, R. K. McGregor Wright, would turn "results of reciprocity" into the negative of "accommodating the assumption of human autonomy" (*No Place for Sovereignty*, InterVarsity Press, 1996, 12). In recent years, however, the relational dimension has been brought out by William W. Klein, *The New Chosen People: A Corporate View of Election* (Grand Rapids: Zondervan, 1990).

1. **No "Terrible Decree."** John Calvin had used the phrase "terrible decree" in relation to his belief that God as a sovereign act had destined some people to eternal lostness (*Institutes* 3:23). God wills all things; since some will be lost according to his reading of the Bible, logic compelled Calvin to conclude that God wills such lostness. But with the premise of reciprocity, Pinnock now could see and accept the apparent biblical teaching that God's desire and will are that *all people be saved* (1 Tim. 2:4; Titus 2:11; Rom. 5:18). Lostness is only by human choice, not by divine decree.

2. **Corporate View of Election.** What, then about divine election? It is a corporate category, Pinnock concluded. God has chosen *a people*, and individuals enter into God's election as they choose by faith to join the elect body in Christ (Eph. 1:3-14). Election thus encompasses all people, at least potentially, and is a cause for rejoicing rather than for stumbling in mystery and having to defend God from the charge of acting in a morally intolerable way by choosing some people and damning others. Pinnock was helped to see this corporateness of God's election by the writing of Robert Shank.[45]

3. **Predestination and Theodicy.** If the biblical narrative reflects a dynamic and interactive pattern of God's dealing with people, then predestination focuses on God setting goals rather than enforcing preprogrammed decrees. The primary goal for those elect in Christ is that they be conformed to the image of God's Son (Rom. 8:29). The future is a realm of possibilities for believers who are to be co-workers with God. This view helps greatly to relieve theodicy of the apparent conclusion that God is the author of evil.[46] Here is the personal witness of Pinnock: "In the past I would slip into my reading of the Bible dark

---

[45]Robert Shank, *Elect in the Son* (Springfield, Mo.: Westcott, 1970).

[46]See Gregory A. Boyd, *God At War: The Bible and Spiritual Conflict* (Downers Grove, Ill.: InterVarsity Press, 1997). Boyd assumes the reality of an active reciprocity between God and a fallen world that has the freedom to choose against the will of God. Boyd argues that theologians still draw too heavily on Augustine's approach to the problem of evil, an approach that attributes pain and suffering in this world to the mysterious "good" purposes of God. Pinnock is highly appreciative of this extensive work of Boyd.

assumptions about the nature of God's decrees and intentions. What a relief to be done with them!"[47]

4. **Free Will of the Sinner.** Calvinists had defined human sinfulness as total, leaving no room at all for human freedom to function in relation to potential salvation. But, if there is a divine-human reciprocity, would there not be some room for human free will? Pinnock was appreciatively aware of John Wesley's doctrine of universal prevenient grace (God graciously compensating for a fallen humanity unable to respond otherwise)[48] and recognized that the Bible treats people as though they were responsible and able to respond to God. The gospel of Christ and the evangelistic efforts of the church certainly address people as though they are free and responsible. Therefore, Pinnock concluded that such is actually the case.

5. **Atoning Work of Christ.** What then about the very source of human salvation, the atoning work of Jesus Christ? Put simply, Jesus really did die for the sins of the *whole* world, contrary to Calvinian logic. Given the premise of reciprocity, where does human response fit in? If Christ died for all and no human response is possible or necessary, one would be at the stance of universalism (all will be saved) or at the old Calvinism (those who are saved must be by God's choice and that alone). But such are not the only options if stress is placed on the needed human appropriation of the saving act of Christ. Those who are finally saved are those who, in their relative freedom granted by prevenient grace, choose in faith to reach out and accept and continue to appropriate the divine grace offered.

During his years at Trinity, Pinnock concluded that this cluster of insights deserved a broader hearing. He took the initiative to assemble and edit the essays of writers whose work soon comprised the contents of *Grace Unlimited*.[49] These theological results of the reciprocity premise were not well received by all at Trinity. One of Pinnock's own students, R. K. McGregor Wright, found the shift unacceptable and revisited the

---

[47]Clark Pinnock, "From Augustine To Arminius…," 21.

[48]See Randy Maddox, *Responsible Grace: John Wesley's Practical Theology* (Nashville: Kingswood Books, Abingdon Press, 1994).

[49]Clark Pinnock, ed., *Grace Unlimited* (Minneapolis: Bethany Fellowship, 1975).

subject many years later in the writing of his own *No Place for Sovereignty*.[50] Another critic, Norman Geisler, would later characterize Pinnock's shift as finally arriving at "extreme Arminianism." The danger of this "neotheism" is that, according to Geisler, it exalts human free will "at the expense of divine sovereignty."[51] Even so, the meanings of reciprocity continued to expand for Pinnock and a growing group of others. The results quickly came to include a non-Calvinistic view of church and state and a range of dramatically altered views of the nature and work of God generally. The first of these is addressed below, with the second explored in the following chapter.

Pilgrimage in Political Theology

One aspect of traditional evangelicalism, its view of church and state, was generally affirmed by Clark Pinnock in his earliest and then his later years, with, as he says, the "exception of one enormous zigzag in the middle." At first he tended to believe that significant social problems could only be solved by widespread conversions to Jesus Christ. This stance went beyond the traditional stance of fundamentalism which tends to dismiss politics as "dirty business." It hopes, prays, and sometimes even crusades for the public reality of a "Christian nation." Pinnock always had a sensitive social conscience and resisted settling into the caricature of evangelicals as socially indifferent and ineffective Christians. Vernon Grounds criticized evangelicals in 1969 as sometimes

---

[50]R. K. McGregor Wright, *No Place for Sovereignty* (Downers Grove, Ill.: InterVarsity Press, 1996). Pinnock was a member of Wright's Th.M. thesis committee at Trinity. Pinnock speculates that InterVarsity Press may have published this Wright book to balance its having published the work by himself and others titled *Openness To God* (1994). However that may be, Wright recalls Pinnock as "very kind and helpful to me…considerate and patient, thoughtful and irenic." He also recalls, however, that Pinnock was not pleased when Wright chose to develop a thesis based on the conviction that "apologetics had to be based on a consistent Calvinism" (38). Wright did not realize at the time that "Pinnock was already in a determined retreat from his earlier Calvinist convictions" (39).

[51]Norman Geisler, *Chosen But Free*, 104. Geisler defines divine sovereignty as God's "complete control of all things" (113). Pinnock was coming to judge that such a definition is biblically unjustified and theologically destructive. Complete control certainly lies inherently within the divine capacity; but the question is whether God chooses to function in this manner in relation to humans.

too conservative (sanctifying the status quo), quietistic (naively trusting Providence to remedy social injustice), pietistic (focusing only on the spiritual needs of individual souls), perfectionistic (only supporting the unqualified good), legalistic (righteousness usually defined as abstinence from particular evil practices), nationalistic (nearly equating the American way of life and Christianity), and pessimistic (real hope lies only at the end of the age with the return of Christ).[52]

The enormous zigzag in the middle came around 1970. Pinnock, obviously influenced by the spirit of those volatile times, began to recognize that, beyond the apologetic task of defending the gospel, evangelicals need to risk actually practicing the demands of the gospel in public affairs. In fact, "a defending of the gospel which is not matched by a living of it is hollow and inauthentic.... We do not wish to think that the gospel might have radical life-changing implications for the entire range of our existence."[53] The word "radical" was gaining prominence in some Christian circles, aided greatly by the publishing of John Howard Yoder's *The Original Revolution* (1971) and *The Politics of Jesus* (1972).

Pinnock began exploring the possible appropriateness of a Christian political "radicalism." At the time he was on the faculty of Trinity Evangelical Divinity School near Chicago, having been appointed to a post in systematic theology in 1969. This school was gathering a growing number of avant-garde young evangelical scholars and had noted the growing reputation of young Professor Pinnock. Although Pinnock to that date had seen himself as politically conservative, he now experienced a "total transformation." Before the big shift in 1970, Billy Graham's approach to social change—through individual conversions—was Pinnock's own. He had learned from Francis Schaeffer in the early 1960s to emphasize theological over political issues (although Schaeffer identified with alienated youth in ways seeming to support their social concerns). During the 1960s Pinnock respected Bill Buckley's "feisty" way of defending capitalism (Buckley having a personality similar to

---

[52]Vernon Grounds, *Evangelicalism and Social Responsibility* (Scottdale, Pa.: Herald Press, 1969), 4-6.

[53]Clark Pinnock, "A Call for Liberation of North American Christians," *Sojourners* (September 1976), 23. Pinnock comments that the requirement of a "living sacrifice" in Romans 12:1 certainly is "radical."

Pinnock's in some ways). He himself was more preoccupied with the issue of biblical inerrancy than with racial justice, although he had taken appreciative note of Carl F. H. Henry's ethical writings that sought to prick the conscience of evangelicals in the direction of increased social responsibility.[54] Then came the transformation around 1970.

Pinnock absorbed with appreciation the eschatological stance of dispensationalist premillennialism, in part through influences from Dallas Theological Seminary. He admitted that, while "dispensational premillennialists are notoriously passive politically, it is also true that such an eschatology puts one in radical opposition to the powers that be and makes one a potential radical."[55] Radicalism, in fact, was very much in the air among many American youth in the late 1960s. The prominent German Christian theologian Dietrich Bonhoeffer was lost to the Nazis in 1945 and then gained a wide North American readership with his books *Life Together, The Cost of Discipleship, Letters and Papers from Prison,* and *The Way to Freedom.* The urgency of this call for Christians to be serious about the implications of their faith got to Pinnock when a Trinity student, Jim Wallis,[56] gathered and helped motivate a small group of deeply concerned people on the campus. The seminary made clear in its catalog that it sought "to inspire devotion to Jesus Christ as divine Savior and Lord, to the Bible as His inerrant Word, and to consistent Christian living in both personal and social ethics, guided by the Holy Spirit." The new group on campus was focusing on "consistent Christian living in both personal and social ethics." Wallis had been in the "new left," was converted to Christ at Michigan State University, came to Trinity as a student, and promptly formed the "Peoples Christian Coalition." Professor Pinnock was in good touch with students

---

[54]See, e.g., Carl Henry's *The Uneasy Conscience of Modern Fundamentalism* (Grand Rapids: Eerdmans, 1947). For a good overview, see Robert Johnston, *Evangelicals at an Impasse* (Atlanta: John Knox Press, 1979), chapter 4.

[55]Clark Pinnock, "A Pilgrimage in Political Theology," in *Liberation Theology,* ed. Ronald Nash (Milford, Mich.: Mott Media, 1984), 108.

[56]Jim Wallis was born in 1948, was raised in a devout Plymouth Brethren family, and was radicalized by the blatant racism he saw as he was growing up in Detroit. He came to Trinity Evangelical Divinity School after his earlier education at Michigan State University.

and sought to be open to new movements of the Spirit. He sensed biblical legitimacy and timeliness in the fresh call to authentic and relevant Christian living.

Those in this Coalition, recalls Pinnock, were "deeply critical of America and supportive of radical politics and Anabaptist herme-neutics."[57] Such a "radical" hermeneutic involved taking literally the Sermon on the Mount, including pacifism. This was attractive to a quasi-fundamentalist like Pinnock who always was inclined to take the Bible seriously. *Christianity Today*, the prominent evangelical mouthpiece, took President Nixon's word on the Watergate affair and at least tacitly backed his stance on Vietnam until as late as May, 1972. It supported the American political system as the best available in the world. Pinnock had shared this general mindset. Drawn increasingly, however, by what he now saw as God's favor on anti-racism and anti-Vietnam rhetoric, his disturbing new vision was dominated more by the awful disparities in wealth between nations, the enormous investments in weapons of war, the pattern of frantic material consumption in the West, the obviously irresponsible pollution of the earth's limited resources, and the North American indifference to the cries for help from the Third World. What he now felt was "shame and outrage at the moral callousness involved in our collective North American behavior."[58] He helped Wallis and others recognize that the work of John Howard Yoder was the Christian countercultural support they needed.

It now was becoming much easier for Pinnock to associate in his mind "the socialist utopia and the promised Kingdom of God."[59] From the Wallis group at Trinity emerged the periodical *Post American*, soon to become the influential *Sojourners*. Wallis, Pinnock, Yoder, Catholic

---

[57]Ibid. The "how" of being socially responsible as Christians was debated in a 1977 series of articles and editorials in *Sojourners* and *The Reformed Journal*. In some ways it was a twentieth-century reflection of the same debate that raged between sixteenth-century Anabaptism and Calvinism. Pinnock had been nurtured in the latter and now was moving toward the former. For extended orientation to the "radical" option, see Barry Callen, *Radical Christianity* (Nappanee, IN: Evangel Publishing House, 1999).

[58]Clark Pinnock, "A Call for Liberation of North American Christians," *Sojourners* (September 1976), 23.

[59]Clark Pinnock, in Nash, op. cit., 111.

radicals like Dorothy Day, and others were the frequent writers. Behind these publications was a vision of committed Christians yielding their social privileges and embodying a new humanity that truly serves the poor and oppressed. The focus of God's action in history was seen as intended to be through the distinctive and sacrificial life of God's sojourning community, the church, not in the general political arena from which Christians must distance themselves so that they are not merely absorbed by mainstream secular values, agendas, and methods.[60] Real social change, according to these Christian visionaries, comes through the witness of a prophetic minority that refuses to meet "the system" on its own terms, but acts out of an alternative vision, the vision of Christ on the cross. The solution to society's deep ills is God's "original revolution" which brings into disrepute the evils of individualism, capitalism, and patriotism. Pinnock later described his new social stance as standing on three legs: (1) a deep alienation from North American culture; (2) a resurgence of the radicalizing theological foundations of Anabaptism; and (3) a new left radical movement far beyond any Christian commitments.

Pinnock was quickly caught up in the strong anti-war and anti-establishment sentiment of the early 1970s. Christian socialism was a new consideration for him, one he saw filled with the beauty of an idealism that glowed with apparent biblical authenticity. The social leftists at Trinity "imbibed" works like Arthur Gish's *The New Left and Christian Radicalism*.[61] In the late 1960s the word "revolution" had become common in some segments of Christian thought. What it tended to mean is summarized by John Howard Yoder: "The system is

---

[60]Summarizes Robert Johnston (*Evangelicals at an Impasse*, 1979, 92): "*Sojourners* is suspicious of, if not downright opposed to all expressions of society based on political power and governmental institutions. Because all secular structures are demonically influenced, because all forms of power breed their own abuse of the poor and powerless, because the use of power not only invites, but demands compromise with evil—Christians must distance themselves from the public political arena. But this is all right, for 'the state is never intended to be an instrumentality for bringing in the new order.'"

[61]The word "imbibed" is Pinnock's (interview with Barry Callen, April 18, 1998). See Arthur Gish, *The New Left and Christian Radicalism* (Grand Rapids: Eerdmans, 1970).

rotten. Those whom it oppresses should submit to its tyranny no longer. It deserves nothing other than to collapse in upon itself, a collapse we will engineer."[62] Christian radicalism moved in a similar direction, although it sought to clarify how the faith should shape a distinctive form of radicalism.

In seeking the "original revolution" of Jesus as the proper model for any time, and especially for the 1970s, Yoder reviewed the options Jesus faced and rejected (establishment order of the Herodians, violent revolution of the Zealots, outward emigration of the Essenes, inward emigration of the Pharisees). Beginning with the first promise to Abraham, says Yoder, God's original revolution is "the creation of a distinct community with its own deviant set of values and its coherent way of incarnating them." Jesus did the same, calling together a unique society with a new way of living. It included voluntary suffering as its way of responding to violence. When this Jesus community is true to itself, it is "the most powerful tool of social change." War is not the way to save a culture. The call of Jesus to his community is for it to be "an active missionary presence within society, a source of healing and creativity because it would take the pattern of His own suffering servanthood."[63] This Christian vision was appealing to people like Pinnock because it was simultaneously Christ-centered and biblically founded, thus addressing the evangelical instinct while also confirming the cultural alienation being felt.

Hope was being expressed in *Sojourners* magazine that the Viet Cong would prevail over American imperialist forces in Southeast Asia. There was open admiration for what was thought to be happening in the new China under Mao. Pinnock called for Christians to become downwardly mobile, to be liberated from bondage to Mammon and accept lives of costly and thus credible discipleship. The new emphasis on "church growth" at the time was, according to Pinnock, to be affirmed as long as numerical growth was much more than "the proliferation of pseudo-disciples who can hardly distinguish the cross from the flag."

---

[62]John Howard Yoder, *The Original Revolution: Essays on Christian Pacifism* (Scottdale, Pa.: Herald Press, 1971), 14.

[63]Ibid., 28, 31, 180.

Beyond the appropriate evangelistic quest for many new believers, the North American church was said to need real growth "in the knowledge of the biblical God who loves justice and mercy and who calls us all without exception to costly discipleship."[64] Rather than "bourgeois" Christians, the church needed a radicalized evangelism that dared to call converts to more than individualistic spirituality. Believers should accept the full lordship of Jesus over all aspects of life. Pinnock, remaining an evangelical at heart despite his new social radicalism, spoke favorably of the passion for justice evident by the now prominent Latin American "theologians of liberation." He cautioned, however, that salvation should never focus on "social justice to the exclusion of the human need to be saved from sin through faith in Jesus Christ."[65]

Soon, the scene of living and teaching shifted for Pinnock from Trinity Evangelical Divinity School in the Mid-Western United States to Regent College in Vancouver, British Columbia (where he would remain for only three years, 1974-1977). During the five years he had spent at Trinity, his theological style had become more irenic, he felt "less threatened" as an evangelical thinker in a predominately non-evangelical world of scholarship, and he became convinced that the inerrancy doctrine of biblical inspiration, held widely among evangelicals, must be matched by a "profound exegesis of the text."[66] The Watergate tragedy in American national politics had only confirmed for him the rightness of the radical critique of U. S. society made by the Peoples Christian Coalition and its *Post American* (*Sojourners*) publication. He had been impressed by the peace witness in the face of the war in Southeast Asia and in particular the work of John Howard Yoder. Before him was an aggressive writing schedule as he returned to his native land (although on the opposite end of the continent from his place of birth and in a quite different cultural environment).

Once back in Canada, he was quickly in touch with "radical" movements and people, Christian and otherwise, himself voting Communist

---

[64]Clark Pinnock, "A Call for Liberation…," 24.

[65]Clark Pinnock, "Liberation Theology: The Gains, the Gaps," *Christianity Today* (January 16, 1976), 14.

[66]Clark Pinnock, "Five Years at Trinity," *The Scribe* (student publication of Trinity Evangelical Divinity School), 1974, n.p.

in the 1974 Vancouver city election. Mother Teresa of India came to town, and he knew well the ideals of the Mennonite community in Western Canada. However, the Vietnam War finally ended, and the culture that had moved left in the 1960s and early 1970s began to move right.[67] Pinnock soon went with it, admiring a figure like President Ronald Reagan in the United States. While he now admits that "it does worry me a little" to reflect on the apparent influence that culture has on Christian perspective, he surely was not alone in his mirroring of shifts in general social perspective. He now read people like Richard John Neuhaus whom he characterizes as "a man of the left coming to his senses and shaking off the social romanticism without giving up his deep social conscience."[68] There came an end to Pinnock's thrust into the arena of radical Christian socialism, an ending of the "enormous zigzag." He soon came to judge himself to have been "a babe in political thinking," even though somehow it seemed evident at the time.

What caused the big change away from Christian social radicalism? Pinnock recalls reading appreciatively the work of Michael Novak and awakening from "my radical dream." Now he could see the other side of the coin—the positive features of free speech, limited government, an independent judiciary, and genuine pluralism. These positive aspects of a good society had been substantially realized in the American experience; in fact, they now were affirmed by him as the very reasons why it had been possible for the radicals to express and try to live out their concerns. The radicals had been calling for liberation in the one society where more of it already existed than nearly anywhere else on earth. Pinnock's new judgment was this: "What really endangers liberty and justice in our world is not a flawed America, but that political monism, whether of the Fascist right or the Communist left, which declares itself to be absolute and answers to no transcendent value."[69] The peace movement meant well, but in the end he concluded that it had been wrong about Vietnam. He went so far as to say that peace advocates

---

[67]See Barry Callen, *Seeking the Light: America's Modern Quest for Peace, Justice, Prosperity, and Faith* (Nappanee, Ind.: Evangel Press, 1998), chapters 5 and 6.

[68]Clark Pinnock, Interview with Barry Callen, April 19, 1998. See, e.g., Richard John Neuhaus, *The Naked Public Square: Religion and Democracy in America* (Grand Rapids: Eerdmans, 1984).

[69]Clark Pinnock, in Nash, op. cit., 112.

helped inadvertently to enable the enslavement of large parts of South-east Asia.

Where, then, did Pinnock end up after his major zigzag in Christian social vision? His mild millennialism now hardly exists. He tends to lean slightly toward the older post-millennial model which anticipates the faithfulness of the church leading to a greater realization of God's reign on earth before the return of Christ and the eschaton. This continues his social radicalism, but in quite a different vein. It has come to be his view that the church does not always need to function counterculturally in places like North America where the Christian gospel already permeates many areas of public life. Rather, the task of the church in such a privileged place can be to encourage the fuller christianization of the culture and to call the nation to the will of God, assuring people that God will bless the nation whose God is the Lord. Pinnock had moved back in the direction of a vision that contrasts with the Anabaptist model—moving from the countercultural existence of the church itself as the core social strategy for building a new society to seeking to bring the general society under God's law by a combination of evangelistic and political initiatives.[70]

Given the reciprocity principle, Pinnock now sees the future as genuinely open. The Lord intends to reclaim the whole of creation.[71] In the process, democratic capitalism offers the best political and

---

[70]Jim Wallis proceeded over the coming decades to share and live a prophetic witness to the intended "radical" implications of true Christian faith. In the 1980s, for instance, he sometimes directed his critique against conservative Christians who seemed prepared to sell their faith for a share of President Reagan's patriotism and prosperity. By the 1990s Wallis was "just as uncompromisingly Christian as ever, but he is less angry, less self-righteous, and more alert to opportunities for common action with erstwhile ideological foes" (John Wilson, "Mr. Wallis Goes to Washington," in *Christianity Today*, June 14, 1999, 41).

[71]In his 1996 book *Flame of Love*, Pinnock developed his growing pneumatology in the context of the whole of creation. Salvation becomes new creation. The life of the church is to be directed outward in cooperation with what God is doing in the world. The work of the Spirit is God's ongoing work of opening the creation to the full breadth of the renewing potential of divine grace. He insists: "God is present to us in the creation, and the world is a natural sacrament.... The whole creation is a field of the Spirit's operations and thus sacramental of God's presence.... If the whole world is the field of Spirit activity, recognizing Creator Spirit gives us the opportunity to relate theology to origins and environment in fresh ways" (62-64).

economic opportunity for widespread liberty, justice, and prosperity, thus deserving the clear although not uncritical support of Christians. In fact, "no system [other than democratic captialism] has been so helpful to the poor and provided such opportunity to rise out of suffering."[72] While the earlier socialist ideal turned out to be a cruel delusion in Pinnock's eyes, in a sense he has never left this idealism. He has only decided that it is fulfilled better by relying less on countercultural isolationism and one-sided criticism of contemporary Western capitalism and democracy. Christians now must help democratic capitalism to stop its slide into self-centered materialism so that the hope it offers will not be lost.

In the area of the Christian approach to social change, Pinnock has found himself on a sometimes jolting journey. In 1970 it dawned on him that there is a biblically revealed reciprocity between God and the world which classical theism had diminished and even denied. He came to believe that God is interactive with humans in the midst of history, responding to what happens, even altering the divine course of action in response to human decisions. He found himself being drawn to a love-centered theology that makes room for real human freedom and joyfully affirms a divine providence that is prepared by sovereign choice to take real risks on behalf of ultimate goals. The result, beyond the changes in his own thinking, was the issuing of a challenge to the larger evangelical community to "grow up and recognize that evangelical theology is not an uncontested body of timeless truth.... Like it or not, we are embarked on a pilgrimage in theology and cannot determine exactly where it will lead and how it will end."[73]

One place it has ended, after an early time in the conservative mainstream of relative disinterest in political matters and then a time sojourning out on the edges in a radical, countercultural activism, is the place of clear concern for Christian involvement in government on behalf of faith-related issues like the right to life, limited government, adequate national defense, and provision for the poor. Pinnock has come to appreciate journals like *First Things* where balanced debate on

---

[72]Ibid., 113, 115.
[73]Clark Pinnock, "From Augustine To Arminius...," 28.

Christian social ethics can occur. He retains his respect for Ronald Sider, seen as less ideological than many Anabaptist, pacifist, and liberationist types. Sider was "not a young turk of the new left and thus has worn well over time."[74] The call to Christians is to be responsible stewards of all resources, the divine gifts of life, finances, and the earth itself. So says Sider,[75] and Pinnock as well.

While he was becoming more Wesleyan-Arminian in matters related to salvation and discipleship, Pinnock has followed his brief period of radicalism by becoming more Calvinistic in a political theology featuring Christ as the transformer of culture.[76] He reported in 1985 that "as a Canadian citizen I grieve over the decline of North America into the secularist abyss and thirst for its Christian reconstruction." In this thirsting he acknowledged deep appreciation for the recent writings of Francis Schaeffer (*The Great Evangelical Disaster*, 1984) and Franky Schaeffer (*Bad News for Modern Man*, 1984), realizing anew "how profoundly the L'Abri themes have affected me ever since I was a worker there in 1966 and a student there in years before that."[77] The social circumstances of the 1980s, as Pinnock judged them, called for starting Christian schools "to stem the tide of secular humanism"; getting vocal about issues like abortion, pornography, and educational brainwashing; making a difference "by laying our bodies down"; engaging in "bread and butter" evangelism; electing godly politicians who support biblical principles; in short, reclaiming "the creation and the culture for God."[78]

While Pinnock has had no direct relationship with Rev. Jerry Falwell or his American "Moral Majority," he certainly has come to appreciate

---

[74]Clark Pinnock, Interview with Barry Callen, April 19, 1998.

[75]See, e.g., Ronald Sider, *Rich Christians in an Age of Hunger* (Dallas: Word Publishing, 4th ed., 1997).

[76]*The Reformed Journal*, e.g., has argued that social responsibility goes beyond benevolence and the assumption that good people will make good societies. Along with evangelism directed at individuals, life has a corporate nature, requiring the church to act directly on and within social and political structures. Social ethics requires concrete political engagement for the Christian.

[77]Clark Pinnock, *Three Keys To Spiritual Renewal* (Minneapolis: Bethany House, 1985), 11, 101.

[78]Ibid., 78.

this kind of society-reclaiming rhetoric, and at points speaks favorably of its agenda. He rejects as unfair overreaction the critics who fear that politically active fundamentalists are a real danger to liberal democracies.[79] In fact, he reports, most such fundamentalists are Baptists who respect the principle of the separation of church and state and do not want to impose their religious beliefs on others. Their usual premillennial theology tells them that evil will not disappear and that victory in worldly political terms should not be expected prior to Christ's return. They just think that the American experiment was based on Christian religious beliefs and is in trouble if systematically divorced from them. Pinnock agrees with such thinking and admires those prepared to insist on the wisdom of the Bible still having a culture-forming influence. Such a "fundamentalist" (Christian) concern, he insists, "is not to take over the United States and turn it into a religious theocracy. The idea is not to make the United States like the Iran of the Ayatollah, but to be responsible Christian citizens in a democracy."[80]

Pinnock's more recent assessment declares that the verdict is in. A utopian vision like Marxism actually functions to betray the poor. Democratic capitalism may not have the seductively romantic appeal that socialistic utopian visions feature, but at least it does not shackle the dynamic creativity of people which is the very source of wealth creation and then replace it with a vast bureaucracy which is notoriously inefficient and basically serves the ruling class in the system. While market economies have been remarkably successful in raising the standard of living of whole populations, welfare states intended to serve the poor primarily increase the material well-being of the administering bureaucracies. The rhetoric involved may be social justice, but the reality turns out to be economic payoffs to the politically favored. Pinnock is quick to say on the other side that Christians should never support

---

[79]Note, e.g.: Grace Halsell, *Prophecy and Politics: Militant Evangelists on the Road to Nuclear War* (Westport, CT: Lawrence Hill, 1986); Lowell Streiker, *The Gospel Time Bomb: Ultrafundamentalism and the Future of America* (Buffalo: Prometheus Books, 1984); and Gary Clabaugh, *Thunder on the Right: The Protestant Fundamentalists* (Chicago: Nelson Hall, 1974).

[80]Clark Pinnock, "Defining American Fundamentalism," in *The Fundamentalist Phenomenon*, ed. Norman Cohen (Grand Rapids: Eerdmans, 1990), 49-50.

capitalism in an unqualified way. The very success of the marketplace can be people's downfall morally and spiritually—currently a major problem in North America. Even so, socialism works very poorly indeed, in part because it wrongly presupposes that citizens are saints.

A market approach is more realistic and thus more successful. Capitalism should be the natural ally of any Christian liberation theology which is serious about political and economic liberty. "Liberal" Christians, Pinnock insists, should stop their notorious attachments to the rhetorically rich pursuit of utopia on earth—which really turns out to be a bowing to the idol of the modern world, statism, and finally functions as a betrayal of the poor.[81] Accordingly, it is time to leave the myth of Marxist theory, to quit foolishly relying on collectivist economic practice and trust that the word and power of Jesus will one day, in Abraham's seed, bless all the nations of the earth with peace, justice, and prosperity.[82] For this vision Christians must work, being shrewd in this fallen world and trusting finally in God alone—and certainly not in any all-powerful state. Unbridled optimism for dramatic progress in this present world is the fool's gold of faith, but pessimistic passivity in the face of rampant evil is sheer irresponsibility in light of the transformative power of the Spirit of God.

The journey of Clark Pinnock has been sobered by the zigzag of his own foray among the various Christian approaches to Christian social ethics. "On both ends I was unwise," he now judges. "I allowed myself to be tempted too far in both directions. Now I know that you can't sanctify any social order." The better stance is to be both "appreciative and critical of Western democracy." He even is appreciative of having gone through this shifting experience, assessing it like this: "It illustrates my tendency to *experience* things rather than stand back to only observe and analyze. I enter enthusiastically, looking expectantly for what God may be doing."[83] He once had loved Ryrie's dispensationalist vision of God's operating in human history, but its shine eventually wore off.

---

[81]Clark Pinnock, "The Pursuit of Utopia," in *Freedom, Justice, and Hope*, ed. Marvin Olasky (Westchester, Ill.: Crossway Books, 1988), 78-79, 82.

[82]Ibid., 83.

[83]Clark Pinnock, Interview with Barry Callen, April 19, 1998.

"Millennialism is hardly a central biblical emphasis," he now sees. Eschatology for him has finally come to this:

> The already/not yet of the New Testament is my real position. When the Lord came, the new age came with him—apart from any speculative apparatus about all things future. I am basically amillennial and always should have been. In my journey of personal and social renewal, I was buffeted by how much of the Kingdom of God is to be *now* and how much will be *only later.* I have explored the continuum of the present pessimism of premillennialism and the optimism of grace of post-millennialism. I stand with the optimism of divine grace, but only with the full awareness of the evil not yet overcome in this present world.[84]

Such remaining evil certainly raises its ugly head when humans go to war with each other. Pinnock was caught up in the anti-war and anti-establishment sentiments that were so strong in the United States in the early 1970s. But by the early 1990s he found himself sobered by the complexity of these issues and the hard choices that sometimes they appear to force on socially responsible and Bible-believing Christians. An example is the 1990 "Desert Storm" offensive against Saddam Hussein's Iraq. Was the liberation of Kuwait worthy of Christians identifying the massive military response of the West as a "just war"? Pinnock was well aware of Christian pacifists who oppose all acts of war as inherently unjust regardless of circumstances. However, by 1991 he was prepared to dismiss such blanket opposition as an unrealistic stance for which "facts do not matter [and] the enormity of the crime is not relevant to their decision." Contrary to such pacifists, he now belonged to what he judged the large majority of Christians who believe that war on some unfortunate occasions is a legitimate function of the state. When it appears necessary to restrain evil by force, rulers

---

[84]Ibid. He identifies the book *Faithful in the Meantime: A Biblical View of Final Things and Present Responsibilities* by Barry Callen (Evangel Publishing House, 1997) as stating his current eschatological position rather well. He also identifies the book *God At War: The Bible and Spiritual Conflict* by Gregory Boyd (InterVarsity Press, 1997) as an excellent exposition of the dynamic in the biblical narrative that views God in an age-long but not eternal battle against Satan.

"may exercise God's wrath against evil doers when required (Rom. 13:1-4)."[85]

The real question is not *whether*, but *when*. According to Pinnock, the determination of when waging war is justified is to be accomplished by the application of classic principles of judgment, principles supported widely in the Christian tradition since the time of Augustine in the late Roman Empire. They are that the cause must be just, undertaken by legitimate authority, with reasonable promise of success, by using means and goals proportional to the circumstance, always respecting the immunity of noncombatants, and chosen as the path of social policy only as a last resort. Pinnock concluded as a concerned Canadian citizen and committed Christian that Desert Storm was a just war. Regarding the pacifist believers, among whom he was once numbered, he now concludes that one should respect their high ideals while not failing to see their naiveté.[86] In fact, at times Pinnock smiles at his own tendency to naively reach for ideals with a rhetoric that later requires toning down. He has been sobered, but not sidelined in the quest for compassion and justice in public life.

Reason Enough

Clark Pinnock had set out on a spiritual and academic journey, sometimes defensively traditional and increasingly fresh and experimental. In terms of political theory and the church's mission, the journey was impacted heavily by both biblical teaching and given times and settings. It moved along a sometimes volatile route that knew its share of idealistic romanticism. Theologically speaking, the path would lead in a relatively consistent direction. Valuing a coherent rationalism employed in the service of faith, he found reason enough to search for a faith paradigm judged more adequate than the one provided by the old Augustinian tradition. To tackle a deeply entrenched pattern of theological logic like Augustinian Calvinism would not prove an easy task for Pinnock and the many others who soon joined him. Easy or not, the task

---

[85]Clark Pinnock, "Desert Storm...A Just War?" *The Canadian Baptist* (March 1991), 17.
[86]Ibid., 18.

has been undertaken and pursued diligently for three decades so far.

Following an initial attempt to re-establish the integrity of the Christian faith itself, with special attention paid to the issue of nature and authority of biblical revelation, Pinnock eventually would attempt to refine mainstream evangelical understandings of some central aspects of this revealed and authoritative faith. His early writing in *Set Forth Your Case* (1967) had been undertaken in the secular 1960s when traditional Christian faith was not fashionable. That book had been sent out with the prayer that it "might lend glory to the Lord, and encourage the people of God to undertake a bold witness for Him which will shake the foundations of our tottering, secular culture."[87] The goal had been to argue that there were important reasons to believe in more than secular materialism and political liberation. By contrast, but still in the apologetic mode, in 1980 Pinnock released *Reason Enough: A Case for the Christian Faith*. He then saw large numbers of people who were struggling with the emptiness of secular life and no longer were passively tolerating the enormous problems facing the world's peoples, including a rapidly eroding faith in the ability of science and dollars to solve the deepest needs of human beings. Many people again were believing in something beyond themselves and their material possessions. Pinnock, naturally pleased at this return of faith, nonetheless insisted that faith by itself is not enough. A wrongly directed faith only leads people into vain superstitions and cruel illusions which cannot ultimately sustain fulfilling life and responsible theological thought. His concern was not just *a* faith, but *the* faith.

His prescription to avoid faith's pitfalls was that people should exercise "critical judgment" in relation to their beliefs so that the faith held is reasonable. He was convinced that such critical judgment would support believers in Jesus Christ and that "the Christian world view is adequate intellectually, factually and morally."[88] About the risen and living Christ, there is reason enough to believe! To build his case he laid

---

[87]Clark Pinnock, *Set Forth Your Case: An Examination of Christianity's Credentials* (Craig Press, 1967, Moody Press edition, 1971), 9.

[88]Clark Pinnock, *Reason Enough: A Case for the Christian Faith* (Downers Grove, Ill.: InterVarsity Press, 1980), 10.

out several circles of credibility or categories of complementary evidence that he saw joining to affirm the Christian understanding of all reality, especially God in Christ who now is making claims on our lives (see Appendix B). The conclusion was that there is adequate reason to believe that the Christian gospel is "the true end to our quest for meaning and our quest for the intelligibility of the world, true to the religious longings of our heart, true to the biblical record, and true to the moral intuition that we need a new kind of human community on this groaning planet."[89] Having faced critical judgment, the Christian faith proves itself truly pragmatic since it offers life real meaning, experiential since it reaches the deepest levels of human life with credibility, cosmic since the heavens really do declare the glory of God, historical since the Son of God actually did come to earth, and corporate since this faith does change lives and bind them together in the new community the world awaits. Is faith still required? Yes, of course, but "we work with reasonable probabilities which, while they do not create or compel belief, do establish the credible atmosphere in which faith can be born and can grow."[90]

The apologetic use of reason, however, was not the same as Pinnock had employed in his 1967 book *Set Forth Your Case*. By 1980 he was actively questioning the dominance and appropriateness of the rationalistic epistemology typical of evangelicalism. He was replacing it with a "softer" rationality, a modified "foundationalism," a less militant frame of mind (see Pinnock's 1999 postscript in Appendix B). Now he came to judge himself a "pilgrim-type theologian who likes to explore territories outside the fortress to see what is out there." As would often become clear to him during the years to follow, "the meanderings of a pilgrim can be infuriating for defenders of a fortress."[91] Nonetheless, he now was seeing that, as a biblical Christian, he was not obligated to a view of knowledge that needs a rationally unshakable foundation, like a Bible which is claimed to have an "inerrant" text direct from God's hand. Knowledge,

---

[89]Ibid., 15.

[90]Ibid., 18.

[91]Clark Pinnock, unpublished paper delivered at the 1997 evangelical-process dialogue convened at Claremont School of Theology, 7.

in fact, is more "web-like," requiring the humility of faith, and yields relative and not absolute certainty. While this softening rationality left him with a "post-modern ambiance," he still maintained that truth is *sought* rather than *created.* It relates to more than the "grammar" of the believing community. Christian claims about truth supersede their contextual settings, influential as these settings always are. We who believe have to do with more than ourselves; there is God and God's truth. It may be apprehended only partially and articulated only tentatively, but divine revelation does exist and enables at least a meaningful apprehension of its essence and intent.

Pinnock has remained a serious evangelical, although one who certainly has considerably softened the hard-rational approach of many of his colleagues. Even so, in the 1980s the Wesleyan scholar Randy Maddox found cause to judge that Pinnock was still retaining a basic "foundationalist" presupposition, seeming yet to accept the assumption that believers must be able to *prove* that Scripture is reliable knowledge or its authority will be called into question.[92] Was John Calvin not right in teaching that the witness of the Spirit is itself the final ground of the Scripture's perceived authority? By the 1990s, especially with his book *Flame of Love* in 1996, Pinnock increasingly had heeded the concern of Maddox and moved farther from the urge to engage in aggressive and rationalistic apologetics. However, while this move would please Maddox, it was causing Donald Bloesch some concern. He now referred to Pinnock as an "evangelical narrative theologian" and expressed his own attitude toward the supposed tendencies of such theologians:

> All narrative theologians are distrustful of discursive thought, preferring aesthetic sensitivity. They prize imagination over abstract or theoretical reason.... In narrative theology the Bible is no longer a record of the mighty deeds of God but a collection of stories that throw light on the universal human predicament.... From my [Bloesch] perspective, to reduce the gospel to a story or a number of stories devalues the apostolic interpretation of the realities described in the stories. The gospel

[handwritten margin note: I think with McFague are a narrative theologian?]

---

[92]Randy Maddox, review of *The Scripture Principle,* by Clark Pinnock, in *Wesleyan Theological Journal* 21 (Spring/Fall 1986), 206.

is not simply a drama played out in history but the speech of
God interpreting this drama to the community of faith.[93]

While Pinnock certainly had not abandoned the necessity of
assuming real divine revelation and a substantive historical context for
the origins of Christian faith, his journey had taken him in dynamic
directions that are uncomfortably destabilizing for many evangelicals. He
has been characterized variously as a post-fundamentalist now become
a mainline evangelical, a Western theologian now drawing from the
deep wells of the Eastern theological tradition, a former Christian
rationalist now more a pentecostal pietist who would rather experience
and be than argue and prove, and a former propositional inerrantist
transformed into much more of a story-oriented narrative theologian.
The Bible has remained central for Pinnock, although he reads it
increasingly with his heart and not merely his head.

The theological task of evangelicals in this postmodern world,
according to Robert Webber, is to maintain the historic biblical faith, but
in a dynamic way. Faithfulness to the ancient tradition must be coupled
with the church's willingness to discover persuasive and relevant new
presentations of it in the present culture. Given the nature of this
postmodern culture, Webber explains that both the maintenance and
presentation should be done with "a healthy, even joyous regard for
mystery," with a freedom "to make mistakes and to take the risk of
thinking out loud—a risk that no one who is a slave to a system can
take."[94] One could hardly find a better description of the theological
work of Clark Pinnock once he had broken free of the rigid system of
scholastic Calvinism. He remains Christ-centered and biblically-rooted,
as before, but now he also is a Spirit-animated risk-taker prepared to

---

[93]Donald Bloesch, *Holy Scripture* (Downers Grove, Ill.: InterVarsity Press, 1994),
211, 213, 344. Bloesch was reacting largely to Pinnock's then latest book, *Tracking the
Maze* (1990), in which he explores in preliminary ways the possible implications of his
emerging narrative approaches to Christian theology. Note, however, that Pinnock
shares much of Bloesch's concern. For instance: "We must contend, in opposition to
the existential theologians, that the heart of the Christian story is fact, not myth. The
message possesses existential value precisely because it is, first of all, historical" (160).

[94]Robert E. Webber, *Ancient-Future Faith: Rethinking Evangelicalism for a Postmodern World* (Grand Rapids: Baker Books, 1999), 199.

hear anew the Word of God on behalf of the church's mission in a post-modern world.

The intellectual journey of Clark Pinnock from the 1960s to the end of the century certainly did pass through its share of debate and struggle. It finally reached its matured highpoints in an "open" view of a gracious God (chapter 5) and a daring commitment to walk with the divine Spirit who brings all real and lasting renewal (chapter 6). These years would witness the rise of a new generation of "postmodernist" evangelical theologians. Pinnock, a primary pioneer of this generation, would lead in the effort to rethink the epistemological assumptions and implications of evangelical orthodoxy. While his shift might be seen as a move from modernity to postmodernity, it also can be seen as his reappropriation of the vital heritage of Christian pietism which incorporates several postmodernist assumptions in real, although always guarded ways.[95]

Gary Dorrien put it well in 1998: "As a respected elder figure in a movement of mostly young theologians, he [Pinnock] supported the 'postmodern' evangelical claim that it was time for evangelicals to move beyond the categories and defensive positions established by the modernist-fundamentalist conflict.... With each book he inched further away from evangelical fundamentalism. One century of overdetermining evangelical debate with modernism was enough."[96] Richard Lints was correct both in his 1993 observation that Pinnock had issued a call for the construction of a "postmodern orthodoxy"[97] and in his assessment that such a call presents a considerable challenge for classic evangelicalism.[98] Pinnock was prepared to face the challenge in ways freshly "open" and "unbounded."

---

[95]Note, for example, Stanley Grenz, *Revisioning Evangelical Theology: A Fresh Agenda for the 21st Century* (InterVarsity Press, 1993), where Grenz encourages a shift in evangelicalism from a creed-based to a spirituality-based identity (37). Grenz reports in his 1994 *Theology for the Community of God* that, "I discovered anew the importance of the pietist heritage in which I had been spiritually nurtured" (x). These volumes and their author are much appreciated by Clark Pinnock.

[96]Gary Dorrien, *The Remaking of Evangelical Theology* (Louisville, KY: Westminster John Knox Press, 1998), 145-146.

[97]See Clark Pinnock, *Tracking the Maze* (San Francisco: Harper and Row,1990).

[98]Richard Lints, *The Fabric of Theology: A Prolegomenon to Evangelical Theology* (Grand Rapids: Eerdmans, 1993), 234.

5

Open and Unbounded

In the relational model God is wise, proficient, resourceful, loving and responsive, even though God does not get everything he desires. This...is God our Creator and Redeemer. It is not a "shrinking of God" as some allege. Rather, it is an enriching view of God, well attested in the biblical material. Such a perspective of God's nature and the risk involved in his project has profound ramifications when applied to the subjects of sovereignty, eschatology, suffering, prayer and guidance.[1]

God, in grace, grants humans significant freedom to cooperate with or work against God's will for their lives, and he enters into dynamic, give-and-take relationships with us.... We respond to God's gracious initiatives and God responds to our re-sponses...and on it goes. God takes risks in this give-and-take relationship, yet he is endlessly resourceful and competent in working toward his ultimate goals.[2]

During the 1970s, the dramatic unraveling for Clark Pinnock of deterministic scholasticism, or the standard Calvinian logic typical of much of North American evangelicalism, had brought him numerous new theological perspectives. He now was seeing increasingly that

---

[1]John Sanders, *The God Who Risks: A Theology of Providence* (Downers Grove, Ill.: InterVarsity Press, 1998), 207.

[2]Clark Pinnock et. al., *The Openness of God: A Biblical Challenge to the Traditional Understanding of God* (Downers Grove, Ill.: InterVarsity Press, 1994), 7.

believers are to be open to questioning the appropriateness of some of the old interpretations of Scripture and to the potential of new meanings of a biblical text that the Spirit might identify in new times. He had moved toward key stances of the Arminian/Wesleyan traditions, at points even going beyond them. Central elements of what now has come to be called "free will theism" are seen in such traditions and often are also reflective of the ancient Eastern tradition of Christianity.[3] To be distinguished carefully are the non-biblical philosophical perspectives that influenced early theologians like Augustine and the biblically compatible perspectives characteristic of the ancient Eastern tradition of Christianity. Now being affirmed by Pinnock as biblically compatible is genuine human freedom granted by God's loving grace; denied is any mechanical operation of an absolute divine control that disallows real relationality between the Creator and the created.

The thirtieth annual meeting of the Evangelical Theological Society convened in December 1978 on the campus of Trinity Evangelical Divinity School—something of a homecoming for Clark Pinnock who had left the faculty of that campus in 1974 and now was back as a featured ETS speaker. According to the editors of the subsequent publication of select papers from this historic meeting:

> "Evangelicalism" is currently very visible and the "in thing" on the North American scene.... [However] much that goes by that label is shallow and shoddy. But evangelical scholarship is alive and well, coming to grips with the tough questions of the present and facing the future.[4]

---

[3]The annual meeting of the Wesleyan Theological Society that convened at Nazarene Theological Seminary in Kansas City in November 1991 focused on the topic of "Wesley and Eastern Orthodoxy." The general importance of the early church, especially its Greek theologians, on Wesley's theological understandings is now widely recognized by Wesley scholars. Randy Maddox, e.g., reports this: "My ongoing dialogue with Wesley convinced me that he is indeed best understood as one fundamentally committed to the therapeutic view of Christian life [characteristic of the Eastern tradition]. Demonstrating this primacy, and reflecting on how Wesley integrated the juridical convictions of Western Christianity into his more basic therapeutic viewpoint, has become another major goal of this book" (*Responsible Grace: John Wesley's Practical Theology*, Nashville: Kingswood Books, Abingdon Press, 1994, 23).

[4]Kenneth Kantzer, Stanley Gundry, eds., *Perspectives on Evangelical Theology* (Grand Rapids: Baker Book House, 1979), ix.

Pinnock's specific assignment was to explore intellectual issues related to classical theism. He addressed the "classical synthesis" of revelation and rationalism, insisting that biblical theism and classical theism (infused as it is with Greek philosophic ideas) are *not* the same thing. The problem is "the attempt to interpret a [biblical] message which is historical and personal at its core by means of [Greek] metaphysical categories which are ahistorical and impersonal at their core.... The dynamic ontology of the Bible clashes inevitably with the *static* ontology of the Greek thinkers...."[5]

Jacobus Arminius and John Wesley, while love-centered and appreciative of relational categories of theology,[6] nonetheless had remained rather Western in their traditional definitions of the supposed divine perfections of unchangeability, eternity, etc., which contemporary free-will theists believe bring into question the genuineness of real divine/human relationships. Thus, free-will theism calls for a more radical modification of aspects of the Western theological tradition than the Arminian/Wesleyan tradition typically has done. For instance, Pinnock's Eastern view of salvation focuses on the Holy Spirit through whom people can participate in the merits of the Christ event. This view highlights the inadequacy of the Western (Latin) teaching of substitutionary atonement and the related satisfaction theory (Christ satisfying the wrath and righteous requirements of a holy God). The atonement in Pinnock's view has its basis in the love, instead of the wrath, of God. Note the Eastern emphases of spiritual journey, transformation, the divine likeness formed in believers, and human destiny as union with God. Accordingly, Pinnock came to affirm this:

---

[5]Clark Pinnock, "The Need for a Scriptural, and Therefore a Neo-Classical Theism," in Kantzer and Gundry, op. cit., 41.

[6]Note, for instance, the Wesleyan systematic theology of H. Ray Dunning (*Grace, Faith, and Holiness*, Beacon Hill Press of Kansas City, 1988). Here there is clear appreciation for loving relationalism as key to Christian theology. Reports Dunning: "I have adopted the relational model of ontology in contrast to substantial modes of thought.... Justification is a change of relation in the external sense (the person is not changed by the relation), whereas sanctification involves a change of relation in the internal sense (the person is really changed by this relation).... The primary categories of Hebraic-Christian belief are all relational" (14-16).

Humanity was transformed by Christ through the power of the Spirit and can share in his representative journey through death to life. God revealed the goal of creation in Christ and offers it as a gift to us. His longing is for the divine likeness to be formed in us.... The work of the Spirit of creation converges on the incarnation of the Son, in which creation finds fulfillment. Through the incarnation we glimpse the destiny of our union with God, because it has implemented the goal of creaturely existence.[7]

For Pinnock, the implications of the unraveling of the Reformed and scholasticized theological logic of the Reformed tradition had begun with issues surrounding biblical inspiration and authority, but expanded in the 1970s into the territory of Christian theism itself. Briefly, Pinnock came to believe that Augustine, influenced heavily by Greek philosophy, had long ago distorted the biblical portrait of a personal, interactive, and self-giving God to one of a timeless, changeless, unmoved, and unmovable sovereign—a view to have a profound, long-term, and largely adverse impact on Christian "orthodoxy."[8] As he left Trinity for Regent College in 1974 he explained:

I have come to be increasingly skeptical of the value and truthfulness of Calvinistic theology. I find that it tends, at least in its conservative versions, to reduce the dynamic quality of the relations between God and his creatures which the Bible everywhere assumes (cf. Luke 7:30). Even more seriously, I am concerned that it threatens the integrity of the gospel which is offered in the New Testament without reservation to *all* sinners, and not to an arbitrarily selected number (cf. 1 Tim. 2:4).[9]

---

[7]Clark Pinnock, *Flame of Love: A Theology of the Holy Spirit* (Downers Grove, Ill.: InterVarsity Press, 1996), 100-101.

[8]Ironically, as Pinnock lays at Augustine's feet a considerable distortion of Christian thought rooted in elements of an alien Greek philosophy, so R. K. McGregor Wright accuses Pinnock. The doctrine of human free will, claims Wright, "is a development of the Greek assumption of the autonomy of human consciousness." To Pinnock's claim that humans are personal agents, made free as God is free, Wright responds by calling such an assertion "Greek mythology, not biblical exegesis" (*No Place for Sovereignty*, InterVarsity Press, 1996), 13, 223.

[9]Clark Pinnock, "Five Years At Trinity," *The Scribe* (student publication of Trinity Evangelical Divinity School), no issue no., 1974, 12.

Pinnock has demonstrated an instinct for addressing problem areas with courage, even with a risky abandon at times. The perceived problem with classical theism would be no exception. It was time to boldly broach the question of the "openness" of God by a daring recognition of the implications of a belief that God is not inert and immobile, a metaphysical iceberg, but a personal agent who desires loving relationships with fallen creatures and chooses the risks and costs of dynamic give-and-take interaction. Pinnock now wanted to bear convincing witness to God's relationship to a fallen world as a relationship of *dialogue*, not *monologue*. Why would God make choices involving cost and risk to the divine being? They are made because of the nature of divine love and for the redemptive purposes inherent in this magnificent love. Since Pinnock understands the operations of such love to be Spirit oriented, he criticizes the atrophied pneumatology of the West (common in evangelicalism) and enriches his own Christology by placing the person and work of Christ within the Spirit's global operations.[10]

In preparation for considering this "opening" of God, it is crucial to understand Pinnock's emerging theological method generally, the context for understanding his revised theism.

An "Open" Way of Doing Theology

Dealt with variously across his career, the question of the proper evangelical way of doing theology has always been central for Clark Pinnock. In the early phase of his work he espoused this view from which later he would depart:

> Each proposition of the Bible amounts to a divine assertion, and theology exists to organize these assertions as a botanist might collect specimens of plants. Good theology according to this ideal is a correct summarization of biblical truth. Truth is thought to be unchanging and capable of being stated in timeless and culture-free ways. Theology aims at a set of universally valid propositions.[11]

---

[10]Clark Pinnock, *Flame of Love*, 80-82.

[11]Clark Pinnock, "New Dimensions in Theological Method," in *New Dimensions in Evangelical Thought*, ed. David Dockery (Downers Grove, Ill.: InterVarsity Press, 1998), 202.

Reference here to McFague "and systematic".

In the midst of Pinnock's pilgrimage into political "radicalism" in the 1970s, he had published what he called "an outline of a systematic theology for public discipleship." Remaining "evangelical" because it sought to be faithful to the good news as biblically defined, it sought especially to "display forcefully the strength of the biblical witness to social justice and human liberation."[12] Then in 1990, now focused somewhat differently, Pinnock published *Tracking the Maze*, his most comprehensive attempt to that date to articulate a systematic approach that reflected the results of his emerging theological perspective. Actually, given the dynamic, less rationalistic, and still tentative nature of his new thinking, the word "systematic" is somewhat misleading. What he now envisioned was a *via media*, a middle way between what he called the *text* and *context* poles of any adequate Christian theology.

The search now was to find the best way to move beyond both the extremes of a doctrinally rigid and often socially irrelevant fundamentalism and a reductionistic and compromising modernism. Recently Roger Olson said that Pinnock and his Canadian colleague Stanley Grenz had become pioneers of "a cautious, biblically-committed evangelical reformism." Pinnock's response? "We are being called," he says, "to strive for the dynamic equilibrium of continuity and creativity that characterizes great theology.... More like a pilgrim than a settler, I tread the path of discovery and do my theology en route."[13] This pilgrim image was inspired in part by the narrative focus of Gabriel Fackre, a respected theological colleague of Pinnock's.[14]

The stance of the later theological work of Pinnock has been called a postmodern orthodoxy that consciously balances faithfulness and

---

[12]Clark Pinnock, "An Evangelical Theology of Human Liberation," *Sojourners* (February 1976, 30-33, and March 1976, 26-29).

[13]Roger Olson and Clark Pinnock, "A Forum: The Future of Evangelical Theology," *Christianity Today* (February 9, 1998), 42-43. Pinnock refers approvingly to Stanley Grenz as "a postmodern, soft-rational, simple biblicist type of theologian who does not discuss inspiration until page 494 [of his 1994 book *Theology for the Community of God*]" (Pinnock in Dockery, ed., op. cit., 200).

[14]See Gabriel Fackre, *The Christian Story: A Narrative Interpretation of Basic Christian Doctrine* (Grand Rapids: Eerdmans, 1984), especially pages 250-265. Also see Fackre's "An Evangelical Megashift: Promise and Peril of an 'Open' View of God," *Christian Century* (May 3, 1995), 484-487.

relevance, text and context. To get there, he proposes "to allow revelational norms to exercise control over any and all philosophical influences. . .[and to recognize] the 'sola scriptura' principle in the realm of theism."[15] Christian theology should turn away from any captivity to timeless propositions of revealed truth and any standardless vacuum of radical relativity. Rather, Christian theology should be turned toward the importance of the Bible in the midst of the faith community. For instance, in his 1996 book, *Flame of Love*, Pinnock discusses the church before the subject of salvation because of his conviction that Christian formation occurs fundamentally within the life of the church. When faithful to her intended identity and functions, the church is an event in the ongoing history of the Spirit's ministry.[16] He explained in 1985 what it had come to mean for him to write as an evangelical theologian:

> This means that my insights come from the perspective of one who stands within the stream of historic Christianity, and confesses the great truths of incarnation and atonement, of salvation by grace through faith, and of our everlasting hope only in Jesus Christ. I am committed to the infallibility of the Bible as the norm and canon for our message, and stand staunchly against the modern revolt against all these truths. Finally, I am not writing theoretically or abstractly.... As a theologian I work where the battle for gospel truth rages fiercely. As a church member and deacon, I long for the church to come alive unto God.[17]

---

[15]Clark Pinnock, "The Need for a Scriptural, and Therefore a Neo-Classical Theism," in Kantzer and Gundry, op. cit., 42. Pinnock was not ruling out the potential positives of using philosophical tools and perspectives, only warning that they should not be allowed to dominate and reshape Scripture. He notes, for instance, his appreciation for the critique of traditional Christian theism by process theology [e.g., David Griffin, *God, Power, and Evil*, 1976], while countering the "monistic" ideas used by some process theologians to "mute the biblical witness" (37).

[16]Clark Pinnock, *Flame of Love*, 114. Pinnock certainly does not limit the Spirit's ministry to the walls of the church, but seeks to recognize the special significance of the church where believers are to be formed mystically and sacramentally into Christ's humanity and thus enabled by the Spirit to participate in Christ's journey (p. 120).

[17]Clark Pinnock, *Three Keys to Spiritual Renewal* (Minneapolis: Bethany House, 1985), 11.

The divinely revealed nature of Christian truth is still assumed to be basic. He says, for instance, that "theology for evangelicals is the task of articulating the content of revelation mediated in the Scriptures."[18] While the fact of real revelation remains something not up for negotiation, the focus of Pinnock's personal passion has shifted from a vigorous rationalistic defense of this revealed theological resource. After all, evangelicals who continue to insist on a rationalistic systematizing of propositions that presumably are themselves of divine origin may turn out to be the last remaining "modernists"! By contrast, Pinnock's central goal has become helping the church to read the Bible more biblically, to worship this self-revealed God "with freedom, to experience the truth of the Bible in fresh ways, and to be able to share the gospel in a more effective and natural manner."[19] This "open" approach has real advantages, according to Pinnock. It benefits from the "vitality and diversity" of evangelicalism and looses the potential of theological creativity. Indeed, "it is an enjoyable experience to live under this tent [broad spectrum of evangelicalism] with so many who love God sincerely and want to share their faith. Living here is "less restrictive theologically and more open ecumenically" than aligning evangelicalism with a precise Reformed theology.[20]

Pinnock once quoted Ecclesiastes 3:8 about there being a time for war and a time for peace. In the 1960s he had judged that there was a great threat from religious liberalism, and thus it was the time for war. By the 1980s, although the liberal threat certainly was not wholly conquered, it was more the time to build. Since then he has been building on a particular understanding of the nature of Christian truth. It is not some simple post-Enlightenment recitation of spiritual facts, but a combination of information divinely revealed and a Person to be directly experienced. Revelation is addressed to the whole person, not merely to the intellect. Thus, truth is not just external to us, something

---

[18]Clark Pinnock, in Dockery, ed., op. cit., 200.

[19]Clark Pinnock, *Three Keys to Spiritual Renewal*, 55.

[20]Clark Pinnock, "Evangelical Theology In Progress," in *Introduction to Christian Theology*, ed. Roger Badham (Louisville: Westminster John Knox Press, 1998), 78. He added (p. 79): "It took me decades to get free of the shackles of old Princeton, but this is a diminishing problem for younger people."

to be retrieved, catalogued, and communicated, but it is also internal because of the illuminating and transformational work of the Spirit. Being also internal, however, does not mean that it is merely subjective and without objective content; nor does it mean that it is *private*, since Christian truth is known best as the Spirit of God works in the community of faith to instruct the common understanding of the contemporary meaning of the biblical text.[21]

The increasing moderation in Pinnock's previously aggressive style can be seen in the published dialogue between Pinnock and Delwin Brown (*Theological Crossfire*, 1990). Here the ability to listen, learn, and change was featured over the vigorous attempt to win an argument through rational dominance. Remaining nonetheless was something of Pinnock's old apologetic fire. For instance, he made this comment in 1985 about his liberal church upbringing and his deepest concern as a theologian:

> I remember feeling appalled at the omission of the central gospel themes both in my church and in other churches like it.... It has been about thirty years since I was saved, and I have never been able to shake off the feeling of outrage at the arrogance of the liberal decision to revise the New Testament message to make it acceptable to modern men. I suppose that my deepest concern as a theologian today is to expose and refute this deadly error.[22]

Despite such lingering combativeness of style, Pinnock's way of doing evangelical theology was now much more irenic, open, and unbounded. The foundational principle remained firm, namely that the Bible is *alone* in the sense that it finally is the only infallible norm for Christian understanding of truth. But it is *hardly alone* in the way it functions normatively—tradition, reason, and culture are constant handmaidens of hermeneutics, inevitable and useful contexts and tools of interpretation. Accordingly, "what is open to change and growth in understanding is the many and varied ways in which God speaks in Scripture and in the way theology listens."[23]

---

[21]Clark Pinnock, *Flame of Love*, 231-238.
[22]Clark Pinnock, *Three Keys to Spiritual Renewal*, 18.
[23]Clark Pinnock, in Dockery, ed., op. cit., 203.

Given this persistent concern, and reflecting an appreciative acceptance of the general thesis of Stanley Grenz and Roger Olson in their review and analysis of twentieth-century Christian theology,[24] Pinnock proceeded in the 1980s and 1990s to lay the careful groundwork for a fresh approach to Christian theology. This approach centers in what he sees as a truly biblical understanding of God which overcomes the perceived distortions caused largely by the entry into the Christian theological bloodstream long ago of an excessive hellenization (adopting a philosophy alien to the biblical one). When biblical ideas about God got coupled with contrasting views of the divine nature drawn from ancient Greek thought, the result was a theological virus that soon came to so permeate Christian theology that many came "to take the illness for granted, attributing it to divine mystery."[25] The needed antibiotic for reintroducing a more thoroughly biblical view is said to involve the "opening" of our human view of God. Once open, the result should be enhanced awareness of the possibility of humans having real relationships with a truly transcendent, yet a wonderfully loving God. The needed correction is reversing the typical tilt toward extreme divine transcendence (God seen as a "metaphysical statement about abstract being") with a measured move in the direction of an enriched under-standing of the coordinate truth of divine immanence. Pinnock's intent is to make this shift in a limited way, always under biblical control, so that it does not turn out to be the overcorrection common to "liberal" theologies and avoids falling into the trap typical of most "process" theologies.

---

[24]Stanley Grenz and Roger Olson, *20th-Century Theology: God and the World in a Transitional Age* (Downers Grove, Ill.: InterVarsity Press, 1992). Their general thesis is: "We believe that one significant theme that provides an interpretive tool and a means for bringing to light the unity and diversity of theology in this transitional century [20th] is the creative tension posed by the twin truths of the divine transcendence and the divine immanence.... Twentieth-century theology illustrates how a lopsided emphasis on one or the other eventually engenders an opposing movement that in its attempt to redress the imbalance actually moves too far in the opposite direction" (10, 12). Pinnock, while sharply opposed to the extreme immanence of classic liberalism, nonetheless came to judge that traditional evangelicalism had faulted excessively in the opposite direction. He seeks to correct this without overcorrecting.

[25]Clark Pinnock et. al., *The Openness of God*, (Downers Grove, Ill.: InterVarsity Press, 1994), 9.

The result of the needed correction, to quote prominent evangelical theologian Millard Erickson who has only limited appreciation for it, is the following:

> The free will theists see their view as quite different from the classical view in many ways. They see the latter view as being that of an absolute, perfect God, who is outside of time, knows everything, and controls or causes all that occurs. Further, he is something of an aloof monarch. He is not affected by anything that transpires in the world he has made. In contrast, their view of God is that of a loving, caring parent. He experiences the world, interacts with his children, and feels emotions. He takes risks and, in response to developments in the world, changes his mind and his actions. He does not arbitrarily and unilaterally control the world. He shares that control with humans. He is a partner with them, rather than a tyrant. Unlike a God whose experience is closed because he knows and has determined everything that will happen, this kind of God has an open experience of the world.[26]

Erickson, more generous than some of his colleagues, admits that such free-will theism "deserves careful evaluation," even though he lists his perception of its values and "its dangers." While Erickson's statement of the heart of free-will theism is terse and mildly misleading at points, it is generally accurate. There indeed are dangers when engaging in significant theological alteration, but a risky alteration accomplished many centuries ago brought about what now may need altering again. Doing Christian theology is an ongoing process that never has been free of difficulty. The risks are tolerable if one believes that the Bible and its illuminating Spirit are leading toward the proposed alteration. Pinnock had arrived at such a belief and was prepared to face the challenge.

Revising Classical Theism

Clark Pinnock was barely a teenager when theological trouble began to brew at Asbury Theological Seminary in Wilmore, Kentucky. He was not involved in any way, of course, being just a boy living in Toronto at

---

[26]Millard Erickson, *The Evangelical Left: Encountering Postconservative Evangelical Theology* (Grand Rapids: Baker Books, 1997), 93, 103-107.

the time. Only much later would he move toward the Wesleyan theological tradition that was at the center of this trouble and himself become active in leading in innovations similar to what shook the Kentucky campus in 1948-1950. A brief review sets the stage for increased present understanding.

That shaking in the late 1940s involved a popular Asbury professor, Claude Thompson, and his alleged views, as well as those of his teacher, Edwin Lewis of Drew University.[27] Lewis had published *The Creator and the Adversary*, a book that to many readers contained more theological innovation than could be tolerated easily.[28] He wrote about the problem of evil in relation to a God of goodness and love. His obvious commitment to an Arminian notion of human free will led Lewis to question the Calvinist reliance on the absolute sovereignty of God as the right assumption in relation to which one must solve the problem of evil's pervasive presence. The resulting unwillingness to make God responsible for evil took Lewis—according to his critics—to the edge of dualism. Was God, in fact, limited, even finite, a struggler in this world of evil? There certainly was in the Wesleyan theological tradition an understanding that God is self-limiting, voluntarily granting genuine human freedom for the sake of a true love relationship. But in the case of the trouble surrounding Thompson and Lewis at mid-century, influential elements of the North American Wesleyan-Holiness tradition associated with Asbury seminary had begun looking toward classic evangelicalism, then being defined by the young National Association of Evangelicals as a primary theological paradigm.[29] This partnership brought shockwaves to Asbury. Thompson finally resigned under pressure, and the seminary soon lost its accreditation for a short time. This tragic episode helped define the need for a fresh openness in

---

[27]See Scott Kisker, "The Claude Thompson Controversy at Asbury Theological Seminary," *Wesleyan Theological Journal* 33:2 (Fall 1998), 230-248.

[28]Abingdon Press, 1948.

[29]For the last half of the twentieth century, whole denominations within the Wesleyan-Holiness theological tradition would face identity crises arising in part from a dominant "evangelical" culture in which they found themselves participating— and into which they increasingly feared significant absorption. Note, e.g., Luke Keefer, "Brethren In Christ: Uneasy Synthesis of Heritage Streams," *Wesleyan Theological Journal* 33:1 (Spring 1998), 92-110.

theology that champions key elements of the Wesleyan theological tradition in contrast to a rigorous and rationalistic evangelical alternative.

Clark Pinnock had begun his Christian life in the paradigm of classic evangelicalism, but his personal and theological journey had taken him in the direction of the Wesleyan tradition. By the late 1970s he had moved to a position of openness similar in some ways to that of Thompson decades earlier. In 1977 he returned to his home area as Associate Professor of Systematic Theology at McMaster Divinity College in Hamilton, Ontario. Here his evolving pattern of theological innovation and sometimes boldness entered their more mature stages. To one observer he appeared to function as a "more spiritually sensitive theologian than at any time in his career."[30] He had come to a more relational, responsive, and personally satisfying understanding of who God is and how God relates to this fallen world. Having invested the early stage of his professional career in dealing largely with the nature and authority of the Bible, he now found himself directly addressing the largest subject of all, Christian theism.

Adequacy in a Christian doctrine of God, he said, would be "a distillation of what we believe God has told us about himself.... Although the Bible does not present a systematic doctrine of God that can be easily reproduced, it provides building blocks for such a doctrine."[31] In order to formulate what he was coming to accept as an adequate view, he gathered these building blocks that both criticized elements of classic Christian theism and warned that the popular "process" alternative did and did not better represent the broader biblical vision of the divine that now was enriching his thought and Christian life. God surely is more than the earthbound gods of modern thought. The Divine is transcendent in a way that can really satisfy today's urgent questions about meaning and significance with answers that have roots in a reality

---

[30]Robert Rakestraw, "Clark Pinnock," in *Baptist Theologians*, eds. Timothy George and David Dockery (Nashville: Broadman Press, 1990), 664. Pinnock's current local church membership is at Westmount Baptist Church, Hamilton, Ontario, where he and his wife Dorothy function as active laypersons.

[31]Clark Pinnock, in Pinnock and Delwin Brown, *Theological Crossfire: An Evangelical/Liberal Dialogue* (Grand Rapids: Zondervan, 1990), 61, 63.

beyond the restricted and momentary horizons of this world. God clearly rules over the world, but in a way that does not negate its basic character and structure, including its divinely-given freedom to be and choose. Indeed:

> To say that God is the sovereign Creator means that God is the ground of the world's existence and the source of all its possibilities. But he is not necessarily the puppet master who pulls all the strings. It is possible for God to make a world with some relative autonomy of its own, a world where there exist certain structures which are intelligible in their own right and finite agents with the capacity for free choice. Thus, God gives a degree of reality and power to the creation and does not retain a monopoly of power for himself. His sovereignty is not the all-determining kind, but an omnicompetent kind. God is certainly able to deal with any circumstances which might arise, and nothing can possibly defeat or destroy God. But he does not control everything that occurs. God honors the degree of relative autonomy which he grants the world.[32]

How is God best understood? The answer to this question lies at the foundation of all Christian theology and, for Pinnock, is explained well in his essay titled "From Augustine To Arminius: A Pilgrimage in Theology."[33] Biblically speaking, God at least is the Lord, sovereign and free, the mystery who transcends all time and worlds and all that they contain. But "classic" orthodoxy came to add to such affirmations that God's glory is the ultimate purpose that all creation serves, that God controls all that happens, and that God's sovereign will is irresistible. According to the Westminster Confession (1646): "God from all eternity did, by the most wise and holy counsel of his own will, freely and unchangeably ordain whatsoever comes to pass" (3:1). After World War II, evangelicalism in North America was dominated by this classic view that God is best understood as the One who is all-controlling and

---

[32]Clark Pinnock, "God Limits His Knowledge," in *Predestination & Free Will: Four Views of Divine Sovereignty and Human Freedom*, eds. David and Randall Basinger (Downers Grove, Ill.: InterVarsity Press, 1986), 145-146.

[33]This pivotal Pinnock essay appears in *The Grace of God and the Will of Man*, ed. Clark Pinnock (Minneapolis: Bethany House Publishers, 1995, original edition 1989), 15-30.

ordains all things, the One who is timeless, changeless, passionless, unmoved, and unmovable. This was the very teaching environment of Clark Pinnock's earliest years as a Christian, and a view he later would refer to as "a power-centered theology requiring deterministic freedom and no-risk providence" [no risk to God].[34] This classic characterization of the divine…

> …emphasizes God's sovereignty, majesty and glory. God's will is the final explanation for all that happens; God's glory is the ultimate purpose that all creation serves. In his infinite power, God brought the world into existence in order to fulfill his purposes and display his glory. Since his sovereign will is irresistible, whatever he dictates comes to pass and every event plays its role in his grand design. Nothing can thwart or hinder the accomplishment of his purposes. God's relation to the world is thus one of mastery and control.[35]

One finds this "classic" view of God defended and expounded in Pinnock's early writings. But by the 1970s the theological landscape was shifting for Pinnock. In the stimulating environment of Trinity Evangelical Divinity School he prepared a major manuscript he titled *The Living God and Secular Experience.* Explaining that it was *for* and not *of* the times, he resisted the common call to reformulate the Christian gospel without the hypothesis of a transcendent God. His wish was to "maintain that the doctrine of God is meaningful simply because it alone is capable of illuminating large areas of human experience" (Introduction). He assumed that theological answers need to be connected with the questions emerging from the contemporary human situation. While biblical norms are not to be subservient to modern

---

[34]Clark Pinnock, "Evangelical Theologians Facing the Future: An Ancient and a Future Paradigm," *Wesleyan Theological Journal* 33:2(Fall 1998), 22. In 1998 there appeared *The God Who Risks: A Theology of Providence* by John Sanders (InterVarsity Press). Pinnock refers to this book as a competent and detailed argument that God indeed is relational in nature, and in the manner of working with the creation God is relational and loving to the extent of taking real "risks." Says Sanders: "The almighty God creates significant others with freedom and grants them space to be alongside him and to collaborate with him" (137).

[35]Richard Rice, "Biblical Support for a New Perspective," in Clark Pinnock et. al., *The Openness of God: A Biblical Challenge to the Traditional Understanding of God,* (Downers Grove, Ill.: InterVarsity Press, 1994), 11.

ideas, theology needs to be clear, intelligible, and its relevance to real life made explicit. What then, he asked, is the biblical understanding of God and how God relates to ordinary human life?

Trinity had granted him a sabbatical in 1972 to write this work. The school provided what he called an "open atmosphere which enables a person to develop his thinking in the service of the Lord Jesus Christ" (Introduction). Its initial use was to have been as the basis of a lectureship to be given at Conservative Baptist Theological Seminary in Portland, Oregon. But when they saw the text, they cancelled the engagement! Here was an early warning signal about Pinnock's Arminian turn, and the negative reactions that on occasion would result.

The manuscript was submitted to InterVarsity Press, with more frustration being the eventual result. The decision was not to publish. The editor affirmed that Pinnock's position was a legitimate evangelical option and that the writing had the potential of real significance that might be worthy of wide consideration one day, but the editor also thought it was just not yet ready to be released. Specifically: "We are not rejecting the manuscript because it is Arminian, too 'radical' or too far away from the main stream of evangelical thought. Rather, our hesitancy has to do with the manner in which the theological and philosophical argument is mustered."[36] Pinnock indeed was emerging as an Arminian[37] in a Calvinism-dominated evangelicalism. He was a theologian increasingly sympathetic to the Eastern mentality of Christianity while yet rooted in Western language and still wishing to address an evangelicalism that remains quite Western in its general mentality.[38] How he would go about mustering his arguments for the change would remain

---

[36]Letter to Clark Pinnock from James W. Sire, Editor, InterVarsity Press, October 3, 1972.

[37]To be more precise, Pinnock had come to affirm certain key elements of Arminianism, while in the process gaining considerable sympathy for categories and insights of the Eastern tradition of Christianity not necessarily affirmed by Jacobus Arminius.

[38]This sympathy of Pinnock with teaching themes of Eastern Orthodoxy was less the result of concentrated study of Eastern theologians and more the fruit of fresh biblical study through the eyes of a warmhearted pietism that suggests more relational and dynamic theological categories than has been typical of much theology in the West. For more detail on Pinnock's shift toward the Eastern mind, especially by way of Wesleyanism, see chapter 4.

controversial for many, although InterVarsity Press, true to its word, would become one of his main publishers.

By the 1980s he was identifying key aspects of the classical theism found in Augustine, Aquinas, and Reformed scholasticism as a significant theological problem. The problem was said to be that God is understood as a closed, immobile, and unchanging structure, rather than the more biblical view of God as a dynamic personal agent who by choice is deeply and vulnerably involved in human joys and sorrows. To many ancient minds, a god who is immutable and impassable suggested a divine being who is stoic, stable, even untouchable. But the divine determination of all things, meaning that the future is already settled and divinely known, "has a definite tendency to diminish the dynamic dimension of God's nature and to threaten the reality of creaturely freedom."[39] Such diminishing and threatening were now being judged by Pinnock as serious theological and practical matters. The classic tendency is to "prefer to speak more of God's power than of weakness, more of God's eternity than of temporality, and more of God's immutability than of living changeableness in relation to us."[40] But he had come to believe that the Calvinist argument for God's exhaustive foreknowledge was tantamount to predestination since it implies the fixity of all things. Further, the rigid categories of scholastic Calvinism were now seen as inadequate to contain the radically relational God revealed in the Bible. After all, the Word *became* flesh—a dramatic statement of God's changing unchangeability!

For Pinnock this classic tendency for fixity is a serious distortion that needs to be corrected—without the equal danger lurking in an over-correction. Avoiding such an equal danger was the central burden of Gabriel Fackre's essay review of the books *The Openness of God* and *Unbounded Love*, each by Pinnock and others. According to Fackre, "Evangelicals pursuing the agenda of immanence and openness would benefit from studying the mainline's previous engagement with this

---

[39]Clark Pinnock, "Between Classical and Process Theism," in *Process Theology*, ed. Ronald Nash (Grand Rapids: Baker Books, 1987), 315.

[40]Clark Pinnock, "Systematic Theology," in Pinnock et. al., *The Openness of God: A Biblical Challenge to the Traditional Understanding of God* (Downers Grove, Ill.: InterVarsity Press, 1994), 105.

subject." To clarify the points of wisdom gained in this previous engagement, he highlights five subjects, each intended as a point of current caution for free-will theists like Pinnock. They are the areas of: (1) human freedom and divine sovereignty where it is easy to stumble on oversimplifications that lead to both predestinarian determinisms and libertarian Pelagianisms; (2) the need to avoid cultural captivity when celebrating divine immanence; (3) dealing adequately with a necessary political witness when underscoring divine compassion and vulnerability; (4) being adequately sober about the depth and intractability of sin when insisting on the limitations of the Augustinian-Reformation tradition that may limit excessively divine relationality and human responsibility; and (5) not forgetting that God also is holy when one seeks to correct a pattern of "retributive absolutisms" unfairly attributed to God. Fackre is appreciative of Pinnock's central concerns and only calls for caution that in the proper recovery of certain biblical accents too often lost by Christian theologians there remain "the importance of the closure as well as the openness of God."[41]

Not unmindful of the necessary cautions to be honored in the midst of significant corrections, Pinnock proceeded to initiate fresh thought about the "social Trinity." Reluctance to recognize a truly social model of Trinity is judged a major theological problem over the centuries. While making the doctrine of the Trinity central to his theology, Karl Barth, for instance, elevated unity over diversity, insisting on speaking of three modes of divine functioning rather than three persons in God. For Pinnock, "such agnosticism regarding the immanent Trinity has led some of his [Barth's] disciples into unitarianism" and has deprived Christians of "the revolutionary insight concerning God's nature represented by the social analogy of the Trinity." Naturally one wants to make it easier for Jews and Muslims to appreciate Christianity in the context of monotheism; thus, in order to avoid any suggestion of tri-theism, "we say that the Trinity is a society of persons united by a common divinity. There is one God, eternal, uncreated, incomprehensible, and there is no other. But God's nature is internally complex

---

[41]Gabriel Fackre, "An Evangelical Megashift? The Promise and Peril of an 'Open' View of God," *Christian Century* (May 3, 1995), 485-487.

and consists of a fellowship of three. It is the essence of God's nature to be relational."[42]

In this dynamic but still biblical context of a relational God who chooses loving reciprocity with creation, it had become possible for Pinnock to engage again in the reconceptualization of God similar to the reforming work of John Wesley two centuries earlier. Wesley argues in his "Thoughts upon Divine Sovereignty" that integral to the divinity of God as God is the necessary association of divine justice and mercy with divine transcendence, power, and sovereignty. By insisting on such a necessary association, Theodore Jennings, Jr., suggests that Wesley "sought to overcome a bifurcation in the conceptualization of the divine being which seemed to be the consequence, on the one hand, of a deistic conception of God and, on the other, of a Calvinist reflection on the divine sovereignty.... [Thus] the question of the poor, of the violated and humiliated of the earth, is decisive for the doctrine of God."[43] After all, the distinctive place where the God of the biblical witness intersected the life process of creation was at the point of pain. Israel experienced great pain in its Egyptian slavery and through it a distinctive discernment of the God who identifies with, shares, and redeems (the exodus) in the midst of the pain. As the classic biblical story reads, God instructs Moses to say to the suffering Israelites who had cried to God in their pain: "I am the Lord and I will bring you out from under the yoke of the Egyptians. I will free you from being slaves to them and will redeem you with an outstretched arm and with mighty acts of judgment. I will take you as my own people, and I will be your God" (Ex. 6:6-7).

Clark Pinnock has not wanted to overdo his criticisms of classical theism—after all, in his judgment the classic view is far better than radically liberal or extreme process views of God. But he had learned a few important lessons from process thinker Charles Hartshorne, for instance. One was the lesson that God, although unchanging in character

---

[42]Clark Pinnock, *Flame of Love: A Theology of the Holy Spirit* (Downers Grove, Ill.: InterVarsity Press, 1996), 33-35.

[43]Theodore W. Jennings, Jr., "Transcendence, Justice, and Mercy: Toward a (Wesleyan) Reconceptualization of God," in *Rethinking Wesley's Theology for Contemporary Methodism*, ed. Randy Maddox (Nashville: Kingswood Books, Abingdon Press, 1998), 65.

and intent, surely is nonetheless able to change operationally in response to a changing creation that possesses genuine freedom of decision. Pinnock confesses that, without being a process thinker himself, "God has used process thinkers to compel me to change certain ideas which I had and bring them up to scriptural standards."[44] He admits that modern culture generally has also influenced him in this matter, encouraging in him a new emphasis on human freedom and a viewing of God as self-limited in relation to this present world. In this case, he is sure that modernity has drawn reflection in the direction of biblical teaching. Further, recovering fresh dimensions of God's immanence helps today's Christians to relate to the new insights into the origin of the universe now being supplied by modern science.[45]

Pinnock shares his fear that "if evangelical theologians refuse to recognize the moments of truth in process thought, they will force many to accept process theology."[46] Such acceptance is viewed as highly negative because the process view of theism is an "extreme correction" to the classical theism it seeks to improve. It so honors the freedom instinct of modernity that God's very being is fundamentally compromised. The reduction leads to a feeble theism deserving of judgment. For process theists:

> God is not the ground of the world's existence and has no final control over what is going on.... God is finite and metaphysically incapable of determining events.... A God who is neither the creator or redeemer of the world in any strong sense does not deserve to be called God, and is vastly inferior to the God of the Bible and evangelical experience.[47]

---

[44]Clark Pinnock, "Between Classical and Process Theism," 317. Another evangelical, Gregory Boyd, embraces elements of the fundamental vision of the process world view and constructs an interpretation of the Trinity with careful modifications of this process vision (see Boyd, *Trinity and Process*, New York: Peter Lang, 1992).

[45]Clark Pinnock, "Systematic Theology," 113. He refers the reader to Hugh Montefiore's *The Probability of God* (London: SCM Press, 1985) which "shows us how to craft a new teleological argument out of the evidences of modern science in relation to the immanence of God the Spirit."

[46]Clark Pinnock, "Between Classical and Process Theism," 317.

[47]Ibid., 318.

Therefore, despite his deep concern about some aspects of classical theism and his appreciation for some aspects of process thought, Pinnock remains a committed and biblically oriented evangelical Christian. Commenting on the "social trinity" of God, Pinnock confesses valuing "the way in which trinitarian theology can match process theology's witness to God as being related to and being affected by the world without requiring one to actually adopt a process metaphysics."[48]

The guarded appreciation of Pinnock for aspects of process thought originated largely with the appearance of Delwin Brown's review of Pinnock's *The Scripture Principle* in 1984.[49] That led to some Brown-Pinnock correspondence, then an invitation for Pinnock to teach in the Aspen summer school sponsored by Iliff School of Theology where Brown was a faculty member and later dean. Brown and Pinnock found that they had much in common[50] and engaged in extensive dialogue that led to their joint book *Theological Crossfire: An Evangelical/Liberal Dialogue* in 1990. In this published dialogue with a well-known process theologian, Pinnock explains his own view:

> I do not think it is quite enough to assign God the role of experiencing and remembering everything, to make God the final organizer of what comes to him from the world. According to the biblical message, God takes the initiative in the history of salvation. So even though I too [like Delwin Brown] want to replace a static view of God with a dynamic view, it cannot just be any dynamic view but must be the dynamic theism of the scriptural witness.[51]

---

[48]Clark Pinnock, "A Bridge and Some Points of Growth: A Reply to Cross and Macchia," *Journal of Pentecostal Theology* (October 1998), 51.

[49]The Delwin Brown book review, including Pinnock's response, appeared in the *Christian Scholar's Review* in 1990.

[50]Delwin Brown had been reared in the Church of God (Anderson) and thus understood well a conservative mindset like that of Pinnock. Pinnock has referred to Brown as "an irenic, wonderful, non-sectarian person," adding: "Brown reached out to me and I reached back" (in the Pinnock interview with Barry Callen, November 21, 1998).

[51]Clark Pinnock, in Pinnock and Delwin Brown, *Theological Crossfire* (Grand Rapids: Zondervan, 1990), 96.

In 1997 Pinnock was an invited participant at an evangelical-process dialogue at Claremont School of Theology. Then in 1998 he participated in a followup Whitehead conference. For this second major meeting he had suggested to the planners that there be a special section where the evangelical-process dialogue could proceed. Such did take place. He then arranged for papers to be prepared on the two sides of this dialogue, papers that he planned to edit and gather into a book to widen the circle of awareness of these important discussions. In Pinnock's judgment, the obvious circumstance that emerged is that there are both affinities and differences that need to be clarified for the process and evangelical publics.[52] He was open to taking the lead in such clarification, although warned that many conservatives would see this very dialogue as evidence that the free-will theism so identified with Pinnock really is a subtle form of process theology—and thus dangerously unbiblical. Since Pinnock was confident that this is not the case, he chose to take the risk of being wrongly characterized by many of his evangelical colleagues.[53]

His approach to the doctrine of God shows his continuing evangelical identity, regardless of his affinity with select insights of process theism. He will not yield the ontological transcendence of God. God *is*, even when the world is not. Contemporary Christians should resist the "interiorization of faith where Christianity becomes an ideal of life rather than a truth claim about an objective God beyond the natural

⌐ contra McFague !

_____

[52]A forthcoming (2000) Eerdmans volume, co-edited by Clark Pinnock and John B. Cobb, Jr., is tentatively titled *Searching for an Adequate God*. In the Introduction, Pinnock highlights a series of important convictions shared by process and free-will or evangelical openness theists. They include: the value of natural theology, the love of God as a central theme and high priority, a dynamic understanding of the world and God's interactive relations with it,rejection of the notion of God being absolute in the sense of being unaffected by the world, and the need to critique classical substantive metaphysics. He goes on, however, to note some important theological differences. His conclusion is to call for a "hermeneutic of charity" which affirms that "differences are not something to be done away with but something to be embraced because, when we embrace them, a larger sense of the truth can emerge."

[53]Millard Erickson, e.g., is prepared to commend free-will theists for clarifying the effect of historical conditioning on Christian theologies. However, he is concerned about what he says is the "amazing lack of acknowledgment or even recognition of the place that philosophical or other presuppositions play in their theology" (*The Evangelical Left*, 1997, 107).

world."[54] He places much responsibility on Kant for the negative trend today that seeks to shift the grounding of theological concepts to the realm of human experience. Further, evangelicals are said to appropriately resist some aspects of the modern trend to use "inclusive" language. Commitment to biblical revelation rather than modern experience and ideology inclines Pinnock toward using biblical language. For instance, Jesus used "Father" in his own prayers. So should we— without naively assuming that God is in any sense gender-specific in human terms. Feminine images of God, of course, are also used on occasion by inspired biblical writers, and thus in some settings are fully appropriate for use today. The controlling criterion of judgment is that

> ...the foundational symbols of the Bible cannot be replaced, though they may be supplemented and interpreted. The symbols cannot be replaced because they are not based upon cultural experience but on a divine intrusion into history.... We do not feel entitled to resymbolize Christian theology to suit ourselves, based in the ostensive authority of human experience.[55]

Contra McFague!

Pinnock's general intent is to retain as much as possible of the biblical portrait of God as taught faithfully in the classical tradition, except at the points where the conserving tradition has been found to be preserving elements not truly biblical. If his critics are right that Pinnock's "openness" views of God are largely reflections of modern philosophical and politically correct assumptions, he would find such criticism devastating.[56] To him, the primary criterion of truth for the Christian is fidelity to the Scriptures. But, in fact, he judges that the critics are wrong in this regard, and that an "openness model" of God is more adequate than several aspects of conventional Christian theism precisely because it expresses better the burden of biblical revelation.

---

[54]Clark Pinnock, in *Theological Crossfire*, 67-68.

[55]Ibid., 72. Pinnock adds: "The female imagery cannot be used to supplant the controlling symbols. At issue is the authority of the Bible. For many feminists it is an androcentric book that deserves their condemnation. They read it in overtly biased ways and accord infallibility to their own experience instead. This places them firmly outside the mainstream Christian community" (77).

[56]One such critic is D. A. Carson. He is sharply critical of domestications of God "in line with what appears acceptable to the contemporary spirit." Process theology, says Carson, "wants to emphasize God's personhood while dismissing his absoluteness." He sees Pinnock as an evangelical theologian who is inclined toward

The God Who Risks the Process

The proper view of Christian theism, then, is now thought by Clark Pinnock to be a carefully balanced model that is both sensitive to select insights of contemporary "process" thought and also retains the core biblical elements of theism that insure true divine transcendence. Calling the new alternative "classical free-will theism," he explains:

> It means that we affirm God as creator of the world as classical theism does and process thought does not, and also affirm the openness of God as process theology does and classical theism does not sufficiently. This leaves us with a model of the divine which sees God as transcendent over the world and yet existing in an open and mutually affecting relationship with the world. It is a doctrine of God which maintains mutuality and reciprocity within the framework of divine transcendence.[57]

Pinnock wishes to be clear that, in projecting this new model of Christian theism, it is really very "old." The Bible and not modernity is being given the primary and final voice. As the whole Bible narrative reflects, history is to be seen as much more than "the temporal unfolding of an eternal blueprint of the divine decisions." In fact, by divine choice, human history is "the theatre where new situations are encountered and fresh decisions are made, the scene of divine and human creativity."[58] God tested Abraham to see what he would do. Only after the test did God conclude: "Now I know that you fear God" (Gen. 12:22). Commenting on the wickedness of Israel, God says in frustration: "...nor did it enter my mind that they should do this abomination" (Jer. 32:35). The flow of human history yields results to which God reacts.

The mistake of classical theism is its denial of the gracious choice of the sovereign God to grant real freedom to humans and to enter the

---

accommodation in ways similar to process thought, although he recognizes that Pinnock distinguishes himself from process theology in a few key ways. What of the book *The Openness of God* with which Pinnock is associated so closely? Carson thinks it is "the most consistently inadequate treatment of both Scripture and historical theology dealing with the doctrine of God that I have ever seen from the hands of serious evangelical writers" (*The Gagging of God*, Zondervan, 1996, 225).

[57]Clark Pinnock, "Between Classical and Process Theism," 321.
[58]Ibid., 323.

human arena vulnerably and redemptively so as to affect and be affected by the flawed human historical process that persists prior to the final triumph of God over all evil. God feels the pain of broken relationships (Jer. 31:20). This surely is at the heart of the meaning of the incarnation and is symbolized dramatically by the cross of the Christ. On that old tree of divine sacrifice it is revealed that love instead of coercive power is the primary perfection of God. God works "not in order to subject our wills but to transform our hearts."[59] There emerges a distinctive view of God, a dynamic theism that sees God as simultaneously sovereign over creation and suffering with creation. God is involved, interactive, responsive, and compassionate. God should not be understood either as immune to the evil and suffering of our world or trapped in an ongoing codependence with this world. Pinnock has come to join John Wesley in understanding God's power

> ...fundamentally in terms of *empowerment*, rather than control or *overpowerment*. This is not to weaken God's power, but to determine its character! As Wesley was fond of saying, God works "strongly and sweetly." That is, God's grace works powerfully, but not irresistibly, in matters of human life and salvation; thereby empowering our *response-ability*, without overriding our *responsibility*.[60]

The doctrine of God as "Trinity" is crucial for reflecting adequately the very nature of God and, consequently, God's chosen relation to the creation. Pinnock now teaches a relational ontology, a social trinitarian metaphysics that views God as both ontologically other (not part of or dependent on creation) and at the same time relating actively and responsively to the creation with unmerited love. God has chosen to create "an echo in space and time of the communion that God experiences in eternity, a reflection on the creaturely level of the loving movement within God." Since God by nature is "socially triune," the creation is designed to be "an ecosystem capable of echoing back the triune life of God." God exists as a communion of love and freedom, is

---

[59]Clark Pinnock, "Systematic Theology," 114.
[60]Randy Maddox, *Responsible Grace: John Wesley's Practical Theology* (Nashville: Kingswood Books, Abingdon Press, 1994), 93.

"an open and dynamic structure" which, while wholly self-sufficient, "delights in a world in which he can interact with creatures for whom his love can overflow."[61] Frank Macchia helpfully summarizes by explaining that Pinnock

> ...views the Godhead as a fellowship of persons. God for Pinnock is not pure "rationality" decreeing eternal ideas and causing all things to conform to their fulfillment. God is rather pure "relationality" which seeks to draw all things into the symphony of love that is played eternally within the divine life. The graceless God who forms covenants in order to exact obedience is replaced by the triune God whose very being is an eternal dance of love into which the Spirit of God attempts to bring the entire creation by grace.[62]

God's involvement with the world is characterized by the unchanging nature, essence, and intent of God, but also by God's responsive and therefore changing experience, knowledge, and action. Never is God subject to change involuntarily, but God allows the world to touch and affect him—the very world over which God is truly transcendent.

For evangelicals, probably the most troublesome implication of this more dynamic view of the divine nature and resulting historical involvement is Pinnock's belief that they necessarily imply a limitation of God's complete knowledge of the future. Here is his assessment:

> Like Philo before him, Augustine had wedded to the biblical portrait of God certain Greek presuppositions about divine perfection, notably God's immutability. This made it impossible for Augustine to think of God's learning anything he had not eternally known or changing in response to new circumstances. He thought of God as existing beyond the realm of change and time, and knowing all things past, present and future in a timeless present. However, if history is infallibly known and certain from all eternity, then freedom is an illusion.[63]

---

[61]Clark Pinnock, "Systematic Theology," 108, 110.
[62]Frank Macchia, "Tradition and the *Novum* of the Spirit: A Review of Clark Pinnock's *Flame of Love*," *Journal of Pentecostal Theology* 13 (1998), 34.
[63]Clark Pinnock, "God Limits His Knowledge," 150.

The reality of human freedom is compromised if God knows in advance what humans will decide. If freedom is real and decisions are not yet made, then Pinnock judges that information about those coming decisions does not yet exist—thus cannot be known even by God. That God must know all things that can be known and knows them rightly, he readily affirms. Nonetheless, divine omniscience need not mean exhaustive foreknowledge of all future events. If that were its meaning, would the future not be fixed and determined, much as is the past? In that case, nothing in the future needs to be decided, and human freedom is an illusion. We make no difference and are not responsible.[64] God faces the future as a partly unsettled matter. It is unsettled because of the human choices not yet made, but also it is settled by what already has happened and certainly by what God promises to do eventually regardless of human choice. God indeed is omniscient, but in a way congruent with the character of the created world—the very character chosen and enabled by God.

By the 1990s Pinnock had participated with four others in producing the book *The Openness of God* as a direct challenge to select aspects of the traditional Christian understanding of God.[65] Recognizing the centrality of the doctrine of God and how it deeply

---

[64]Of course, classic Christian theists seek to uphold both a genuine human freedom and God's power and knowledge as total ("compatibilism"). Pinnock says that this is theological sleight of hand and does not work. Millard Erickson's response is that Pinnock's "incompatibilist" view has not effectively refuted the compatibilist view (*The Evangelical Left*, 1997, 105). Norman Geisler also challenges the incompatibilist view, particularly on the basis of predictive prophecy which Geisler argues shows that God often had specific knowledge of future events before human choice brought them into actual being (*Creating God in the Image of Man?*, 1997, 149). Contrary to Geisler's challenging of the incompatibilist view, Gregory Boyd reads a passage like 2 Kings 20 and asks: "Was God being truthful when he had Isaiah tell Hezekiah he was planning to bring him home? And if so, then must we not believe that God really changed his mind when he decided to add fifteen years to Hezekiah's life?" (Boyd, *The God of the Possible*, 1999, Preface).

[65]In fact, the concept of this book originated with John Sanders, who was encouraged by Pinnock to fulfill his vision and pursue the proposed authors. The eventual publication, while not identifying the editor, put priority on Pinnock's name because of its prominence in the marketplace. Sanders judged this decision appropriate, although it should be clear that he had come to many of his own "openness" insights about God separate from Pinnock's direct mentoring.

affects a believer's understanding of incarnation, grace, creation, election, salvation, security, and even destiny, these five authors were ready to state boldly that classic notions of the divine nature drawn largely from Greek thought constitute a serious distortion calling for careful correction. A growing number of Christian leaders had become convinced of the need for a model of God which preserves God's transcendent distinction from creation while upholding both divine and human agency within the historical workings of creation. What had been lost in Reformed scholasticism was the God of promise and love who acts in human history. Replacing this biblical God was a relatively removed deity described by a set of metaphysical statements.[66] Ancient Greek thinking put the perfect and ultimate in the realm of the absolutely transcendent and immutable. By contrast, Pinnock began attempting to provide a fresh model, said to be the old biblical model, an "open view" of God or a "free-will theism" which has been identified as "a biblically persuasive yet nonetheless breathtaking revision of classical theism."[67]

> The issue of divine sovereignty, understood as "nothing happens except what is knowingly and willingly decreed by him" (John Calvin, Institutes, 1.16.3), can be very troubling for modern people who wonder about the supposed divine purpose in the death camps of the Holocaust or the killing fields of Cambodia. So Clark Pinnock concluded that "history itself seems to call the sovereignty of God into question and to require us to rethink it." Further, the Bible "seems to portray more genuine interaction and relationality in God's dealings with creatures than theological determinism allows." Therefore, "it would seem that we need a better model of divine sovereignty than that of total control." If God is a loving parent, sensitive and responsive,

---

[66]Clark Pinnock said the following in his Azusa Street Lecture at Regent University on April 20, 1999 (unpublished): "The problem of classical theism lies in the fact that it posited an ideal of the divine infinite perfection which is often (not always) at odds with what the Bible says about God. It adopted a standard of what God must be like derived from human reason and it used it to interpret the Bible.... In effect, pagan philosophy dictates what the Bible may say.... Isn't that what we usually call 'liberal' theology?"

[67]Henry Knight III, *A Future For Truth: Evangelical Theology in a Postmodern World* (Nashville: Abingdon Press, 1997), 168-169.

evidently God has chosen "to actualize a world with significantly free agents and to exercise sovereignty in an open manner."[68]

Such divine openness calls for a new view of divine power. God chooses to delegate power to the creature, willing that human history flow from the decisions of free persons who, because of their freedom, are capable of both evil and lovingly responding to a loving God. By a deliberate choice, God thus becomes vulnerable to human choice and normally does not choose to override human decisions—at least not immediately. Jesus says that God's rule is near but not yet in full effect since the powers of darkness still resist. Paul says that the Spirit waits and groans with us on the way to final redemption (Rom. 8:23). God clearly is sovereign, meaning that all ability exists within the divine being, but not that there is any divine tyranny involved. God can and will manage, whatever the resistance to the divine will, and one day will triumph. Even so, risk, frustration, and pain lie along the way. This vulnerability exposes God to genuine suffering, a most unusual and amazing expression of the power of a truly sovereign and wonderfully loving God. Insists Pinnock:

> The power of love, the power that wills genuine relationships, is certainly not a diminished or inferior form of power.... Jesus likens God to a father who lets his son leave home and learn for himself that sin leads to destruction.... God's true power is revealed in the cross of Jesus Christ. In this act of self-sacrificing, God deploys power in the mode of servanthood, overcoming enemies not by annihilating them but by loving them.[69]

With love as God's reigning attribute, the sovereign God, truly transcendent, has chosen to make room for others and to seek real and mutually responsible relationships with them. Accordingly, the

---

[68]Clark Pinnock, "God's Sovereignty in Today's World," *Theology Today* 53:1 (April 1996), 16-18. Richard Muller recognizes that contemporary evangelical theology needs to express the profound involvement of God with creation (just as Pinnock does). Contrary to Pinnock, however, Muller remains convinced that the structure of classical theism is still the best option. He insists that "incarnation and the divine immutability are not contraries" ("Incarnation, Immutability, and the Case for Classical Theism," *The Westminster Theological Journal*, Spring 1983, 25).

[69]Pinnock, "God's Sovereignty in Today's World," 20.

wonderful truth is that "God is so powerful as to be able to stoop down and humble himself, and God is so stable and secure as to be able to risk suffering and change."[70] This sovereign God has created a world populated by free agents who are drawn by the Creator's love, but who also are capable of rejecting God's love. God is willing to relate to and work with this risky historical process, choosing to accept a future that is open and a world that is dynamic rather than one that is static and predetermined.[71]

During 1986 for the first time, this concept of a dynamic God-creation relationship was extended by Pinnock to the issue of divine knowledge.[72] God is sovereign, but sovereignty means the power to create any possible universe, including one in which significantly free agents are involved. Such a universe would owe its existence entirely to God's will, but what happens among created and free agents might or might not conform to God's intentions. In this light it had come to make no sense to Pinnock for one to claim that we humans act freely if we are in fact doing only what God from eternity predestined us to do and knew that we would do. He concludes that God allows the future to be "really open and not available to exhaustive foreknowledge even on the part of God." God certainly is omniscient in that all things knowable are divinely known. But "free actions are not entities which

---

[70]Pinnock, "Systematic Theology," 105.

[71]This line of thought is appreciated and well developed by Philip Meadows ("Providence, Chance, and the Problem of Suffering," *Wesleyan Theological Journal*, Spring 1999). Speaking of the paradox of providence and chance, Meadows explores the resources in John Wesley's theology for constructing a contemporary theodicy. He concludes that God loves the world by setting it free. Seen in the cross and resurrection of Jesus is the deeply personal and relational nature of God's vulnerable love.

[72]The previous year Richard Rice had published his *God's Foreknowledge and Man's Free Will* (Minneapolis: Bethany House, 1985). Also see David Basinger, "Can an Evangelical Christian Justifiably Deny God's Exhaustive Knowledge of the Future?" in *Christian Scholar's Review* (25:2, 1995), 133-145. Basinger concludes: "... proponents of PK [present divine knowledge as opposed to exhaustive future knowledge] retain the right to offer their perspective as a viable alternative for consideration by all sincere Christians, including evangelicals" (145). Evangelical Gregory Boyd, for instance, having studied the issue biblically for years, has come to believe that "the future is, to some degree at least, open ended and that God knows it as such" (*The God of the Possible*, 1999, Preface, published privately).

can be known ahead of time. They literally do not yet exist to be known."[73]

Pinnock had come to agree with theologians like Loraine Boettner that foreknowledge necessarily entails foreordination.[74] He also now reflected key aspects of the thought of John Wesley who had located the primary expression of God's sovereignty in the bestowal of grace and mercy instead of in an abstract concept of divine self-sufficiency and freedom. This grace-mercy focus purged the notion of sovereignty of overtones of domination and arbitrariness. It also projected a concept of God interacting both providentially and effectively with fallen human beings who, in the process of the interaction, exercise a measure of free-agency that does not detract from God's glory. In fact, it enhances the glory of a sovereign and gracious God without undercutting human responsibility. This suggested to Wesley (and now to Pinnock) a concept of divine foreknowledge that does not imply determinism. For example, it probably is better to say that human choices to accept divine grace enter God's knowledge because they take place rather than that they take place because God knew (and presumably determined) them in advance. Christians generally agree that God is omniscient (all-knowing). The real question concerns the nature of this divine omniscience. For John Sanders and a growing number of others, "Omniscience may be defined as knowing all there is to know such that God's knowledge is coextensive with reality." Consequently, "The key issue is not the type of knowledge an omniscient deity has, but the type of sovereignty an omniscient God decides to exercise."[75]

---

[73]Clark Pinnock, "God Limits His Knowledge," *Predestination and Free Will*, eds. David and Randall Basinger (Downers Grove, Ill.: InterVarsity Press, 1986), 145, 150, 157.

[74]While sympathetic to much of Pinnock's thought, the necessity of this particular conclusion is questioned by Barry Callen, *God As Loving Grace* (Nappanee, Ind.: Evangel Publishing House, 1996), 146-147. Agreeing with Pinnock is Richard Rice, *The Openness of God: The Relationship of Divine Foreknowledge and Human Free Will* (Minneapolis: Bethany House Pub., 1985). Also leaning toward agreement is John Sanders who develops an understanding of divine providence which assumes that "God only foreknows what he himself determines to do" ("Why Simple Fore-knowledge Offers No More Providential Control Than the Openness of God," in *Faith and Philosophy*, 14:1, January 1997, 37).

[75]John Sanders, *The God Who Risks: A Theology of Providence* (Downers Grove, Ill.: InterVarsity Press, 1998), 194-195.

Pinnock resonates with this assessment and recognizes that his own criticism of much of the common thinking about God's omniscience is the most controversial feature of the relational model of Christian theism that he now espouses. Some Calvinistic critics have responded to his current view on this subject with what could only be called inflammatory rhetoric.[76] At the heart of the issue for Pinnock is whether God really acts in actual human history or merely exists as a supra-temporal ruler. Is God, by sovereign choice of course, really with us in the rough and tumble of our broken lives or does God rest serenely in a wholly separate realm, unchanging and untouched? Pinnock admits that his critique of the "classic" view of divine omniscience is not a necessary part of the relational model of God—and some of his close colleagues do not fully agree with him on this particular point. Nonetheless, he sees his present view of divine omniscience as a natural part of the model.

Clark Pinnock's spearheading of this fresh and "open" thinking about the nature and functioning of God certainly has sparked widespread response. His direct style of communication is surely one reason. For instance:

> To say that God hates sin while secretly willing it, to say that God warns us not to fall away though it is impossible, to say that God

---

[76]For example, R. C. Sproul has expressed publicly his judgment that Pinnock is a heretic and unbeliever for holding such a view as limited divine omniscience. Others have been critical of Gregory Boyd because of his Pinnock-like views. In March, 1999, Boyd published *The God of the Possible* to explain and document biblically his "open" understanding of the foreknowledge of God and the dynamic nature of the future. He extends words of appreciation to "my dissenting friend John Piper—a true Calvinist if ever there was one" (Preface). In June, 1999, a major resolution on the issue of the foreknowledge of God was introduced at the annual meeting of the Baptist General Conference convened in St. Petersburg, Florida. It insisted that the doctrine of God's exhaustive foreknowledge has been "the orthodox view of the church during the entire history of the church, only being questioned by marginal groups like the Socinians who were eventually regarded as outside orthodoxy for their views of God and salvation." Therefore, the resolution called on that church to declare that the words "every divine perfection" in its *Affirmation of Faith* "shall be construed to include the perfection of God's exhaustive, infallible foreknowledge of all future events, including all future volitions of humans, demons and angels." This resolution was *not adopted* by the Baptist General Conference.

loves the world while excluding most people from an opportunity of salvation, to say that God warmly invites sinners to come knowing all the while that they cannot possibly do so—such things do not deserve to be called mysteries when that is just a euphemism for nonsense.[77]

Well beyond manner of speech, however, is the substance of the subject. Vigorous opposition to such "neotheism" has come from several evangelicals, including Norman Geisler. Rather than a wise correction of classic theism with selected insights from process theology, Geisler sees Pinnock's work as part of "a dangerous trend within evangelical circles of creating God in man's image.... If the logical consequences of neo-theists' unorthodox beliefs about God are drawn out, they will be pushed more and more in the direction of process theology and the liberal beliefs entailed therein."[78] Here is fear of the "slippery slope" syndrome. There also is Robert Morey who equates the more open view of God as finite godism.[79] Pinnock's pastoral response to Morey's criticism is: "What troubles me about his view is not the charge of heresy so much as the distance I feel between his vision of God and the loving heart of the Father."[80]

Obviously, change in "classic" Christian theism will not come easily if at all among the general evangelical community. Pinnock has proceeded nonetheless to journey along a path that he sees as biblically

---

[77]Clark Pinnock, "Systematic Theology," in *The Openness of God*, 115.

[78]Norman Geisler, *Creating God in the Image of Man?* (Minneapolis: Bethany House, 1997), 11-12. The very idea of God not knowing all things, past, present, and future, is unacceptable to many evangelical Christians. In recent years, the Baptist General Conference has struggled with the issues of divine providence and foreknowledge. What should the denomination believe and expect of its professors in this regard? Should the "classic" view of theism be questioned? Should faculty members be permitted the freedom to espouse the "openness of God" model of free-will theism? The issues are basic and the politics of the matter is sometimes hard to separate from the substance of the question.

[79]Robert Morey, *Battle of the Gods: The Gathering Storm in Modern Evangelicalism* (Southbridge, Mass.: Crown, 1989).

[80]Clark Pinnock, in Pinnock, et. al., *The Openness of God* (Downers Grove, Ill.: InterVarsity Press, 1994), 191 (note 8).

pioneered and vital for the credibility and effectiveness of Christian life in the world of the twenty-first century. Out of a heart of love and in the chosen context of freedom granted to fallen and yet beloved humans, God reaches, risks, suffers, relates, and redeems. Committed to belief in a loving and personal God whose Spirit is everywhere present, Pinnock has become convinced that the Spirit of God is striving for life and wholeness among all peoples. This "inclusivist" view is a natural response to belief in the boundless love that God is by nature, and it brings its vision, challenge, and implications forward into today's world of religious pluralism. Pinnock now has pursued these implications extensively.

A Wideness in God's Mercy

The concept of a loving and relational God who is "open" and chooses to risk[81] by granting meaningful freedom to humans began to have some controversial implications for Clark Pinnock beyond the issue of divine foreknowledge. These implications soon were being championed by at least a few other leading evangelicals, but J. I. Packer clearly was not one of them. He may have followed Pinnock in the post in theology at Regent College in the 1970s, but he was not prepared to follow some of Pinnock's innovative views, including select aspects of his emerging eschatology.[82] Packer remained staunchly in the Calvinistic theological mode with its scholasticized tendency to be quite

---

[81]Note especially the significant volume by John Sanders titled *The God Who Risks: A Theology of Providence* (Downers Grove, Ill.: InterVarsity Press, 1998).

[82]In 1999 a faculty position in Christian Spirituality came open at Regent College and, at Regent's initiative, Clark Pinnock became one of the candidates given consideration (by then he had been at McMaster Divinity College in Hamilton, Ontario, for twenty-two years and J. I Packer had maintained a continuing appointment at Regent). Soon Regent dropped the consideration of Pinnock, apparently because Packer was opposed to the candidacy, and some others either did not wish to oppose Packer or had their own concerns either about Pinnock's "openness" theology or his appropriateness for this particular position. Pinnock was saddened by this development. He had a continuing love for the Regent campus and mission and found it difficult to be thought of as "outside the pale" (Pinnock letter to Barry Callen, August 10, 1999).

deterministic.[83] On the other hand, Pinnock was coming to use a key theological concept of John Wesley in a somewhat expanded sense, seeing the work of the Spirit in the world as a form of "prevenient grace." Reformed theology, of course, does recognize the universal operations of the Spirit, a "common" grace. But this grace is thought to assist sinners only in nonsalvific ways.

For Pinnock, it now was appearing that, with appropriate caution that continues to affirm the central significance of the incarnation of God-with-us supremely in Jesus Christ, one must not prematurely restrict the present work of the Spirit to those people who actually hear the Jesus message. In fact, "believing in the finality of Christ does not require us to be arrogant in our claims or closed to grace at work in other people."[84] As he observed to the Evangelical Theological Society in 1999, "A high Christology does not entail narrowness of hope."[85] He now was championing a "catholic" option reflective of some early Christian theologians, some contemporary evangelicals, and the Anglican and Roman Catholic Churches.[86] Amos Yong has provided a helpful overview of Pinnock's wider hope for human salvation, indicating that it presents for evangelicals an "inclusivist" option that does not sacrifice commitments either to biblical authority or high christology. He does call for more detailed work on how the presence of the Spirit can be dependably discerned in non-Christian religious contexts, fearing that without such increased clarity critics will dismiss Pinnock's whole

---

[83]As early as 1955 in England, J. I. Packer was actively opposing the Keswick emphasis that Christians may experience *full salvation* in Christ. Arguing from the traditional Reformed standpoint, he labeled any such teaching Pelagian through and through (see D. W. Bebbington, *Evangelicalism in Modern Britain*, 1989, 257). Similarly, decades later, Packer was prepared to critique Pinnock's championing of the concepts and implications of reciprocity and openness.

[84]Clark Pinnock, *Flame of Love: A Theology of the Holy Spirit* (Downers Grove, Ill.: InterVarsity Press, 1996), 205.

[85]Clark Pinnock, "Toward a More Inclusive Eschatology," unpublished paper delivered to the Evangelical Theological Society (Boston, November, 1999). He had argued the same point as early as 1992 in his *A Wideness in God's Mercy* (Zondervan).

[86]Pinnock documents this "catholic" position by reference to Avery Dulles, interacting with Donald Bloesch in *Evangelical Theology in Transition*, Elmer Colyer, ed. (Downers Grove, Ill.: InterVarsity Press, 1999), 73-74. See also *The Mystery of Salvation: The Story of God's Gift* (London: Church House Publishing, 1995, chap. 7).

approach as vacuous and dangerous to a responsible evangelical stance.[87] Pinnock has responded appreciatively to Yong's writing, agreeing with the call for more work on discernment, admitting that he himself is hardly a leading expert on comparative religions and cross-cultural communication, and explaining how he goes about seeking such discernment.[88]

John Sanders is one evangelical who was moving in the same direction as Pinnock. He highlighted the two most discussed views of the following persistent question: What about the fate of people not consciously identified with Jesus Christ—especially those who never even hear of him? Calling the two views "restrictivism" and "inclusivism," Sanders defined the first as the view that access to salvation is restricted to people who hear and respond appropriately to the gospel of Jesus before their deaths. Inclusivism, the view he favors,[89] is explained this way:

> Inclusivists hold that God makes salvation universally accessible even apart from evangelization. They believe that the un-evangelized may be saved if they commit themselves to the God who saves through the work of Jesus. Appropriation of salvific grace can be mediated through general revelation and God's providential workings in human history. Though inclusivists affirm the particularity and finality of Christ for salvation, they deny that knowledge of Christ's work is absolutely necessary for redemption. They hold that the work of Jesus is ontologically but not epistemologically necessary for salvation. No one will be saved without Christ's atonement, but one need not be aware of that work of grace in order to benefit from it.[90]

---

[87] Amos Yong, "Whither Theological Inclusivism? The Development and Critique of an Evangelical Theology of Religions," *The Evangelical Quarterly* 71:4 (October 1999), 327-348.

[88] Clark Pinnock, "Response to Daniel Strange and Amos Yong," *The Evangelical Quarterly* 71:4 (October 1999), 354-357.

[89] John Sanders, *No Other Name: An Investigation Into the Destiny of the Unevangelized* (Grand Rapids: Eerdmans, 1992). Clark Pinnock wrote the Foreword to this book, saying: "What this book does is to open up a possible understanding of Scripture in which the divine judgment, whatever the surprises, can be contemplated as a judgment that is fair and full of mercy" (xv).

[90] John Sanders, "Evangelical Response to Salvation Outside the Church," *Christian Scholar's Review* 24:1 (1994), 51-52.

While there is a strong tendency among evangelicals to insist that all who die unevangelized are automatically dammed (usually excluding very young children), there now is a growing openness among some evangelicals to considering the belief that God reaches out in salvific love even to the unevangelized. In the forefront of this tendency is Clark Pinnock who has sought to put on the evangelical agenda the pressing issue of religious pluralism. His timely and forthright book, *A Wideness in God's Mercy,* appeared in 1992. There he writes within the framework of two assumptions: (1) salvation is available to anyone only because of and through the redemptive work of Jesus Christ; and (2) it is God's will to save all people even if they have no opportunity in their earthly lifetimes to hear about the gospel of Christ. On the one hand, biblical teaching appears to exclude universalism, the view that eventually all people will be saved. On the other hand, "Surely God judges the heathen in relation to the light they have, not according to the light that did not reach them."[91] Thus, argues Pinnock, universal salvation is not guaranteed; what is guaranteed is the universal possibility of salvation. Pinnock's goal in this 1992 book was to define an authentic Christian alternative to both (1) the reductionist inclusivism of much recent liberal theology of religions and (2) the reactionary restrictivism of much recent theology championed by leading evangelicals.

In 1965 Packer had delivered the Payton Lectures at Fuller Theological Seminary on the theme "The Problem of Universalism Today." By 1988 several leading evangelical writers, while not typically affirming universalism, had affirmed a concept of "conditional immortality" that sees no continuing place for human beings to exist in unending torment once they are unreconciled to God by choice and have died, been judged, and separated from life with God.[92] The bliss of immortality is said to be granted only to those who were saved. So some tentative new thinking had begun about "annihilationism." Packer had been a colleague of three of these cautious innovators, the English

[91]Clark Pinnock, "Toward an Evangelical Theology of Religions," *Journal of the Evangelical Theological Society* 33 (Sept. 1990), 367.
[92]For a brief review of the issues and options here, see Barry L. Callen, *Faithful In the Meantime* (Nappanee, Ind.: Evangel Publishing House, 1997), 228-229.

evangelicals Philip Edgcumbe Hughes, John Stott, and John Wenham.[93] He responded with his Leon Morris Lecture in Melbourne, Australia, in 1990. Packer's chosen topic was "The Problem of Eternal Punishment," and his treatment was intended to dissuade people from any Christian belief in universalism or conditionalism.[94] Did Christ not speak explicitly of the goats being sent away to eternal fire and punishment (Matt. 25:41, 46)? He objected to the sense of moral superiority he detected in critics of the traditional view of hell, a superiority he attributed to secular sentimentalism.[95]

While Packer was lecturing in Australia in 1990, Clark Pinnock in Canada was engaging this issue by publishing a significant article titled "The Destruction of the Finally Impenitent,"[96] soon to be followed in 1992 by his broader treatment of related issues in *A Wideness in God's Mercy*.[97] In line with his general lament over what he viewed as the excessive and often destructive influence of Augustine and Greek philosophy on Christian theology, Pinnock now critiqued such influence on the dominant Christian thinking about divine judgment and hell. This old accommodationist thinking was said to combine belief in God's hatred for sin and a presumed universal and inherent immortality of humans, resulting in the expectation that a large percentage of humanity eventually will be tortured horribly and endlessly in hell by God. Pinnock wondered openly how such an expectation could be

---

[93]See, for instance, Wenham, *The Goodness of God* (InverVarsity press, 1974), Stott, with David Edwards, *Evangelical Essentials* (InterVarsity Press, 1988), and Hughes, *The True Image* (Eerdmans, 1989).

[94]Reported in Alister McGrath, *J. I. Packer: A Biography* (Grand Rapids: Baker Books, 1997), 260-264.

[95]J. I. Packer, "Evangelicals and the Way of Salvation: New Challenges to the Gospel," in *Evangelical Affirmations*, ed. K. S. Kantzer and Carl F. H. Henry (Grand Rapids, Zondervan, 1990), 126.

[96]Clark Pinnock, "The Destruction of the Finally Impenitent," *Crisswell Theological Review* 4(1990), 243-259. Pinnock had earlier argued for annihilation in a *Christianity Today* article (March 20, 1987).

[97] Clark Pinnock, *A Wideness in God's Mercy: The Finality of Jesus Christ in a World of Religions* (Grand Rapids: Zondervan, 1992). Here he clearly rejects universalism by insisting: "Our relation with God, as well as our final destiny, are chosen by ourselves and not thrust upon us. God does not purpose to condemn anyone, but anyone can choose rejection" (156).

reconciled with the revelation of God's nature and intent in Jesus Christ, especially when those poor souls to be so tortured were identified by Augustine as the nonelect, those to whom divine grace had deliberately not been extended, grace that might have helped them to have avoided hell altogether. This line of logic, to which the traditional view of hell belongs, is judged to have extensive and profound problems.[98]

Knowing that he would be criticized as being sentimental and a liberal who determines Christian doctrine on the thin ice of a subjective sense of moral outrage, Pinnock nonetheless began arguing that the finally impenitent wicked, rather than suffering the torture of hell forever, finally pass out of existence. The question is posed: "Does the one who told us to love our enemies intend to wreak vengeance on his own enemies for all eternity?"[99] He now had come to a negative answer and was prepared to argue his case on philosophical, metaphysical, moral, and ethical grounds, all of which he does in the book *Four Views of Hell* (see Appendix F). Recognizing, however, that evangelical theology starts with the Bible, and affirming his own evangelical identity, he makes clear that whatever the Bible teaches he certainly is prepared to accept. He proceeds to find the Bible offering little precise information on the future condition of the lost, but giving a strong general impression of "final, irreversible destruction, of closure with God." The biblical language is that of death and perishing. The "eternal" of the punishment awaiting the unrepentant wicked may well mean that it will be irreversible, not an eternal punishing but a final and never-changing judgment.

Psalm 37, for example, says that the wicked will fade like the grass and wither like the herb (v. 2), will be cut off and be no more (vv. 9-10), will perish and vanish like smoke (v. 20), and will be altogether destroyed (v. 38). Jesus warned of God's ability to destroy body and soul in hell, echoing John the Baptist who had pictured the wicked as dry wood and chaff to be burned (Matt. 3:10, 12). Paul says the wages of sin is death (Rom. 6:23) and speaks of the end of the wicked as "destruction" (Phil.

---

[98]Clark Pinnock, "The Conditional View" in *Four Views On Hell*, ed. William Crockett (Grand Rapids: Zondervan, 1996), 136ff.

[99]Clark Pinnock, "The Destruction of the Finally Impenitent," 247, 259.

3:19). Peter saw the end as like Sodom and Gomorrah that were burned to ashes (2 Pet. 2:6). The Apocalypse of John pictures a lake of fire that will consume the wicked in a second death (Rev. 20:14-15). Suggesting, then, that a fair person would think it reasonable to read such biblical texts as teaching the final destruction of the wicked, Pinnock addresses directly the only four texts seeming to suggest otherwise.

Jesus spoke of Gehenna, the fiery pit outside Jerusalem where garbage was thrown so that it would be consumed and destroyed—becoming a symbol of the fate of the wicked (Matt. 5:22). Mark reports that "their worm never dies, and the fire is never quenched" (9:48). Does this imply by comparison that those consigned to hell will endure everlasting conscious suffering of the most terrible sort? According to Pinnock, not if one goes back to the source of this imagery, Isaiah 66:24, where the dead bodies of God's enemies are pictured as being eaten by maggots and burned up. The fire and worms are destroying the dead bodies, not tormenting conscious persons. This fire indeed is unquenchable, by which the Bible seems to mean that the fire cannot be extinguished until the job is fully done. He also gives attention to Luke 16:23-24, Revelation 14:9-11, and Matt. 25:46. In the verse in Matthew 25 Jesus says, "They will go away to eternal punishment but the righteous to eternal life." In this one case interpretation could mean either that hell is everlasting torment (eternal punishing) or irreversible destruction (eternal punishment). Thus, Pinnock concludes that "the traditional belief that God makes the wicked suffer in an unending conscious torment in hell is unbiblical, is fostered by a hellenistic view of human nature, is detrimental to the character of God, is defended on essentially pragmatic grounds, and is being rejected by a growing number of biblically faithful, contemporary scholars."[100]

William Crockett critiques this conclusion, saying that Pinnock is "opting for possible interpretations rather than the more probable."[101] But Pinnock had concluded that the traditional evangelical position on hell has weak biblical grounding and violates a range of persistent biblical assumptions about the nature and intent of God. The fire of

---

[100]Clark Pinnock, "The Conditional View" in *Four Views on Hell*, 165.
[101]William Crockett, in *Four Views on Hell*, 172.

[handwritten margin note: hell only makes moral sense in an Open universe in which human beings have real freedom of choice]

God's judgment *consumes* the lost. There indeed is a hell, the dark side to divine judgment; nevertheless, the annihilationist or "capital punishment" view of the final judgment "at least does not involve a deity who is endlessly vindictive, and a new creation where heaven and hell exist alongside each other forever. Final judgment is a moral necessity in God's universe."[102] There certainly is a hell. It is proof of how seriously God takes human freedom. The key question for Pinnock is whether the Bible's fire image of hell is a fire meant to torment or consume. He concludes, and he believes on good biblical grounds, that hell is not "the beginning of a new immortal life in torment but *the end* of a life of rebellion.[103] There is no wish on Pinnock's part to create a new division among evangelicals on this controversial subject—he does not challenge the traditional view lightly, but feels forced to do so by his perception of the weight of biblical evidence and the significance of the subject.[104]

The central problem in Pinnock's view moves well beyond the issue of the nature of hell to this: "If God desires to save all mankind, and the only way to salvation is the Christian way [a continuing Pinnock assumption], what about the multitudes who have lived and died outside any knowledge of it?"[105] The current world setting is one of religious pluralism, with a high priority being placed on a leveling toleration, and with no claims to the universal and absolute application of any truth being judged acceptable. How then should Christian theology relate God's saving efforts to this pluralistic arena? Central to the Bible is belief in the comprehensive and all-embracing character of divine sovereignty and grace. Salvation is through Jesus Christ alone. So how can this all be seen and practiced today?

---

[102]Clark Pinnock, "Fire, Then Nothing," *Christianity Today* (March 20, 1987), 40.

[103]Pinnock, "The Conditional View," 137. Emphasis added.

[104]Stanley Grenz (*Theology for the Community of God*, Broadman and Holman, 1994) reviews helpfully what he calls "The Dark Side of the Judgment." He concludes that universalists "simply go too far in their optimism for the outcome of the judgment" (831). Regarding conditional immortality (annihilationism), Grenz reviews the biblical evidence and theological concerns, expresses appreciation that interpreters like Clark Pinnock "do not chafe at the prospect of an eternal punishment for the unrighteous" (834), and then concludes: "While acknowledging the sad reality of hell, we must take seriously the concern annihilationists raise" (835).

[105]Clark Pinnock, "Why Is Jesus the Only Way?" *Eternity* (December 1976), 15.

Pinnock began urging a "hermeneutic of hopefulness"[106] that rests on the presumed generous grace of God in Jesus Christ (any grace by definition is generous). Salvation is made available to all persons, many of whom only have access to this knowledge of God through general revelation. This inclination toward an inclusiveness, wider than has been usual among evangelicals, and the limiting determinism heavily reflective of the Greek influence on Christian theology, prompts Pinnock to ask: " Why do we look so hopefully to Plato and expect nothing from Buddha?"[107] He proceeds to argue that there is the very real possibility of many people being saved even though they have not had the direct benefit of God's special revelation in Christ, but have learned of God nonetheless through the grace of God's general revelation in nature and human experience. Although he wishes that such hopefulness would demonstrate that universalism is true (assumption that all people finally will be saved), the Bible blocks such a view. All will not be saved, but none will be lost because they were denied the opportunity of accepting God's saving grace. Terry Cross is right in observing that Pinnock's approach is often misread as universalism (all people finally will be saved), when Pinnock is actually a "grace-filled optimist."[108] Alister McGrath confirms that Pinnock is hardly a "pluralist": "Even Clark Pinnock, who would be regarded by some as perhaps the most 'inclusive' of modern evangelical theologians, mounts a devastating critique of 'pluralist' approaches to the significance of Christ."[109]

---

[106]Clark Pinnock, *A Wideness in God's Mercy: The Finality of Jesus Christ in a World of Religions* (Grand Rapids: Zondervan, 1992), 20-35.

[107]Clark Pinnock, "The Finality of Jesus Christ in a World of Religions," in *Christian Faith and Practice in the Modern World*, eds. Mark Noll and David Wells (Grand Rapids: Eerdmans, 1988), 159. Pinnock recalls that Abraham was justified by faith without knowing Jesus and Paul holds him up as a model believer for us all (Rom. 4:1-25). Pinnock then reports, "I also respect the Buddha as a righteous man (Matt. 10:41)" ("An Inclusivist View" in Dennis Okholm and Timothy Phillips, eds., *More Than One Way?*, Grand Rapids: Zondervan, 1995, 110).

[108]Terry L. Cross, "A Critical Review of Clark Pinnock's *Flame of Love: A Theology of the Holy Spirit*," *Journal of Pentecostal Theology* 13 (1998), 26.

[109]Alister McGrath, *A Passion for Truth* (Downers Grove, Ill.: InterVarsity Press, 1996), 248. Pinnock presents his view like this: "On the one hand, God's decisive self-revelation took place only in Jesus Christ. There is no other deity revealed in other religions. The one God is the triune God. On the other hand, God is not our property and possession but is active throughout creation and history.... We do not affirm the

For Pinnock, this openness to the possibility of salvation for all persons is in some sense an "inclusivist" view, one that offers "a middle ground between exclusivism and pluralism, holding both to the particularity of salvation through Christ and to the universal scope of God's plan to save sinners."[110] It affirms that the Spirit of God is operative even in the sphere of human religions to prepare faithful people for the gospel of Christ. Religion, Christianity included, often is a mixture of good and evil, truth and falsehood. It is not to be glorified naively, nor do these many religions function as vehicles of salvation in and of themselves. Even so, God is at work in non-Christian persons and surely at times in religious institutions (and with "general" revelation outside them). The Spirit is everywhere graciously present, even if specific witness to Jesus Christ is yet absent (see Appendix E). The Spirit "embodies the prevenient grace of God and puts into effect that universal drawing action of Jesus Christ.... As a result, we may hope that wherever we go as ambassadors of Christ, the Spirit has gone there first. What an encouragement this is for mission!"[111]

Where did Pinnock get such "open" views? The source was hardly the context of North American conservative evangelicalism in which his own faith initially was formed. That context featured a "strongly exclusivist temper." There were, however, a few lines of inclusivist thinking that reached and began impacting him. One in the 1950s was C. S. Lewis whom Pinnock trusted as an orthodox thinker. The inclusivism of Lewis was summed up for Pinnock in an incident reported in *The Last Battle,* the final volume of the Narnia cycle. There Emeth, the pagan soldier, is surprised to learn that Aslan (God) regards Emeth's worship of Tash as directed to himself. This turn of events came to symbolize Pinnock's growing confidence that "the Spirit is operating in every sphere to draw people to God, using religion when

possibility of God's revealing himself outside Christianity begrudgingly—we welcome it! Not only does such a possibility suggest bridges in other cultures to enhance mission, but it also allows us to hear the word of God from others and deepens our own understanding of revelation" (*Flame of Love,* 207-208).

[110]Clark Pinnock, "An Inclusivist View" in *More Than One Way?,* eds. Dennis Okholm and Timothy Phillips (Grand Rapids: Zondervan, 1995), 102.

[111]Ibid., 104-105.

and where it is possible and appropriate."[112] Inclusivism, however, as symbolized in literature such as that of C. S. Lewis, is not to be rooted there. Its justification ultimately must come from the Bible itself.

Early in his Christian life, Pinnock was aware of dispensational eschatology that sees in the Bible God dealing differently with people depending on their circumstances. He also closely followed the dramatic new perspectives of the Second Vatican Council of the 1960s which moved Roman Catholicism beyond its traditional exclusivism to seeing God truly at work outside the Roman church, even in non-Christian religions. Having noted the important inclusivistic symbols of Melchizedek (Gen. 14:17-24) and Cornelius (Acts 10:1-48), Pinnock increasingly emphasized that God never leaves himself without witness among all peoples (Acts 14:17). The conclusion? Jesus is "the fundamental way to salvation as God's eternal Son and sacrifice, but does not confine the saving impact of God's saving work to one segment of history." In fact, "Scripture encourages us to see the church not so much as the ark, outside of which there is no hope of salvation, but as the vanguard of those who have experienced the fullness of God's grace made available to all people in Jesus Christ. The Spirit is universally present in the world as well as uniquely present in the fellowship of the church." Biblical exposition of such inclusivism is provided by Pinnock in his book *A Wideness in God's Mercy*. A local Canadian example for Pinnock is his deep respect for the testimony of Sacred Feathers, a Missisauga Indian who found in Jesus the golden chain that for him fulfilled what God already had taught him in native traditions.[113] In all such instances, Jesus Christ remains the one Savior of the world. He is Lord of all and the "criterion of truth in religion, including the Christian religion."[114]

Some evangelicals like J. I. Packer recognize the possibility of salvation outside of direct witness to Jesus Christ, but are uncertain that many will actually be saved in this extraordinary way. Pinnock is

---

[112]Ibid., 106.

[113]For this testimony, see Donald Smith, *Sacred Feathers* (Toronto: University of Toronto Press, 1987).

[114]Clark Pinnock, "An Inclusivist View," 114.

critical of such hesitancy and suggests that this is a hermeneutic of pessimism, an unjustified tendency to be stingy with and even hoarding the grace of God.[115] He does not suggest that anyone ever earns salvation apart from the grace in Jesus Christ or that the reality of general revelation undercuts the urgency of Christian mission. There is, however, a fullness of experience emerging from a conscious trust in Jesus Christ that is not available to the "mere believer." Pinnock insists that a legitimate opportunity for salvation comes to all people. For some this apparently will be a postmortem encounter with Christ at which they will receive their first and only chance to claim the benefits of God's atoning grace in Jesus Christ. He cites 1 Peter 3:17-19; 4:6 as support for this likelihood, recognizing that the meaning of this passage is exegetically uncertain, although his suggested view of it is held by no less than Cranfield and Pannenberg.

In summary, Pinnock admits that human knowledge about God's dealings with the unevangelized is slight at best; even so, the very nature of God argues that no person will be lost without an opportunity to choose new life by the grace of God. He thinks of those who respond inwardly to the grace of God without yet becoming aware of Jesus Christ as "premessianic believers," concluding:

> By faith, one receives the prevenient grace of God on the basis of an honest search for God and obedience to God's word as heard in the heart and conscience. A premessianic believer is, one might say, latently a member of Christ's body and destined to receive the grace of conversion and explicit knowledge of Jesus Christ at a later date, whether in this life or after death.[116]

Western theology since Augustine has been reluctant to recognize the presence of God's grace outside the church, with John Wesley being

---

[115]Clark Pinnock, *A Wideness in God's Mercy*, 163. Noting that Millard Erickson, for instance, has little salvation hope for those who have not heard and responded to the grace in Christ and in fact doubts that anyone ever has been saved through the agency of general revelation, Pinnock comments: "What does 'evangelical' mean when applied to those who seem to want to ensure that there is as little Good News as possible? The Bible offers them a strong basis for optimism, yet they decline."

[116]Clark Pinnock, "An Inclusivist View," 117.

one important exception.[117] There may be general revelation that at least can provide contact points for Christian missionaries to build on, but such revelation does not of itself create the possibility of redemption. Such a view tends to imply that God reveals himself to all people, not necessarily to redeem them but to make their final judgment more severe. This line of thought Pinnock finds unbiblical, morally repugnant, and not coherent with a gracious and loving God whose will it is to redeem.

In Pinnock's view, Christian missionaries should go to the unevangelized to provide more than "fire insurance." Taking a stance relatively novel for evangelicalism but with a rich history in Christian tradition, Pinnock affirms the redemptive potential of general revelation. He reasons that "it is surely valid to infer that divine grace is prevenient everywhere. God's ever-gracious Spirit is not confined to the walls of the church."[118] His inclusivist view, however, is not understood to undercut the motive for Christian mission. What it does do is take out of the mission the panic that is unnecessarily created by exclusivism. It certainly broadens the missionary purpose to calling all people to the fullness of salvation in the fellowship of the body of Christ. Specifically, "To the one who has already reached out to God in the premessianic situation, we call them to come higher up and deeper in, to know God better and love God more."[119]

The journey to renewal had brought Clark Pinnock to theological stances more open and unbounded than is typical in the evangelical

---

[117]John Wesley argued much like Pinnock that people will be judged in light of their response to God's universal work of grace—and there is good reason to hope that many of them will be saved. Further, Wesley and Pinnock tend to agree that a proper understanding of the nature of God, one in keeping with the revelation in Jesus Christ, necessarily involves affirming God's universal love and mercy for all of humanity. This does not lead to an all-will-be-saved universalism, but to belief in a God of universal grace and holiness who respects and holds accountable the decisions of responding humans. For good perspective on Wesley's views, see Randy L. Maddox, "Wesley and the Question of Truth or Salvation Through Other Religions," *Wesleyan Theological Journal* (Spring/Fall 1992), 7-29.

[118]As quoted in Gary Dorrien, *The Remaking of Evangelical Theology* (Louisville, KY: Westminster John Knox Press, 1998), 179.

[119]Pinnock, "An Inclusivist View," 120.

world. To him these stances are biblically justified, pastorally crucial, and apologetically timely. The fuller wisdom of Christian faith emerges only as one walks with, learns from, and is changed by the Spirit of God. We now turn to a consideration of such life with the Spirit.

6

Walking With the Spirit

Let anyone who has an ear listen to what the Spirit is saying to the churches (Rev. 3:22).

This book [Pinnock, *Flame of Love*] puts on display before the reader my restlessness: in experience to know the living God and in theology to grow as a hearer of God's Word. As a theologian, my aim is always to retrieve more of the treasures of divine revelation and to present them in ever more timely ways.[1]

Clark Pinnock has chosen to walk a lively path during his long and distinguished career. He has encountered—even provoked on occasion—some political turmoil within the evangelical community. He also has enjoyed that rare pleasure of participating in the recovery of some wonderful biblical and theological truths. At times the course of this lively path has wandered through a minefield of traditionalisms not always open to the results of his exploratory and prophetic nature. He has experimented, shifted, and crossed frontiers, often moving ahead boldly and sometimes having to retreat humbly. He finally has assumed what he hopes will prove to be the role of reconciler among evangelicals as he now seeks to help weld this large and diverse body of believers into

---

[1]Clark Pinnock, "A Bridge and Some Points of Growth: A Reply to Cross and Macchia," *Journal of Pentecostal Theology* (October 1998), 49.

a more unified front that is better prepared to represent the gospel of Christ to the worlds of secular humanists, theological liberals, and postmodernists of whatever kind. At a minimum, as Alister McGrath admits with appreciation, Pinnock "has been the catalyst for much rethinking within the evangelical movement."[2] Or as Henry H. Knight III observes, Pinnock's story "provides a window on some of the more central theological issues of our day."[3] Indeed, at a minimum, Pinnock has been a reforming catalyst and his work a revealing window.

A fresh focus that has come to enlighten Pinnock's theological journey is the shift in the root metaphor for God from "absolute monarch" to "loving Parent."[4] As he views his own circumstance, being a reformer does not necessarily mean standing stubbornly aloof from one's associates. Occasionally one may need to speak out in the face of a largely unappreciative crowd, but on critical issues like a more relational model of God and a wider hope for human salvation: "I did not invent them and my answers belong to ancient traditions...."[5] Expressing mixed reactions to Daniel Strange's characterization of him as an "evangelical maverick," Pinnock confessed keen awareness of his own fallibility and observed that appearing to be a maverick depends on the eyes doing the looking. The Wesleyan, Anabaptist, and Pentecostal evangelicals, for instance, would not see him as rashly moving out on his own. Those who would are the "paleo-Calvinists" who "decided to stop growing in their outlook beyond the guidelines of the Westminster Confession, in contrast to Reformed theologians such as Karl Barth who have made many of the changes in Calvinism that I and many others consider essential."[6] Given the essential changes, Pinnock now is filled with a passion to walk with the Spirit, lifting up for our day the divine relationality and tender mercies of a loving God.

---

[2]Alister McGrath, "Response to Clark H. Pinnock," in *More Than One Way? Four Views on Salvation in a Pluralistic World*, eds. Dennis Okholm and Timothy Phillips (Grand Rapids: Zondervan, 1995), 129.

[3]Henry H. Knight III, in his endorsement statement for this present volume.

[4]Clark Pinnock, "Response to Daniel Strange and Amos Yong," *The Evangelical Theological Quarterly*, 71:4 (October 1999), 351.

[5]Ibid.

[6]Ibid., 350.

Along the road, with both its jolts and joys, Pinnock has found his only enduring adequacy in a humble walk with the Spirit of God who calls, enlightens, gifts, and sends. He has developed a resistance to the imposition of any simple and *a priori* theological scheme on the stubborn phenomena of reality, including any pre-set plan for interpreting the biblical text. A dynamic hermeneutic has kept him flexible and searching, always on the road.[7] If, as Robert Price has observed, "this leads him to take positions uncongenial to those of the left, right, or middle, this does not much matter."[8] Pinnock has always been willing to "set forth his case."[9] He is a sincere Christian man trying to hear and share the voice of God's Spirit as the Spirit speaks to the churches today. Whatever the disappointments and challenges, here is one theologian who, because of his determination to be attentive to and honor the Spirit's constant presence, is always ready to search and celebrate, both affirming the biblical tradition rooted in Jesus Christ and innovating what may be new in this tradition's fuller understanding as wisdom arises from the Spirit of that same Christ.

Such creativity and related joy, however, have come in the midst of many questions, much change, and occasionally sharp criticism from some of Pinnock's own colleagues—especially from some evangelical leaders staunchly defensive of the scholasticized Reformed nature of much of the evangelical tradition in recent decades. This complex and sometimes conflicted journey has led Pinnock to a persistent loyalty to his Baptist roots, to an increasing acceptance of core aspects of the Eastern and later Wesleyan theological streams of Christian perspective and commitment, to an appreciative hearing by many Pentecostal scholars, in short, to an openness to the whole of the Christian community as the Spirit has led. The journey has passed from the territory of "canon" to that of "criterion," and now increasingly back to

---

[7]See Clark Pinnock, "Biblical Texts: Past and Future Meanings," *Wesleyan Theological Journal* (Fall 1999).

[8]Robert Price, "Clark H. Pinnock: Conservative and Contemporary," *Evangelical Quarterly* 60:2 (1988), 183.

[9]This phrase that represents well the courageous journeying nature of Pinnock's work over the decades was used as the title of one of his early books (*Set Forth Your Case*, 1967).

"canon" by way of the "underworld of protest" identified well by William Abraham:

> Pietism, early Methodism, and Pentecostalism represent a Protestant underworld of protest which has sought to return to a soteriological vision of the Scriptures. Uneasy with a purely cognitive approach to the Christian faith, its inhabitants have searched the Scriptures for salvation.... Within the Church in the West, how one knew that one knew the truth about God overshadowed knowing God.... Eastern Orthodoxy has a way of reflecting on the nature of knowledge of God which is only now receiving the attention it deserves.[10]

Following Pinnock's path causes one to reflect on the relative priority of the process of knowing in Christian faith. For him, given where he started, it has been a moving eastward toward the more dynamic, relational, and transformational world of the Bible.

Into the Eastern and Wesleyan Streams

Clark Pinnock's choice to return to eastern Canada in 1977 symbolized, at least by its direction of movement, a concurrent theological journey he was on. It was a faithful walking with the Spirit of God that was leading him back to some insights long resident in the select theologies of his English heritage and that of the ancient Eastern church. No conscious decision had dictated that this is the way he would go. He did not, for instance, focus heavily on reading the original texts of Eastern Orthodoxy in search of new perspective. Rather, by immersing himself in the Bible and being willing to critique as necessary the evangelical world he knew so well and loved so much, Pinnock found himself moving almost inexorably down paths well-worn by Eastern and Wesleyan theologians over the centuries.

In his now many years at McMaster Divinity College (1977 to the present), Pinnock has had numerous relationships with the Baptist Convention of Ontario and Quebec and has pressed for stronger evangelical commitment. He once sought the adoption of a "confession

---

[10]William Abraham, *Canon and Criterion in Christian Theology* (Oxford: Clarendon Press, 1998), 474, 471, 479.

of faith," arguing that making no attempt at doctrinal articulation results in a dangerous vacuum.[11] By 1981 such a confession was approved by the Baptist Renewal Fellowship, but failed to be approved by the Convention. Pinnock was not politically motivated enough to try managing some major manipulation of this effort.[12] He was, however, theologically motivated enough to continue pursuing, in this and other contexts, what for him were the growing implications of a biblical and unbounded faith. This pursuit was moving him more into pivotal perspectives of the Eastern and Wesleyan streams of Christian thought and life.

He knew when he first returned to eastern Canada that there was a long history of many Canadian Baptists viewing McMaster Divinity College as a center of mainline Christian liberalism. Consciously returning to this circumstance in 1977, while admittedly "sympathetic with the forces of classical theology in their struggle against the innovations brought in by the modernist impulse," Pinnock proceeded to research the history of this presumed modernist mentality at McMaster between 1887 and 1927, when it had led to a division in Baptist ranks.[13] More than researching the past, he was an active participant in the present. He worked cautiously and sometimes with mixed results in the face of some resistant liberalism among certain of his early faculty colleagues at McMaster. At his coming, the school, at least in his view, was "liturgically formal, academically oriented, and related better to the academy than to the church."[14] But he "stuck it out," and change came. A key part of the change was the arrival in 1989 of Dr.

---

[11]Clark Pinnock, "Baptists and Confessions of Faith," *The Canadian Baptist* (May 1980).

[12]According to Pinnock's colleague and friend John Sanders (interview with Barry Callen, September 22, 1998), Pinnock is a trusting person who tends to engage a circumstance believing that all people involved are honestly open and seeking the truth. His first thoughts are dialogical, not political. Typically he has tried to debate "Christianly" in the academic setting, facing the hard issues courageously with the willingness to model humility and grace as truth comes to dictate and as God guides and empowers.

[13]Clark Pinnock, "The Modernist Impulse at McMaster University, 1887-1927," in Jarold Zeman, *Baptists In Canada* (Burlington, Ont.: G. R. Welch Company, 1980), 193-207.

[14]Clark Pinnock, Interview with Barry Callen, April 19, 1998.

William Brackney to be principal. He brought an authentic evangelical ethos, a moderate and generous orthodoxy, and his own pastoral and teaching heritage in the Believers Church and Wesleyan theological streams.[15]

By the 1990s Clark Pinnock was speaking of three standard profiles of Christian theology—the conservative, moderate, and progressive. He himself had some relationship with all three. His original roots were in the conservative, some of his more recent insights were being inspired in part by the progressive, while by choice his own anchor had been placed in the moderate middle. He offers this clarification:

> To distinguish conservative from moderate one would have to say that, for the conservative, the view of revelation that dominates is cognitive and propositional, which imperils flexibility. Whereas for moderates, the view of revelation is closer to the salvation story itself such that the voices of the present can be given a hearing but will not be able to hijack the enterprise, because it is rooted in the Christian grammar.[16]

This middle position is characterized by recognition of the full range of the three human responses generated and enabled by God's disclosure in Jesus Christ. These responses, the written Word, the church that remembers and interprets the Word, and the ongoing experiencing and rational appropriation of the Word in the midst of the community of faith, had come to represent for Pinnock a measure of fullness, balance, and flexibility thought ideal for the work of *moderate* theologians.

Pinnock's journey to this middle position may be pictured in part as a new turning toward the Eastern tradition of Christian thought. This more Eastern focus became a significant characteristic of Pinnock's integrating perspective, largely replacing the previous Latin focus of the West. By contrast with his earlier rationalistic theological patterns, he increasingly had come to exhibit the characteristics of the relational,

---

[15]For an understanding of the Believers Church tradition, see Barry Callen, *Radical Christianity: The Believers Church in Christianity's History and Future* (Nappanee, IN: Evangel Publishing House, 1999).

[16]Clark Pinnock, *Tracking the Maze* (New York: Harper & Row, 1990), 73.

therapeutic, transformational, and cooperative approaches to Christian faith. Like John Wesley before him,[17] Pinnock had come to relate Christianity's Eastern and Western traditions by giving increased priority to the Eastern while sometimes retaining the language and audience of the West—language like the "inerrancy" of the Bible and an audience like the Evangelical Theological Society. He recognizes a helpful addressing of this altered approach in "the so-called quadrilateral of Wesleyan theology,"[18] which retains biblical centrality while recognizing key roles for the experience of true transformation of the believer and the continuing wisdom of the church's tradition (including that of the ancient East).

In his 1997 keynote address to the Wesleyan Theological Society, Pinnock observed that there is shallowness in the rhetoric of "Scripture only" and announced that over the years he had come to realize "how Wesleyan my moves in method and theism were." His conclusion? "I think we need to move to a larger concept of method (as represented by the Wesleyan quadrilateral) and to a more dynamic model of the nature of God (as intimated also in Wesley's thinking)."[19] This "larger concept" and "more dynamic model" appreciates the Eastern Orthodox emphases on the mystery and relationality of God and the fact that in Orthodoxy

---

[17]Randy Maddox has concluded that "Wesley is best read as a theologian who was fundamentally committed to the therapeutic view of Christian life, who struggled to express this view in the terms of the dominant stream of his western Christian setting, and who sought to integrate some of the central convictions of this setting into his more basic therapeutic viewpoint" ("Reading Wesley As Theologian," *Wesleyan Theological Journal*, Spring 1995, 16).

[18]Ibid., 71.

[19]Clark Pinnock, "Evangelical Theologians Facing the Future: Ancient and Future Paradigms," *Wesleyan Theological Journal* 33:2 (Fall 1998), 12-13. Pinnock had been invited to keynote the 1997 annual meeting of the Wesleyan Theological Society by Douglas Strong of Wesley Theological Seminary in Washington, D. C. Strong was the WTS program chair that year and invited Pinnock in part because Pinnock's "scholarly trajectory places him in close proximity to our [Wesleyan] tradition" and in part because he is recognized as "one of the leading North American theologians today and is viewed as a spokesperson for the broad umbrella of American evangelicalism" (e-mail letter to Barry Callen). His invitation was supported enthusiastically by the WTS Executive Committee and led to the Society's support of this present publication. The keynote address is found in the Fall 1998 issue of the *Wesleyan Theological Journal* under the title "Evangelical Theologians Facing the Future."

"the criterion of truth is not external or dogmatic, a speaking *to* the church, but internal and pneumatic, a living Lord *within* the church."[20]

Of assistance in the early stage of this conceptual move of Pinnock had been Grant Osborne, a student of Pinnock's at Trinity in the 1969-1971 period and later himself a long-term faculty member at Trinity. Osborne completed three extensive guided studies under Pinnock. They were on controversial issues of the time, including Arminianism versus Calvinism. This vigorous young teacher and gifted younger student spent considerable time together reviewing the documentation of Osborne's commitment to a more Arminian approach to Christian theology. Pinnock the teacher was willing to be the learner.

In recent years there have evolved significant similarities between the theological work of John Wesley in the eighteenth century and Clark Pinnock in the twentieth. Both have strong ties to England and significant impact in the "new world." Both in their times grieved over the lostness of the masses and the desperate need for renewal in the church by the power of the Spirit of God. Both wrote extensively without being "systematic" theologians in a technical and rationalistic sense. Both affirmed most foundations laid by the Protestant Reformers, but in their different times also struggled against hardened scholasticisms within the Protestant ranks. Mildred Bangs Wynkoop says that Wesley unlocked "the scholastic doors to allow the vibrant 'Word of God' to illuminate and vitalize the cold, correct Reformation theologies."[21] Philip Meadows explains that, like Pinnock, Wesley was

> ...struggling to find a more acceptable balance between the freedom of nature and the sovereignty of grace that can satisfy a truly biblical life of faith.... [For Wesley] the idea of divine justice involves a limitation of God's sovereignty in respect of

---

[20]Daniel Clendenin, *Eastern Orthodox Christianity: A Western Perspective* (Grand Rapids: Baker Books, 1994), 107.

[21]Mildred Bangs Wynkoop, "John Wesley: Mentor Or Guru?," *Wesleyan Theological Journal* (Spring 1975), 7. See Appendix D where Pinnock reflects on the trauma experienced as he has sought to renew in more relational categories the view of God's nature and way with humans. He observes: "Had I been a Wesleyan, I might have had an easier time of it."

and response to the genuine creaturely freedom of choice between good and evil.[22]

Wesley, much like the contemporary Pinnock, concluded that God is a "loving personal agent whose gracious power is exercised not at the expense of human agency but in order to set persons free to love."[23] The issue of human freedom is key. Traditional Protestant teaching has understood "original sin" to mean total corruption of the image of God in humans, meaning that apart from grace humanity has no freedom to respond to God (leading to the logic of determinism since God alone can and does choose who will be graced with the ability to respond). Again joining Wesley, Pinnock has come to believe that the loving God of the Bible "preveniently" graces *all people*, hoping that all will respond and be saved. He also is open to the Eastern Orthodox position on sin and grace which includes real freedom for humans, so that salvation requires the joint functioning of divine grace and human free will—God's intent, provision, and risk. Randy Maddox has concluded that the closest resemblance between Orthodoxy (early Eastern) and Wesley likely lies in "their respective doctrines of deification and sanctification."[24] Similarly, Clark Pinnock has been on a journey of renewal that has come to the centrality of relational theological categories that focus on actual transformation into Christlikeness and the importance of walking closely with the Spirit.[25]

Wesley was and Pinnock again is an active innovator, one with literary skill, sincere passion for the transforming faith, and a prophetic voice focused on the present without losing deep roots in the classic Christian tradition. They both are men of "one book," defending the revelational nature and central authority of the Bible for Christians in

---

[22]Philip R. Meadows, "Providence, Chance, and the Problem of Suffering," *Wesleyan Theological Journal* (Fall 1999), 72, 62-63.

[23]Henry H. Knight III, *A Future For Truth: Evangelical Theology in a Postmodern World* (Nashville: Abingdon Press, 1997), 172.

[24]Randy Maddox, "John Wesley and Eastern Orthodoxy," *Asbury Theological Journal* 45:2 (1990), 39.

[25]Note H. Ray Dunning, *Redefining the Divine Image: Christian Ethics in Wesleyan Perspective* (Downers Grove, Ill.: InterVarsity Press, 1998). He writes chapters on the "Image of God" as relation to God, others, the Earth, and self.

the face of serious challenges. They also are focusing more on the role of Scripture in leading readers to the salvation intended by God and less to preoccupation with rational arguments about a necessary errorless perfection of the biblical text itself. Randy Maddox, in reviewing Pinnock's 1984 *The Scripture Principle*, observed that this "highly-nuanced articulation of a constructive position" was the most "critically aware exposition of Biblical inerrancy available." He saw it as especially sensitive to "the typical weakness of the inerrancy position" and setting forth a "more functional understanding...[that] should prove amenable to most conservative Wesleyans...." Perhaps the most interesting point of all for Wesleyans, reports Maddox, is Pinnock's view that the dictation approach to biblical inspiration (said to be implicit in the claims of many inerrancy advocates) is an "outgrowth of the tendency of Calvinistic orthodoxy to construe all God's actions in terms of total divine control."[26] Further, regarding the thesis argued by some that John Wesley was himself an inerrantist, Maddox responds: "...it is a long way from Wesley's embryonic comments to the intricate theorizing of contemporary inerrancy.... Contemporary inerrancy is predicated on a commitment to total divine control in inspiration, which radically contradicts Wesley's conviction about responsible grace." Maddox then refers to the "insightful discussion of Clark Pinnock" (in *The Scripture Principle*) and judges: "I would expect a present day Wesley to come down closer to Pinnock than to the Council on Biblical Inerrancy!"[27]

A more "resistible" view of God's presence and power is said by Pinnock to lead to a more positive appreciation of the human side of the Bible.[28] Such a view has a comfortable home in the Wesleyan tradition. He already had seen this in 1978 when observing that an evolving new evangelicalism was gaining greater sophistication in its historical perspectives, finally reaching beyond the relatively recent perspective of fundamentalism. He saw within the English Puritan, Wesleyan, and

---

[26]Randy Maddox, review of *The Scripture Principle*, by Clark Pinnock (1984), in the *Wesleyan Theological Journal* (Spring/Fall 1986), 204-205.

[27]Randy Maddox, *Responsible Grace: John Wesley's Practical Theology* (Nashville: Kingswood Books, Abingdon Press, 1994), 269, note 96.

[28]Clark Pinnock, *The Scripture Principle* (San Francisco: Harper & Row, 1984), 101-103.

American revivalism streams less preoccupation with "precise inerrancy" and "a healthier concern for the spiritual power and authenticity of Scripture instead."[29] As in the Eastern Christian tradition, the goal is more the journey to renewal, actual transformation by divine grace (sanctification), and less an almost singular focus on being justified of past sin for the sake of safety and bliss in the next life. Wesley certainly believed that the intended work of divine grace involves more than pardon, a legal transaction that removes the guilt of sin. Grace especially is the transforming power of God in human life. It is a power associated closely with the presence of God as believers journey by faith toward real renewal in the Spirit. Pinnock's book *Flame of Love* (1996) radiates the same belief and hopes to set the reader on a journey with the Spirit, a journey of true transformation.

The passion that has driven the theological work of Wesley and Pinnock has hardly been an intellectual elitism,[30] although their educations certainly allowed that. Pinnock has joined Wesley in being a genuine churchman and a "practical" theologian who is deeply concerned about church renewal.[31] This renewal is related closely to the sanctifying work of the Spirit of God through both established "means of grace" and the sometimes unexpected manifestations of the Spirit that are uncontrolled by rigid definitions, structures, and traditions. In fact:

> As Christ's body, the church is filled with the Holy Spirit and can experience the presence of Christ in both sacramental and charismatic life. Often we are required to choose between sacramental and charismatic modes of the real presence of

---

[29]Clark Pinnock, "Evangelicals and Inerrancy: The Current Debate," *Theology Today* 35:1 (April 1978), 68. Pinnock pointed with appreciation to the example of the letter of Timothy L. Smith to *The Christian Century* (March 2, 1977).

[30]Clark Pinnock once defined Christian theologians as "the pastoral leadership team which is charged with giving good counsel to the churches. Theology gives us access to the memory bank of the community, and makes it possible to discover old forgotten keys which can unlock some of our stubborn rusty locks today. Theology exists to jog the church's memory of truths it is in danger of forgetting but is in need of recalling because they can serve her well in the church's life and mission in our contemporary society" (*Three Keys To Spiritual Renewal*, 1985, 11).

[31]See Randy Maddox, "Reading Wesley as a Theologian," *Wesleyan Theological Journal* 30:1(Spring 1995), 7-54. Also see Maddox, "The Recovery of Theology as a Practical Discipline," *Theological Studies* 51:4(December 1990), 650-672.

Christ, which is unfortunate because both are valid and should be integrated.... As if to mimic the secular rejection of mystery, we [Protestants] have often turned away from the means of grace in which the Spirit renders material things and actions graciously efficacious to faith.[32]

Both men experienced a theological journey that led away from scholastic Reformed determinism with its rationalism that commonly pictures God in ways other than the way Jesus portrayed the Father—loving, gracious, sacrificial, wounded by human transgressions, and prepared to risk on behalf of all who are lost. For Pinnock the tight Calvinistic logic had unraveled in the 1970s. Two centuries earlier, as Colin Williams observes, Wesley "broke the chain of logical necessity by which the Calvinist doctrine of predestination seems to flow from the doctrine of original sin, by his doctrine of prevenient grace."[33]

John Wesley and Clark Pinnock also have shared in evolving a particular Christian characteristic that appears appropriate when faithfully walking with God's Spirit. It may be called the "catholic spirit." It is an intense love for God and all humankind that tends to drive out bigotry and sectarianism. While certainly not indifferent to matters of truth, it is a spirit that respects those who disagree and prods all sincere seekers after God to love, quest, and build instead of freeze where they are, berate and tear down. Note this analysis of Wesley that bears striking resemblance to Pinnock:

Wesley's emphasis expressed itself historically in ways that are exasperating to many evangelicals [of the non-Pinnock type] down to this day. Thus it led Wesley to set no theological standards for membership in the Methodist societies. The only condition required was that one desired to flee from the wrath

---

[32]Clark Pinnock, "The Great Jubilee," in *God and Man: Perspectives on Christianity in the 20th Century*, ed. Michael Bauman (Hillsdale, MI: Hillsdale College Press, 1995), 97.

[33]Colin Williams, *John Wesley's Theology Today* (N. Y.: Abingdon Press, 1960), 44. Wesley remained on the edge of Calvinism in that he also attributed all good to the free grace of God and denied the presence of all natural free will and human power antecedent to divine grace.

to come. Even where Wesley did impose standards, they were deliberately imprecise. He did not…impose a system of formal or speculative theology but…set up standards of preaching and belief that would secure loyalty to the fundamental truths of the gospel and ensure the continued witness of the church to the realities of the Christian experience of salvation. This is a far cry from the five points of Calvinism or of fundamentalism.[34]

Across the eighteenth century John Wesley experienced spiritual renewal, theological development, and what can be read as a range of occasionally conflicting theological viewpoints. Typically identified are the early Wesley (1733-38), the middle Wesley (1738-65), and the late Wesley (1765-91).[35] Across the last half of the twentieth century Clark Pinnock also has grown spiritually, innovated and experimented theologically, and at times changed in attitude and perspective. Interpreting such change in relation to the works of John Wesley is insightful and of historical interest. But trying to communicate it persuasively within the embedded inflexibilities of large segments of contemporary evangelicalism has been and remains a complex and controversial business.

Interpreting Theological Change

Theology is a process that occasionally involves change. How should change be viewed within the faith community? How should one proceed within given faith traditions? How, for instance, would one engage in authentic *Wesleyan* theological activity today? Randy Maddox is clear that it certainly would *not* mean a "simple collation and repetition of Wesley's theological pronouncements as a scholastic authority." Instead, it at least would mean "to bring theological activity into the service of nurturing contemporary Christian life and witness, just as he did."[36] How would one rightly engage contemporary theological challenges in

---

[34]William J. Abraham, *The Coming Great Revival: Recovering the Full Evangelical Tradition* (San Francisco: Harper & Row, 1984), 65-66.

[35]See Randy Maddox, "Reading Wesley as a Theologian," *Wesleyan Theological Journal* (Spring 1995), 16-26.

[36]Randy Maddox, *Responsible Grace: John Wesley's Practical Theology* (Nashville: Kingswood Books, Abingdon Press, 1994), 256.

a way instructed by the wisdom gained from the long pilgrimage of Clark Pinnock? To begin, the very fact of his theological alterations over the decades works against any simple gathering and repeating of his teachings as though they were a singular and authoritative whole. Also contrary to any such mechanical repetition of his work is his own opposition to rationalistic and speculative system building. The proper way forward is seen by Pinnock as being modeled well in the work of fellow Canadian theologian Stanley Grenz. This work, he says, "places theology in the postmodern setting, it adopts the motif of community, it integrates theology and apologetics, it works with narrative, not with timeless propositions, it is nonrationalist in method, it discusses scripture under pneumatology, and so on."[37]

Partly because he has seen the collapse of Communism and the beginning of a new century as an excellent time for major advance in the task of Christian mission in the world, Pinnock now has developed a passion for the kind of theological renewal that would better enable such mission. This passion for theological and personal renewal on behalf of Christian mission has fostered in Pinnock a particular style of evangelical "inclusivism" that recognizes the reality of religious pluralism in today's world, affirms that God is at work with saving intent among all peoples, and encourages "a willingness to be seriously global in our work—to do theology in public, not in a ghetto."[38] He calls for an increased dialogical relationship among the religions of humanity. True dialogue, he judges, does not rule out sturdy and even particularistic commitments by the dialogue partners, but it does require mutual respect for fellow human beings who are seekers after truth, whatever their religious heritages and associations. We Christians dialogue, Pinnock insists, "not because we are indifferent to truth, but because we care so much for it." We testify and learn in religious

---

[37]Clark Pinnock, "Evangelical Theology In Progress," in *Introduction to Christian Theology*, ed. Roger Badham (Louisville: Westminster John Knox Press, 1998), 81. The two Grenz books of particular significance to Pinnock are *Revisioning Evangelical Theology* (InterVarsity Press, 1993) and *Theology for the Community of God* (Broadman, 1994).

[38]Clark Pinnock, "An Inclusivist View," in *More Than One Way?*, eds. Dennis Okholm and Timothy Phillips (Grand Rapids: Zondervan, 1995), 113.

dialogue. We "watch for bridges and points of contact," expecting to find "evidence of God's grace at work in the lives of those who do not know Jesus."[39] To be global and public in theological work, to be affirming of whatever God is doing and wherever God is doing it, to be prepared to learn and not merely "preach at" people, these are stances that combine to bring the possibility of some needful change in a theologian as he or she proceeds in honesty and humility.

For decades now, Pinnock has been prepared to raise pressing questions, investigate possible answers, and risk thinking fresh thoughts—even when the response from establishment evangelicals is predictably negative. John Sanders, for example, reports that Pinnock faithfully attends meetings of the Evangelical Theological Society even though his work is often criticized there.[40] He "knows he needs to listen and thinks his evangelical colleagues also should be listening."[41] Recalled especially was an ETS meeting of the 1990s convened in Philadelphia when Sanders and Pinnock led a seminar responding to their critics on the subject of God and the unevangelized. An unusually large crowd appeared. One seminary professor spoke from the floor, reading part of Romans 10 and openly calling for the seminar leaders to "recant." A "soft" answer came from Pinnock, bringing often unspoken appreciation from many evangelical scholars and denominational officials who affirm the right of all evangelicals to think, believe, and publish their honest views of apparent biblical teaching. Admittedly, this disarmingly gentle response of Pinnock is in some contrast with a certain stridency that occasionally characterizes his writing style. He admits: "I have a tendency to operate out of an enthusiasm, sometimes being a little excessive in language or illustration, not always thinking in advance whether some

---

[39]Ibid., 113.

[40]Clark Pinnock has belonged to the Evangelical Theological Society since the 1960s and in the 1980s became the first leader of the Canadian section of this Society, now the independent Canadian Evangelical Theological Association (CETA). Concerning his continued involvement in ETS, he reports in a 1998 interview with Barry Callen: "I now am an older and honored member, but one who is thought (at least by some in the Society) to have crossed over the line of orthodoxy as the ETS understands it."

[41]John Sanders, Interview with Barry Callen, September 22, 1998.

readers might misunderstand or even be offended."[42] Increasingly, however, he has developed appropriate sensitivity at these points.

Fresh thinking sometimes pioneers viable new paths and sometimes launches experiments that soon prove to be premature and inadequate. Since Pinnock has made several rather dramatic shifts in viewpoint across his long and colorful career, it would have been appropriate in the judgment of some to title this intellectual biography *Always In Motion.* But such a title, while recognizing the dynamic aspect of Pinnock's theological pilgrimage, would convey too high a degree of implied instability. Being on a journey to renewal is not necessarily to be without meaningful roots, consistent concerns, and real stability even in the midst of change. In fact, Christians are supposed to be continually in the process of being "transformed by the renewing of your minds" (Rom. 12:2). Quite unfairly, then, Pinnock often has been dismissed by inflexible evangelicals with little more than a cynical "well, he has changed his mind again!" At a minimum, one can say that this man is often fluid, although not fickle, and sometimes so alive with fresh thoughts that inevitably he will appear to staunch conservatives as intellectually unreliable.

There has been a consistent evangelical middle for Pinnock, a stable biblical base, even though obviously there has been considerable question about some of the structures that he has judged appropriate for placing on this foundation. The consistency can be seen, for instance, even as he argues for his guarded brand of inclusivism. Wanting to carefully qualify what to some appears to be an excessively open stance in regard to God's work in and through religions other than Christianity, Pinnock says that, as an evangelical, "I am concerned that the model be shown to be congruent with the Scriptures.... I want the model to be not only theologically coherent, but also exegetically well founded."[43] He

---

[42]As example of Pinnock's perceived "excessive" language is seen in this confession of D. A. Carson (*The Gagging of God,* Zondervan, 1996, 529-530): "By contrast, it takes considerable grace to listen sympathetically to Pinnock's passionate pleas that his view [on annihilationism] be granted legitimacy, when his own purple prose condemns as sadists devoid of the milk of human kindness all those who disagree with him."

[43]Clark Pinnock, "An Inclusivist View," 109.

certainly has tested various dimensions of numerous lines of thought and has not been afraid to keep his own thinking flexible for the sake of truth and spiritual renewal for himself and the church—even if the results of such flexibility become quite controversial. All the while, he has been determined to remain biblically grounded and evangelistically motivated, and thus be a true evangelical.

To some interpreters, motion in theology means confusion of conviction, drifting somewhere rather than standing solidly on unchanging conviction. For instance, Roger Nicole offered this to conclude his review of Pinnock's book *The Scripture Principle*:

> Open-mindedness and stability are two great qualities that theologians must hold in tension: open-mindedness so that they continue to remain subject to correction where they may be wrong; stability so that some real confidence may be placed in their conclusions. Clark Pinnock has certainly shown considerable open-mindedness through the years, but this is flawed by the instability that has led him to shift his stance repeatedly, even long after he began teaching theology.[44]

Donald Bloesch speaks of the "early Pinnock" for whom biblical inerrancy was presumed to be a necessary inference drawn from the fact that the Bible is *God's* Word. He then speaks of a later Pinnock who affirms the confluence of the divine and human in Scripture, even with what Bloesch sees as his later tendency "to treat Scripture as a totally human book with a divine focus."[45] R. K. McGregor Wright

---

[44]Roger Nicole, "The Scripture Principle: Clark Pinnock's Precarious Balance Between Openmindedness and Doctrinal Instability," review of *The Scripture Principle* by Clark Pinnock, *Christianity Today* (Feb. 1, 1985), 71.

[45]Donald Bloesch, *Holy Scripture* (Downers Grove, Ill.: InterVarsity Press, 1994), 320, 312. He bases his "later tendency" concern on Pinnock's book *Tracking the Maze* (1990), 173-176. Despite this concern, Bloesch himself has been critical of Protestant scholasticism, that is, those rationalists whose static concept of revelation too readily equates the Word of God with the words of Scripture. Much like Pinnock, he affirms that the Bible in and of itself is not the revelation of God, but the divinely appointed means of conveying the revelation. The connection between Word and the biblical text is dependent on the Spirit of God who speaks to the reader through the text. See Stanley Grenz, "'Fideistic Revelationalism': Donald Bloesch's Antirationalist Theological Method," in *Evangelical Theology in Transition: Theologians in Dialogue with Donald Bloesch*, ed. Elmer M. Colyer (Downers Grove, Ill.: InterVarsity Press, 1999), particularly 41-42.

echoes this concern. Pinnock's "highly public progress toward a shifting form of liberal evangelicalism has caused much puzzlement and misgiving among those of us who knew him formerly as a reliable defender of the faith." He concludes: "We quite reasonably fear for what he might give up next."[46]

In fact, however, Pinnock has hardly been an unpredictable disposer of one truth after another, an aimless drifter in the midst of his openmindedness and "highly public progress." He has never been without the persistence of vigorous conviction that has meaningful continuity with his evangelical heritage, a heritage he has sought to reshape and renew while always refusing to abandon. He has remained staunchly biblical in orientation. Donald Bloesch rightly credits him with the willingness "to alter his position on the basis of a deeper immersion in Scripture."[47]

Whatever else might be said about Pinnock's sometimes exploratory and experimental forays across theological frontiers thought fixed by classic evangelicals, it cannot be said that Pinnock has lacked a consistency of direction and intent. The direction has been toward a renewed spiritual identity that enlivens a biblically-defined faith which is concerned with Christ's mission in this world. As Pinnock put it in his 1977 inaugural address at McMaster Divinity College: "My concern for theology…is for it to be *evangelical, conservative,* and *contemporary.*"[48] One consistent intent has been to respect Christianity's traditional authority sources without being victimized by any classic theorizing about them which is found to be inconsistent with the whole biblical witness and the present work of God's Spirit. Recognizing profound paradoxes on nearly every theological hand, Pinnock has

---

[46]R. K. McGregor Wright, *No Place for Sovereignty: What's Wrong with Freewill Theism* (Downers Grove, Ill.: InterVarsity Press, 1996), 230. Wright, himself mentored by Pinnock when Wright was a masters student at Trinity Evangelical Divinity School, observes with alarm that Pinnock's "theological views seem to progress further away from orthodoxy every time he publishes" (39).

[47]Donald Bloesch, *Holy Scripture* (Downers Grove, Ill.: InterVarsity Press, 1994), 366.

[48]Clark Pinnock, *Three Keys To Spiritual Renewal* (Minneapolis: Bethany House, 1985), 85.

shown this consistent determination: "In so many areas of theology we have to seek balance and try to avoid falling into a pit on one side or the other."[49] To him theology is always an unfinished enterprise. There always is more to be known about God and God's ways. Surely, in his view, believers would want to keep growing in their knowledge of God (2 Peter 3:18).

He finds it unfortunate that many people think of him as the one who has changed his mind repeatedly over the years rather than the one focusing carefully and consistently on the actual merits of the positions he develops. Admittedly he has risked publishing in-process thinking, something seen by some as a lively and dialogical approach to constructive theology and seen by others as premature and even irresponsible. For instance, J. I. Packer, after looking over a manuscript copy of Pinnock's *The Scripture Principle* (1984), is said to have commented that Professor Pinnock, in spite of his considerable knowledge of the issues and relevant literature, has a tendency to "walk by himself," which Packer found disconcerting.[50] On an issue like annihilationism, Pinnock decided in the 1980s to risk openly opposing a dominant Christian position despite the price he knew he likely would pay, namely the diminishment of his own reputation among many evangelicals. He would be classed with awkward company since, it surely would be said, "only heretics or near-heretics deny the doctrine of everlasting punishment and defend extinction."[51] More recently the controversial frontier issues have usually been related to aspects of Christian theism like God's omniscience. Pinnock has hardly hesitated. He has shown himself to be a committed theological reformer who believes that sometimes, in order to recover a lost treasure, even in Christian theology there is "a time to plant and a time to pluck up what is planted" (Eccles. 3:2). He has both plucked and planted over the final decades of the twentieth century.

---

[49]Clark Pinnock, "Between Classical and Process Theism," in *Process Theology*, ed. Ronald Nash (Grand Rapids: Baker Books, 1987), 87.

[50]Roger Nicole,"The Scripture Principle" (book review), in *Christianity Today* (February 1, 1985), 71.

[51]Clark Pinnock, "The Destruction of the Finally Impenitent," *Criswell Theological Review* 4:2(1990), 248.

To Pinnock, however, his experience of theological change says something important and quite positive about his attitude toward Christian theology itself. He would prefer to be known "not as one who has the courage of his convictions, but one who has the courage to question them and to change old opinions which need changing." He asks: "Is it not better to learn and to grow, even if that means changing earlier views which have not withstood the test of time, rather than clinging stubbornly to them?"[52] Writing appreciatively about Bernard Ramm's unusually productive lifetime of Christian theological work, Pinnock once observed that Ramm was one of those rare theologians who was prepared to change his mind. Here was one conservative Baptist being admired by another because, as Pinnock put it, Ramm was "dynamic and flexible" and embodied the maxim: "To live is to change, and to be perfect is to have changed often."[53]

Pinnock is well aware of the following kind of negative and all-too-common characterization of himself:

> This theologian [Pinnock], a lucid and trenchant commun-
> icator, seems to thrive in an adversary posture. He moves into his
> subject like a man cutting a trail through a thicket with great
> machete slashes on the right and on the left.... He maintains that
> the use of the term "inerrant" in reference to Scripture is
> warranted and manifests the continuity of evangelicalism with
> the Reformation.... [But] in the assessment of Carl F. H. Henry,
> with which I [Roger Nicole] am inclined to agree, Pinnock
> "retains inerrancy as a concept, but seems to thin it out almost
> to the breaking point."[54]

---

[52]Clark Pinnock, foreword to *Clark Pinnock on Biblical Authority*, by Ray Roennfeldt (published Ph.D. dissertation, Andrews University, 1990), xv.

[53]Clark Pinnock, in *Perspectives on Theology in the Contemporary World: Essays in Honor of Bernard Ramm*, ed. Stanley Grenz (Macon, GA: Mercer University Press, 1990), 17.

[54]Roger Nicole, "The Scripture Principle" (book review), in *Christianity Today* (February 1, 1985), 68. Paige Patterson offers this criticism: "I must grieve over my professor [Pinnock] who has forsaken the prophetic pulpit of Luther for the indecisive desk of Erasmus and the certainty of Paul for the vacillation of the Athenians who must always 'hear some new thing'" (*The Proceedings of the Conference on Biblical Inerrancy, 1987*, Nashville: Broadman Press, 1987, 93).

At times Pinnock has responded defensively to such criticism. At other times he has simply moved on in the awareness that being fully understood and appreciated by all is hardly to be expected. There have even been times when he has engaged in serious introspection, wondering if his own personality and professional track have contributed inordinately to the appropriateness and quality of his theological work. For instance, when considering a move from New Testament to theology as his primary teaching field at the seminary in New Orleans in the 1960s, he was warned by a more "liberal" colleague that he should not make the move. After all, he was told, moving away from one's developed area of specialization would doom the mover to always being a self-taught amateur. The move was made anyway.[55]

Should this advice have been heeded? In the many years to follow, Pinnock occasionally would reflect on this. Was his work in theology all that it should be? Was it "sound enough"? Such reflection has helped to keep him quite modest about his own work—even as he has pursued it with conviction and passion.[56] He recalls that during his New Orleans teaching years he liked the program *Firing Line,* featuring conservative journalist William Buckley, Jr. Much later he likewise appreciated Buckley's autobiography, *Nearer My God.* Pinnock's observation was that Buckley had been so stable in his views over the decades. He mused that it would have been more ideal if he himself could have been more stable.[57] However, the controversial surroundings, the developmental path of his own thinking, and the perceived needs of the evangelical community had spawned numerous changes along the way. Good or bad, that is how it had been.

It has taken courage to embrace fresh theological insights and be willing to champion them among colleagues, many of whom were likely

---

[55]In an unpublished 1997 address to an evangelical-process dialogue convened at Claremont School of Theology, Pinnock repeated this colleague's warning decades earlier and said that "in a sense he was right.... What this means for our subject is that the pressure to change my mind on different items over the years has been felt more intuitively than philosophically.... Having done graduate work in New Testament, I did not have the benefit of formal training in philosophy (or even in theology)."

[56]Clark Pinnock, Interview with Barry Callen, April 18, 1998.

[57]Ibid. The Buckley autobiography is *Nearer My God To Thee: An Autobiography of Faith* (N.Y.: Doubleday, 1997).

to respond negatively. Pinnock has consistently had such courage and sometimes has worried about the courage of others. For instance, in his 1999 Azusa Street Lecture at Regent University, he again affirmed the relational model of God and also observed that Pentecostals are "strong relational theists." As such, and only recently becoming active in the construction of formal theologies, they have, in Pinnock's view, the opportunity to "help us turn the tide" in the struggle to overcome the entrenched theism of deterministic scholasticism in the evangelical community. But caution and courage are required. Pinnock expressed his fear that an evolving evangelical/pentecostal "love affair" will require Pentecostals to intentionally resist the certain pressure of the "paleo-Reformed evangelicals." Pentecostals, he observed, have the theological instincts and opportunity to help in the reform of evangelicalism through a revival of relational theism. He fervently hoped that they would be true to themselves and persist in their distinctive witness "to the dynamism and beauty of God and stand behind the relational model that is biblically, apologetically, and practically so true and so important."[58]

We learn as we remain open in the Spirit and engage in honest dialogue with the larger believing community. Pinnock is anxious to hear the voice of the Spirit in the church today. He has found constructive common cause with "liberals" like Delwin Brown in whom "I sense a Christlike attitude" and with whom he has dialogued on behalf of the fuller truth. "How else," Pinnock asks, "can we honor both the Word and the Spirit?"[59] We are to work for bridges that can span the divides in the church. In this context, one may say that Pinnock has evolved into a thoughtful liberal-conservative and a convictionally conservative-liberal. He is a biblically committed theologian who also is deeply concerned about contemporary relevance and exhibits an inclination to function intuitively on occasion in his search for hearing the fresh voice of the Spirit. He is "catholic" by instinct and conviction. He is

---

[58]Clark Pinnock, "Divine Relationality: A Pentecostal Contribution to the Doctrine of God," the unpublished 1999 Azusa Street Lecture, Regent University, Virginia Beach, Virginia, April 20, 1999.

[59]Clark Pinnock, "Response to Delwin Brown," *Christian Scholar's Review* 19:1(1989-90), 73, 75.

appreciative of an attitude he detected in Francis Schaeffer, one of his own early mentors. Schaeffer's 1970 book *The Church at the End of the 20th Century*[60] included an appendix that argued for love as the defining mark of the Christian community. The world has a right to judge the church on the presence or absence of this distinctive mark (John 13:33-35). Apart from living in the Spirit of love, even the truth somehow becomes a lie. Here Pinnock has chosen to stand. He has been able to do no other.

Flame of the Spirit

From the earliest phase of his career, Clark Pinnock has focused on the meaning and significance of the Holy Spirit in the Christian life. His doctoral work under F. F. Bruce at the University of Manchester in England concluded with his 1963 dissertation on the Pauline concept of the Holy Spirit. In *Truth on Fire*, his 1972 exposition of the message of Galatians, Pinnock argues that this teaching of Paul "has ignited theological revolutions and reformations." He argued that a "Spirit filled life" is central to authentic Christianity and that the only way a believer "can find victory and bear fruit to God is to line up behind the Spirit and allow himself to be led by him."[61] Since the 1960s he has participated in a series of prayer groups of spiritually serious Christians. His motivation has not been an interest in "tongues speaking"; it has been his continuing passion for authentic and transforming life in the Spirit. Increasingly he came to believe that the Spirit clearly is doing something special for our times, and he has wanted to be available to the Spirit on behalf of the church's renewal.

Over the years Pinnock has found himself becoming less rationalistic and Calvinistic and more open, appreciative of and receptive to the work of the Spirit. In 1984 he was insisting in *The Scripture Principle* that there is a dynamic relationship between the Spirit and the Word, one that calls conservative Christians to recover a proper appreciation of the

---

[60]Francis Schaeffer, *The Church at the End of the 20th Century* (Downers Grove, Ill.: InterVarsity Press, 1970). This book was reviewed by Clark Pinnock in *Christian Scholar's Review* (1971), 370-372.

[61]Clark Pinnock, *Truth on Fire: The Message of Galatians* (Grand Rapids: Baker Book House, 1972), Preface.

work of the Spirit in understanding and applying the truths of Scripture. By 1990 he was saying: "We all need to get over a bad case of cultural accommodation and experience freedom in God's Spirit."[62] The accommodation he had in mind was in large part the easy identification with the Enlightenment adoption of a scientific mindset with its rationalistic and literalistic constraints that have greatly impoverished Christian theology.

Later, in what the publisher of his *Flame of Love* refers to as his "magnum opus," Pinnock concludes that the Charismatic/Pentecostal movement is clearly a pivotal reality in modern Christianity and has been a welcome nourishment to his own life. He confesses: "The spiritual vitality so evident in Scripture is rare and thin in the religious circles I inhabit. The atmosphere is restrained and the style highly cognitive; expectations are rather low regarding the presence of the kingdom in power." This relative spiritual vacuum had left him with a thirst for experiencing the reality of the Spirit. Thus, *Flame of Love* reflects much of his own spiritual journey toward renewal in the Spirit. He remains careful, however, to be critical at selective points. For example, he says that "one hears of a 'health and wealth gospel' coming from the charismatic fringes, which is surely heretical."[63] Even so, this book contains his maturing theological thought and is almost a beginning systematic theology that consciously integrates Christian belief and practice by viewing them together through the lens of life in God's Spirit.

Encouragement for the spiritual journey had come to him over the years from several sources. It had come from Pope John XXIII, who in 1959 announced plans for the historic Second Vatican Council by praying that the windows of the church be opened to God's breath, the breath that was needed to sweep away deadness and unleash refreshing renewal in the church. Then in 1986 Pope John Paul II issued the encyclical *On the Holy Spirit in the Life of the Church and the World* which urges Christians to be newly attentive to the Spirit as the third mil-

---

[62]Clark Pinnock, in Pinnock and Delwin Brown, *Theological Crossfire* (Grand Rapids: Zondervan, 1990), 69.

[63]Clark Pinnock, "Response to Delwin Brown," 76.

lennium after Christ approaches.[64] Pinnock used the emphases of this encyclical to organize his own presentation "The Great Jubilee" at the 1994 seminar "God and Man: Perspectives on Christianity in the 20th Century" sponsored by Hillsdale College in Michigan. He reports that, in preparation for writing his book *Flame of Love,* he and his wife spent two months on retreat with the community at Schloss Mittersill, Austria, where their souls were nourished. Also, he acknowledges the influence on him of the "Toronto Blessing" during his time of writing. He found himself marveling at "the flow of grace and love in this remarkable awakening."[65] Then with gladness he finally reports that, in the course of writing this 1996 book on the Spirit, "my heart has been blessed. I have caught the fire again."[66] He was continuing actively on his own journey toward renewal, both of Christian theology and personal transformation.

Pinnock originally had found his own Christian faith in the midst of modern evangelicalism. However, this 1996 book about theology and the Holy Spirit continues his struggle with aspects of this tradition and his search for a more "nondeterministic theology."[67] Now he was prepared to acknowledge Pentecostalism "as a mighty twentieth-century

---

[64]Pinnock soon spoke and wrote appreciatively of the Pope's thought, reflecting on it by saying: "The Spirit is a mysterious power revealed mostly by symbols such as water and fire, not in abstract formulae. While the mind should be active in searching out the meaning of these signs, a knowledge of the Spirit does not come only by way of the intellect but arises in hearts which wait upon God in poverty of spirit.... It is important that our hearts be open to being drawn into the mystery of God's love" (Pinnock, "The Great Jubilee," 92).

[65]Clark Pinnock, *Flame of Love: A Theology of the Holy Spirit* (Downers Grove, Ill.: InterVarsity Press, 1996), 250. He reported in an interview with Barry Callen (April 18, 1998) that he first attended the Toronto Blessing in the summer of 1994. The people were so receptive to God that he found it a time of true refreshment for himself. It was like "living water" that met his need for additional "joyfulness and spiritual expression." The experience ministered helpfully to "my two persistent hungers," being an effective Christian scholar/apologist and being a man full of Christ's love. For Pinnock, love, not a gift of tongues, is the sign of true baptism in the Spirit. He thus keeps a certain distance from some elements of Pentecostalism (which some Pentecostals also do).

[66]Clark Pinnock, *Flame of Love,* 247-248. Recall the personal experience Pinnock himself earlier had reported when he also recaught the fire of the Spirit (New Orleans, 1967).

[67]Clark Pinnock, *Flame of Love,* 18.

outpouring of the Spirit." He recalls that Karl Barth, near the end of his life, had seen the lack of his own theological work in relation to the Spirit. Appreciative of Jürgen Moltmann's obvious distancing of himself from Barth's excessive polemic against religious experience,[68] Pinnock now was prepared to proceed in the direction of Moltmann's correction of Barth, announcing that "it is time for us to heed the East's complaint that Western Christianity has confined the Spirit to the margins of the church and subordinated it to the mission of the Son."[69] Such confinement must end.

What is a Christian? Pinnock now says that being a Christian "is knowing Father and Son and walking along the pathway of cross and resurrection through the power of the Spirit."[70] It is not mere knowing and believing—cognitive functions. It also is journeying with the Spirit along Christ's path. It is discipleship and mission for Christ by the Spirit. It is receiving, nurturing, and using divine gifts for ministry and witness. What gifts has Pinnock come to believe are his own by God's grace? Although he is hardly one to lead with such a list (for fear of seeming arrogant), when asked he listed the gifts of wisdom and discernment in the church's theology and mission, the ability to think new thoughts and try them out (like C. S. Lewis), and the will to put old things in new ways (like Francis Schaeffer).[71]

Effective Christian mission in today's world has remained a prime motive for Pinnock. With people at the end of the twentieth century hungry for spirituality that is meaningful and transforming, a hunger largely the result of the extreme dryness of secularistic modern culture, Pinnock has come to view the beginning of the twenty-first century as a time of special opportunity for Christian mission. Specifically:

> With the demise of Marxism, no belief system is better placed than ours [historic Christianity] is to provide a compelling faith and promising vision of the human future. With the crisis of Darwinistic materialism, there is the possibility again of mutual, beneficial relationships between religion and science being

---

[68]See Jürgen Moltmann, *The Spirit of Life* (Minneapolis: Fortress Press, 1992).
[69]Pinnock, *Flame of Love*, 10.
[70]Ibid., 47.
[71]Clark Pinnock, Interview with Barry Callen, April 19, 1998.

restored and the modern mind being re-opened to the truths of religion. With the waves of pentecostal renewal, the prospect exists for a world-wide outpouring of the Holy Spirit.[72]

People today want to *know* God as much or even more that they want or need to know *about* God. Thus Pinnock prays: "Welcome, Holy Spirit, come and set us free! Let each one catch the living flame and be ravished by your love! Let our souls glow with your fire. Help us overcome our forgetfulness of Spirit."[73] After all, it is the Spirit who epitomizes the nearness of the power and presence of God. Pinnock recalls appreciatively the analogy used by Tertullian that it is helpful to think of the Father as the orb of the sun, Jesus as the beam of light emanating from it, and the Spirit as its present warmth and energy.[74] Why would any Christian resist this "latter rain," the contemporary pentecostal impulse that may be the key revitalization of the churches today? Pinnock asks this question and then identifies five reasons for hesitation that are common among Baptists (and others).[75] If these hesitations can be overcome, he insists, reluctant Christians can rejoin the journey of Christian renewal in our time.

Does this focus on experience subtly undercut evangelicalism with its traditionally strong emphasis on objective divine revelation, even revealed doctrinal propositions about God? Pinnock would say both no and yes. His "no" would come from his firm and continuing conviction that religious experience needs good theology that is rooted in divine revelation the way any traveler needs a reliable map. The crucial dynamic of life in the Spirit is not some subjective source of new and superior theological information that supersedes the biblical record. But he also would tend to say "yes" in that being truly alive in the Spirit of Christ does lead a biblically-grounded believer to "a deeper acquaintance with

---

[72]Clark Pinnock, "Evangelical Theologians Facing the Future: Ancient and Future Paradigms," *Wesleyan Theological Journal* 33:2 (Fall 1998), 7.

[73]Clark Pinnock, Flame of Love, 9.

[74]Tertullian, *Against Praxeas*, 8, as in Clark Pinnock, "The Great Jubilee," 93.

[75]The objections are said to be: (1) hermeneutical; (2) cultural inhibition; (3) block of tradition; (4) fear of pentecostal follies; and (5) the Laodicean complex—being satisfied with a form of godliness with little spiritual vitality. Source: Clark Pinnock, "Baptists and the 'Latter Rain'," in Jarold Zeman, *Costly Vision: The Baptist Pilgrimage in Canada* (Burlington, Ontario: Welch Publishing Company, 1988), 258-265.

the divine mysteries and a finer sensitivity to their timeliness,"[76] potentially releasing evangelicalism from its frequent problems with rationalism and determinism. It is hard to sustain any rigid "isms" when the Spirit blows as the Spirit wills and is "the ecstasy of the divine life." So Pinnock in *Flame of Love* is seeking to nourish evangelicalism with a fresh focus on the dynamism and religious accessibility of the divine Spirit, doing so consciously within a classical frameworks of biblical revelation and Christian orthodoxy. In this way he could foresee a spiritually enlivened evangelicalism becoming the needed bridge to the largely defunct liberal theologies that have yielded to theological revisionism in pursuit of a crucial goal, showing "a continuity between God and the world, the dynamic nature of creation, and the nearness of God to every human soul."[77]

One arena for probing Clark Pinnock's instincts and commitments is the contemporary and controversial Christian renewal phenomenon called the "Toronto Blessing." Pinnock's hometown is Toronto, Canada, the home of this renewal movement since its beginning at the Toronto Airport Vineyard Fellowship in January 1994. Living in nearby Hamilton, Ontario, since 1977, Pinnock has done more than merely be aware of this spiritual revival that has been drawing thousands every week from that area and from around the world. He has attended on occasion and offers this personal testimony of its impact on him personally:

> I go to the meetings in order to wait on God and listen. There is an abundance of faith and expectancy there and the environment is conducive to encountering the Holy Spirit.... I have found myself made more radically open to God's presence and have come away with my faith enhanced.[78]

---

[76]Clark Pinnock, *Flame of Love*, 13.

[77]Ibid., 250. Pinnock insists that evangelicals need to "get over their fears born in the fundamentalist/modernist controversies. The specter of liberalism has kept us long enough from celebrating new possibilities and has robbed us of confidence in our imaginations. It has made us suspicious of new suggestions and even grumpy and mean-spirited at times" (in "Evangelical Theologians Facing the Future: Ancient and Future Paradigms," *Wesleyan Theological Journal* 33:2 [Fall 1998], 22).

[78]Clark Pinnock, "Should Baptists Catch the Fire?" *Canadian Baptist* (March, 1995).

Why his interest in this spiritual revival? The concern leading to his personal participation comes from his awareness of the possibility that this is an authentic divine visitation at a time when life in so many Christian congregations causes him to long for a fresh outpouring of God's presence and power. Knowing God in a personally transforming way is much different than affirming mere theoretical abstractions about God, however "orthodox" and "in good order" they may be.

If there is reason to be open to the possibility of divine visitation, are there also reasons for caution? Indeed there are. Some are unworthy reasons, like the fear of the unknown or refusal for any upsetting of the status quo of the routines of the institutionalized faith. The fact is that God's Spirit is not limited to human control. Bystanders on the day of Pentecost accused Jesus' disciples of drunkenness. There are, however, worthy reasons for caution. Pinnock points out that "people in our culture are craving exciting experiences as an end in themselves and we must not encourage their addiction to high-voltage spiritual highs." Other worthy concerns include the possibility of any of the following:

> One would be disturbed, for example, if the cross were bypassed in favour of resurrection, or if there were an attitude of elitism in relation to other churches, or if there was an emphasis upon physical manifestations as an end in themselves, or if inspired utterances were not tested, or if aspects of the gospel were notably absent, or if there was manipulation to achieve an emotional response, or if people were allowed to think that Christian experience can always exist on the level of exuberance.[79]

In 1995 Pinnock's view was that, at least in what he personally had observed, these serious potential pitfalls were not central characteristics of the Toronto Blessing. He had, however, noted a weakness in its teaching ministry since sometimes it fails to deal adequately with the purpose of an outpouring of the Spirit, namely advancing God's reign by inspiring and empowering a serious following of God's servant Jesus. On the other hand, if the Toronto Blessing is effectively encouraging people not to fear Easter life, then it indeed is a blessing, one that

---

[79]Ibid.

Pinnock hopes will spread into established Christian communities far beyond Toronto, Canada.

Evangelicalism, especially in the 1970s and 1980s, generally perceived the charismatic emphasis on "tongues" to be a big problem. But as early as 1971 Pinnock had been offering a "truce proposal" for the tongues controversy, a controversy he judged an acrimonious debate that "divides our ranks and saps our energies."[80] He called for each side to reconsider their stereotypes of the other and to recall the biblical definitions and governing principles. Of course there were real problems in how some Christians were dealing with "special gifts." Even so, to overreact was judged a major problem itself. As Pinnock boldly said in 1981:

> My own denomination suffers as much from dead orthodoxy as it does from lifeless liberalism, yet it is deathly afraid of what might happen if the Spirit came sweeping over us.... It is not a new doctrine we lack. What we need is a new dynamism that will make all of the old evangelical convictions operational.... It is not a *doctrine* of the Spirit that we need, but a *movement* of the Spirit pervading and filling us, setting our convictions on fire.... May we not be too proud or too fearful to recognize the testimony of our Pentecostal brethren, and add their dynamism to our doctrine.[81]

Like the ancient Hebrew prophets, Pinnock has sought to be an available voice of God's Spirit to the more significant issues of his time. Admittedly, his voice often has been characterized as having about it a certain over-againstness. Rarely has he hesitated long to confront any perceived threat to the integrity or evangelistic effectiveness of Christian faith, whether that threat was arising from inside or outside the Christian community.[82] The targets of his active opposition have been numerous. Note, for instance:

---

[80]Clark Pinnock, "A Truce Proposal for the Tongues Controversy," *Christianity Today* (October 8, 1971), 6-9.

[81]Clark Pinnock, "Opening the Church to the Charismatic Dimension," *Christianity Today* (June 12, 1981), 16.

[82]Said John Sanders (Interview with Barry Callen, September 22, 1998): "I hope Clark Pinnock will be remembered as a serious Christian man who had the intellectual integrity to say what he thought and who identified some burning issues in the church and academy and dared to ask what evangelicals were going to say about them."

Pinnock has opposed liberals among the Southern Baptists by arguing for inerrancy; he has opposed liberals in the wider church for compromising the facticity of the Jesus event. Given the closed-mindedness of many evangelicals, he has pled for space for New-Pentecostalism. In the face of evangelicalism's Reformed theological establishment he has argued for a neo-Arminian soteriology. He has pitted his evidentialist apologetics over against both secularism and presuppositionalism. He argued first for radical politics when the evangelical church seemed quiescent and then for democratic capitalism when progressive evangelicals became enamored of politically correct liberalism. He has questioned classical theism as too static a model, argued against strident inerrancy when the evangelical church was threatened with division and a deflection of its mission, and opposed liberals and conservatives alike on the subject of the place of other religions.[83]

Whatever the time, issue, or public needing addressed, he has sought to hear the Spirit's present voice and with directness speak the Spirit's message.

It may be the case that, at least among evangelicals, dominance still rests with Reformed and quite rationalistic theologians, with varying degrees of inflexible fundamentalist mindsets. Such mindsets include those with anti-Spirit attitudes that fear subjectivism more than they are prepared to risk honoring the pursuit of truth, however that pursuit might come to relate to their fixed creeds and cherished traditions.[84] But if this still is the case, the dominance of such elements is increasingly yielding to the persistent rise of an alternative. No longer, for instance, do strict Calvinists control the boundaries and concerns of the evangelical discussion. Gary Dorrien is right:

---

[83]Robert K. Johnston, "Clark H. Pinnock," in *Handbook of Evangelical Theologians*, ed. Walter Elwell (Grand Rapids: Baker Books, 1993), 442.

[84]In 1997 Pinnock addressed an evangelical-process dialogue at Claremont School of Theology and suggested there that Pentecostals may be good partners in pioneering a new day beyond the dominance of "hard" rationalisms. He expressed appreciation for their focus on real and very present life in the Spirit, for their use of stories (narrative Bible reading and testimonies), and for their relative lack of need for abstract proofs to support their faith.

> The defining debates in present-day evangelicalism are being shaped by thinkers who want to make their tradition less deterministic, less forensic, more open to pluralism and spiritual experience, and, especially, more open to the biblical picture of God as relational, vulnerable, and personally affected by the world.[85]

When one thinks of the tendency toward this paradigm shift in the evangelical community, the name of Clark Pinnock emerges immediately. For some three decades now he has been a primary pioneer of the new way. He has stood in the middle, critiqued all sides, forged the general contours of a fresh path, and nourished a new generation of thinkers who both love their faith roots and express little fear of approaching promising frontiers of biblical understanding and present practice. This fresh approach exudes a sense of freedom, the joy of a journey, the hope of renewal, and the sense that the ongoing illumination of God's Spirit is yet opening new dimensions of biblical meaning that are especially relevant to Christian ministry in our times.

One graphic image brings clarity to the attempt to understand Clark Pinnock. As John Sanders puts it: "Most evangelicals are followers who move into new theological territory only after it is thoroughly explored, tested, and secured. Pinnock is more like a paratrooper who chooses to drop behind 'enemy' lines to really learn the territory and establish a base camp that shifts the action to newly defined arenas."[86] Switching to basketball as a working metaphor, Pinnock is not the center who stands and guards the basket, but more the point guard with the ball who moves quickly and sets the pace and location of play. He searches for places of opportunity and need in the theological community and for points of weakness in whatever obstructs credible Christian life and witness. Finding such places, he then hurries to the spot to make a difference. Being first to the scene can be awkward sometimes; it also can open the way for important achievement.

---

[85]Gary Dorrien, *The Remaking of Evangelical Theology* (Louisville, KY: Westminster John Knox Press, 1998), 182.

[86]John Sanders, Interview with Barry Callen, September 22, 1998.

New Dimensions of Biblical Meaning

The Spirit of God always seeks to breathe new life into the church, and Clark Pinnock has come to relish the renewing warmth of the flame of God's ministering Spirit. Given a continuing commitment to biblical authority as the ancient text is illumined by the Spirit for the community of faith in each new generation, Pinnock has concluded that a biblical text has a "fullness of meaning,"[87] meaning beyond its original historical context and cultural application. Here he joins Donald Bloesch in recognizing that, beyond a biblical text's "objective" or immediately intended authorial meaning, there is true and currently relevant meaning that emerges from the work of the Spirit who "breathes on the text" and still speaks to faithful readers and listeners. This divine breathing adds to the biblical text a "fluidity of meaning within certain parameters," a "pneumatic or revelatory meaning that the text assumes when the Spirit acts on it in bringing home its significance to people of faith in every age."[88]

The very suggestion of new dimensions of biblical meaning, of course, can be threatening to many conservative persons. Does the very idea not verge on an anti-biblical subjectivism, a modernistic arrogance, a politically correct contemporizing of the ancient biblical message? The cautious question is understandable and worthy of being addressed with care. Even so, Clark Pinnock has come to champion the legitimacy and even urgency of penetrating more deeply into the biblical revelation with the help of the Spirit of God and in the context of the cultures that dominate at the opening of the twenty-first century. The Bible remains basic for him, but the Spirit remains active on behalf of its contemporary meaning.

---

[87]Clark Pinnock, *The Scripture Principle* (San Francisco: Harper & Row, 1984), 191. He speaks of the "depth of truth" which opens to current biblical readers "the holistic realm of truth that transcends the merely propositional." Speaking of Israel's ancient deliverance from Egypt, for example, he says: "The wider meaning of exodus, such as the new exodus of the gospel, or the release of modern peoples from slavery, rests upon the proven fact of God's ability to deliver. These mighty acts of God are both facts and symbols—they made a difference to an actual historical experience, and they continue to have impact upon our lives in pointing to ongoing divine activity of delivering" (191).

[88]Donald G. Bloesch, *Holy Scripture* (Downers Grove, Ill.: InterVarsity Press, 1994), 178, 190.

Pinnock judges that evangelicals tend to fear new interpretations of beloved biblical texts largely because of the trauma they have known with certain excesses of liberal theology. Even so, he insists, "God is calling us nonetheless to grow as hearers of the Word of God."[89] Few would question the principle of helping the Bible to come alive in new times and contexts with fresh hearing and applications. Many, however, become quite hesitant when someone like Pinnock calls for going beyond the first interpretation in the text's original setting by seeking the truth toward which that text now is pointing. Pinnock remains firm on the affirmation of biblical authority, but he has come to stress the responsibility of the contemporary reader to listen for "fresh meanings" from the Spirit. Being rooted in the Bible and skilled as careful textual exegetes is essential, of course. So is being riveted to the trajectories of the flow of God's ongoing historical project. The Spirit is still journeying with us humans, and we who choose to be pilgrims following the Spirit must remain open to fresh insight and guidance that are divinely given along the paths not traveled previously. The Bible is a dynamic narrative of ongoing divine activity, not primarily a book of fixed concepts to be perpetuated mechanically and exclusively. God is to be experienced in the pattern of the biblical story. The Spirit-filled community of faith is always to be open to the living God whom they know as personal, dynamic, relational, and amazingly loving.

To be avoided in the quest to be more mature hearers of God's Word in our time is the debilitating problem of Spirit-less blindness and deafness, the hermeneutical disease that blocks fresh perception of how the gospel of Christ is being worked out in our own generation. This interpretive disability was the problem of the Scribes of Jesus' day. The first-century Scribes "were not sensitive to the fact that the reason we engage the narratives of Scripture is not just to refresh our memories about what they said, but also because the history of salvation of which they speak is not finished and we anticipate greater actualizations of the promises of God."[90] Post-biblical existence, primarily by virtue of divine

---

[89]Clark Pinnock, "Biblical Texts: Past and Future Meanings," *Wesleyan Theological Journal* (Fall 1999), 137.
[90]Ibid., 139.

revelation in Scripture, knows much about God's nature, intent, and partial promise fulfillments—and thus knows at least the right road along which to watch and wait for God's likely next steps.

Adequate hearing of the biblical voice is a crucial and complex process. Historical description blends with the contemporary extension of the story. The early church was privileged to know the foundations of the Christian message, but not all of its eventual implications. To grasp these, the believing community must always be growing as sensitive hearers of God's Word. Consequently, Christian theology is an ongoing venture in hope and always is capable of Spirit-guided enrichment and reform. The Bible itself is full of "untapped potentiality of meaning," meaning that is "waiting to break forth as it engages real life situations by the Spirit."[91] Disciples of Jesus in the twenty-first century, then, are not prisoners of the biblical text in some mechanical and antiquarian sense, but are privileged partners of the Spirit of the biblical text as God continues to unfold to the faithful the richness yet unseen in the sacred text.[92] The Spirit is not in the business of communicating new information not congruent with the Bible, but the Spirit's ministry is essential to the search of believers for deeper understanding of the truth already in the text.[93] The quest is for understanding the Bible in new contexts, penetrating the text more deeply rather than going *beyond* the text. The current meaning resides in the text, affirms Pinnock, not in the reader, so that all valid interpretation must come within the range of possible meanings created by the inspired text itself.

Rather than denying biblical inspiration, this "open" stance affirms both the Spirit's *inspiration* yesterday and the Spirit's *illumination* today,

---

[91]Ibid., 140.

[92]For elaboration, see Clark Pinnock, "The Work of the Spirit in Hermeneutics," *Journal of Pentecostal Theology* 2 (1993), 3-23, and "The Role of the Spirit in Interpretation," *Journal of the Evangelical Theological Society* 36 (1993), 491-497.

[93]Clark Pinnock is well aware of the dangers of uncontrolled subjectivity that simply sets aside biblical authority in favor of some "fresh word" received individually, presumably from the Spirit, and not confirmed by a broad consensus of the believing community. However, he is quick to identify as another and equally destructive danger the placing of a fence around the Bible that virtually excludes the Spirit from the process of fresh interpretation and application.

with the inspiration and illumination necessarily linked closely. Rather than a mere once-for-all deposit of abstract truths, the Bible is to be viewed best as a meta-narrative of what God has done and is yet doing on the human scene. Far from a dead letter from a distant yesterday, the Bible is a dynamic vehicle for the relational realities of God's grace that are forever full of fresh and future meanings. This view leads to a grateful *revering* of Scripture, but, it is important to note, it leads to a *reverencing* only of the God who is conveyed by the biblical story and yet is living today and always. The text is to be treasured, while the God of the text is to be worshipped. Henry Knight appreciatively affirms this stance of Pinnock because "it takes account of both the humanity and divinity of Scripture.... There is a single divine Author whose intentions transcend those within the awareness of the inspired writers; it is the fullness of God's intentions which is to be found within the inspired text."[94] Barry Callen has insisted that affirming this ongoing illumination of the Spirit of God does not need to be an open door to unchecked subjectivism among Bible-believing Christians. Reflecting Pinnock's stance, he explains:

> The divine dimension of the biblical materials is bound closely to the present illumination provided by the Spirit of God. This was the case when these materials were first written, when later they were edited and then compiled and canonized within the church's life, and when still later they were freshly understood and newly applied. Rather than the truth of God in Scripture being restricted narrowly to fixed concepts and their exact way of statement and precise point of application, there is a more Spirit-oriented dynamism inherent in the process of inter-pretation. According to 2 Timothy 3:16-17, God "inspires," breathes into the Scripture, thereby keeping it alive, faith producing, and church directing as times and cultures change.... The significance of a biblical text sometimes changes, but not its meaning.[95]

---

[94]Henry Knight III, *A Future for Truth: Evangelical Theology in a Postmodern World* (Nashville: Abingdon Press, 1997), 115.

[95]Barry L. Callen, *God As Loving Grace* (Nappanee, Ind.: Evangel Publishing House, 1996), 318-319.

Pinnock's career could be said to stretch from an early phase of vigorously defending the "inerrancy" of the biblical text to the later matured phase of also honoring the dynamic of the Spirit's illumination of that text. Such illumination enables "current openings" of God's Word. Pinnock has tentatively set forward several such apparent openings, with the caution that each gains increased credibility as a consensus seems to grow about it in the larger Bible-studying and Spirit-listening Christian community. In a recent academic journal article[96] several were identified and explored briefly by him, including: the universality, justice, and non-human creation implications of the saving will of God, a relational interpretation of the doctrine of God and, in that realm of grace-enabled relationship, the full range of spiritual gifts to believers, including to women. He concludes such a consideration of fresh Bible "openings" with this, so typical of his personality and theological method: "We are on an interpretive road, not yet at the end of the journey, and we pray to the Lord for an ever more fruitful discernment of God's meaning for us and our times."[97]

What are believers to do along the road to fuller biblical under-standing and more fruitful Christian ministry? Celebrate! God is; God is good; God is gracious; and God is always present.

Invitation to Celebration

Clark Pinnock has sensed some nostalgia for the "beautifully tight system of deterministic theology" as he has sought to help the evangel-ical community to consciously leave it behind. But any nostalgia has been overwhelmed for him by the realization that the welcome departure from rationalistic determinism can initiate a day of great opportunity for the gospel to be heard in exciting new ways and to become effective as never before. The needed change is seen by him as a path of theological renewal. Among other things, it is an invitation to be liberated from the darker side of the old orthodoxy that "makes hell as much the divine purpose as heaven and the fall into sin as much God's

---

[96]Clark Pinnock, "Biblical Texts: Past and Future Meanings," *Wesleyan Theological Journal* 34:2 (Fall 1999).
[97]Ibid., 151.

work as salvation is."[98] He sees better news than Augustine's rendition of Christian faith. Orthodox Calvinism continues to have great appeal because it "delivers such a delicious sense of security and gives us such a great platform from which to assail those dreadful liberals who are such historicists."[99] But Pinnock has concluded that such security, while hard to give up, can and should be replaced by a more biblically appropriate and pastorally meaningful awareness that, by divine grace, "there is true comfort in the gospel and in the promise of our Lord to preserve his church through time and give to her the Spirit of truth to guide her in the midst of her struggles."[100]

Jesus assured faithful disciples that the Paraclete would be with faithful believers forever and would guide them into all the truth. Such divine presence and wisdom constitute the bond, beauty, power, and even ecstasy that should characterize every fully graced and Spirit-related Christian. To really know the Spirit is to join the joyous journey of redemption and re-creation. Accordingly, Pinnock issues an invitation:

> I invite us to view Spirit as the bond of love in the triune relationality, as the ecstasy of sheer life overflowing into a significant creation, as the power of creation and new creation, as the power of incarnation and atonement, as the power of new community and union with God, and as the power drawing the whole world into the truth of Jesus.[101]

So far as Pinnock is concerned, enduring wisdom comes from the book of First Thessalonians. Early Christians are instructed to rejoice, giving thanks in all circumstances (4:18). The joy comes as believers hold fast to what is truly good. And what is that? It is the enduring and enabling paradox of Christian truth, the text-context poles of Christian believing and living. The *text*, the fixed givenness of the faith, has been

---

[98]Clark Pinnock, "From Augustine To Arminius: A Pilgrimage in Theology," in *The Grace of God and the Will of Man*, ed. Clark Pinnock (Zondervan, 1989, rev. ed., Minneapolis: Bethany House, 1995), 28.

[99]Ibid.

[100]Ibid., 28-29.

[101]Clark Pinnock, *Flame of Love: A Theology of the Holy Spirit* (Downers Grove, Ill.: InterVarsity Press, 1996), 247.

expressed by the "will of God in Christ Jesus" (4:18). A critical *context,*
the dynamic ongoingness and contemporaneity of the faith, resides in
the presence and power of Christ's Spirit which are not to be despised or
quenched (4:19-20)—although they always are to be measured by the
text of God in Christ. Christian celebration, to be authentically Christian,
must remain both anchored in the text and enlivened in and for the
context, rooted in the Word of God in Christ and open to the work of
God in Christ's Spirit. How wonderful that there is such a Word and that
it does not lie only in a distant past or consist only in a set of orthodox
and largely abstract theological assertions. God's Word is *now,* and it is
life! Christian believers celebrate best by becoming better hearers of the
Word of God in Scripture and then better bearers of the life of God's
Spirit in today's world.

The continuum between form and freedom, anchors of tradition
and the immediacy of the Spirit, rational supports and experiential
spontaneity, is an important one for Clark Pinnock. Keeping a good
balance is crucial for his understanding of the genuine substance of
true faith. To be both rooted and open, apostolic and on contemporary
journey, is the holistic dynamic that stimulates a properly informed
and Spirit-inspired Christian celebration. He readily joined Pope John
Paul (*Dominium et Vivificantem,* 69) in affirming that the beginning of
the third Christian millennium will be marked by a great jubilee of
renewed and joyous focus on the Spirit of God in the midst of the
church's life.[102] Can this happen within the confines of today's
evangelical community? Pinnock is hopeful. He remains committed to
the large and diverse coalition of Bible believers that make up the
evangelical world. Despite all of its shortcomings, he sees this coalition
as a vital community of faith,[103] and he enjoys the enrichment of its

---

[102]Clark Pinnock, "The Great Jubilee," 91.

[103]"…we are beginning to see a number of theologians who resemble, not settlers
with a fortress mentality as before, but pilgrims searching for more truth…. Nowadays,
if you want to find the two types, the settlers tend to congregate at the Evangelical
Theological Society, while the pilgrims like to gather in various sections of the
American Academy of Religion. Fortunately, for those like myself who want to mix
with both types, the societies meet back to back in the same cities" (Pinnock, in
Introduction to Christian Theology, 81).

various theological traditions and interdenominational settings. See Appendix G, especially Pinnock's 1999 postscript.

Hans Frei once told Carl Henry that his deepest theological desire was for there to emerge a "generous orthodoxy" that would both blend and transcend previously quarreling elements of liberalism and evangelicalism.[104] Here finally would be a speaking the truth in love that joins commitment and compassion, text and context. One astute observer concludes: "Today [1998], within a significant segment of evangelical theology, the conception of theology as polemic or tournament is receding. The confrontational spirit of fundamentalist evangelicalism is giving way to the discourse of a generous orthodoxy."[105] Should this truly be the case, Clark Pinnock will have played a key role—although he would insist that it really would be the result of the grace of an amazingly faithful God who chooses in love to risk and suffer, and finally will overcome in triumph. And in Pinnock's view it already is happening. Theology among evangelicals is "improving" and might "even reach the point when it will be of help not only to us [evangelicals] but even to others." He envisions the building among evangelicals of "a larger and ever more ecumenical coalition" that offers hope that believers will find increased unity "on the basis of a living faith in mere Christianity in a holy catholic church."[106] He offers this word of reconciliation in the service of the emergence of such a coalition among evangelicals:

> There is room in evangelicalism for many voices, for Wesley as well as Edwards, and for Finney as well as Hodge. It is good to discuss our differences. Might it not even be that God leads theologians in different ways to help different kinds of people? Some people prefer Lewis to Packer, others prefer Henry to Ramm. But there is no doubt that all of them are committed to the good news of God in Christ. The evangelical movement is bigger and richer than any of our schemes, including my own.

---

[104]Hans Frei, "Response to 'Narrative Theology: An Evangelical Appraisal'," *Trinity Journal* 8 (Spring 1987), 21-24.

[105]Gary Dorrien, *The Remaking of Evangelical Theology* (Louisville, KY: Westminster John Knox Press, 1998), 209.

[106]Clark Pinnock, in *Introduction to Christian Theology*, 82.

So let the conversations continue and let us all grow as hearers of the Word of God.[107]

Pinnock has journeyed to the belief that downgrading the relative importance of rationally supported doctrinal systems yields a greater freedom to think, experiment, and grow as hearers of God's Word. It opens one to the contextual nature of theology and thus to new possibilities of meaning, including the crucial awareness that the Word of God did not come as a philosophy to be discussed dispassionately and debated in abstract terms disassociated from the full realities of everyday life. God's Word came as a person to be followed, loved, and enjoyed. He observed that his book *Flame of Love* (1996) "puts on display before the reader my restlessness: in experience to know the living God and in theology to grow as a hearer of God's Word."[108] This book signaled a significant turn in his life, a turn "from preoccupation with the mind to the more apopathic—to mystery, to silence, to experience, to celebration, to prayer."[109]

All we humans are caught in the web of historical limitations that tend to relativize what we think or do. This leads to caution and sometimes despair. From where, then, can there come relief and release, real insight, reliable authority, an adequate foundation for authentic Christian celebration? For Pinnock the answer is clear, even exhilarating. "The joy of traditional theology is to be able to proclaim salvation *from* the Lord in and through a historically attested divine disclosure.... The way ahead for systematic theology is simply to recover the incredible relevance and sheer excitement of revelational Christianity."[110] For him, this is at the heart of what it means to be an "evangelical," and he is not prepared to sit quietly and allow those who

---

[107]Clark Pinnock, "Response to Daniel Strange and Amos Yong," *The Evangelical Quarterly*, 71:4 (October 1999), 357.

[108]Clark Pinnock, "A Bridge and Some Points of Growth: A Reply to Cross and Macchia," *Journal of Pentecostal Theology* (October 1998), 49.

[109]Clark Pinnock, unpublished paper, evangelical-process dialogue, Claremont School of Theology, 1997, 10.

[110]Clark Pinnock, *Toward a Theology for the Future*, eds. Clark Pinnock and David Wells (Carol Stream, Ill.: Creation House, 1971), 118.

are heavily Reformed and inflexibly rationalistic to define the territory otherwise and then reign unchallenged.

At the change of the centuries Clark Pinnock believes it as strongly as when he first put the thought into print some thirty years ago. Singing and joy characterize biblical religion. The grand announcement from heaven still stands: "Fear not: for, behold, I bring you good tidings of great joy, which shall be to all people" (Luke 2:10). In Christ is found "a peace that passes all understanding and a joy which the world system can neither give nor take away."[111] If theology has a tendency to be stodgy and impersonal, abstract and even boring, something is wrong, and Pinnock has chosen to go another way. For him, the Spirit "choreographs the dance of God and also directs the steps of creatures entering God's dance." Theology, he says, "ought to be beautiful because its subject is so beautiful."[112] God's reign is intended to bring peace and joy in the Holy Spirit (Rom. 14:17). Therefore, it is time to celebrate the amazing grace and love of an amazing God! In fact, any time should be a wonderful time to enter into the joy of the Spirit who is illumined by the bright light of Jesus Christ which is faithfully available to all people in the inspired text of the Bible. Those who would be disciples of this Christ must walk the way of the Spirit, journey in the joy of the Spirit, and witness to the wonder of the Spirit.

Pinnock's 1996 book, *Flame of Love,* is clearly a benchmark of the mature Pinnock. Hardly a scholastic theology neatly outlined in any tight propositional framework, here is constructive theology emerging from a pneumatologically informed perspective. The call goes forth for contemporary Christians to more properly balance the historic subordination of pneumatology in relation to christology and soteriology and to rethink classic Christian doctrine in light of this needed rebalancing. Pinnock wants to refocus the faith through the eyes and ongoing work of the Spirit, encouraging evangelicals to lessen their fear of Christianity's broad historic streams, especially those rich in insights

---

[111]Clark Pinnock, *Live Now, Brother* (Chicago: Moody Press, 1972), 41.
[112]Clark Pinnock, *Flame of Love,* 37, 43.

into life by and in the Spirit of God.[113] To be on an authentic life pilgrimage with the God of creation, history, judgment, and redemption, one must be on a journey of renewal with the Spirit. If one longs for a fresh articulation of the spontaneity of a living God who desires above all to breath new life into modern people who seem to know only broken relationships and lost communities, *Flame of Love* would be an excellent place to begin.

Dare one say that there should be a certain "romance" associated with Christian theology, a "flame of love" that should flavor the meaning of Christian "orthodoxy" and keep revealed truth alive, transforming, commissioning? Clark Pinnock responds here with a resounding and inspiring "Yes!"

---

[113]In reviewing Pinnock's *Flame of Love*, prominent Pentecostal scholar Frank Macchia was not always sure that Pinnock had been "attentive enough to the radical implications of Pentecostal pneumatology," but Macchia's significant appreciation of Pinnock's provocative work is made obvious in the extensive review, leading to his judgment that Pinnock "represents an important dialogue partner for us" ("Tradition and the *Novum* of the Spirit: A Review of Clark Pinnock's *Flame of Love,*" *Journal of Pentecostal Theology*, 13, 1998, 34). Pinnock is pleased whenever he is perceived as being both biblically faithful and provocative, Spirit-honoring, and an encourager of the journey of faith and life to which the Spirit always calls.

APPENDIX A

What is a Baptist?

Original Source: Clark Pinnock
A New Reformation: A Challenge to Southern Baptists
(Tigerville, S. C.: Jewel Books, 1968), pages 15-19.

The decisive question which Southern Baptists are going to be forced to answer in the near future is this one: "Is a Baptist a believer in the evangelical truths of an inerrant Bible, or is he a person of any persuasion who happens to hold to adult baptism?" Today the word "Baptist" is loosely applied to anyone, however remotely attached to a denominational program without regard for his private doctrinal beliefs, even in fundamental tenets. Believer's baptism is undoubtedly an important part of evangelical belief, but it is not the whole. Indeed, apart from other cardinal concepts of the Scripture baptism is quite meaningless. Spurgeon confronted the Baptist Union of his day with the searching question: "Are we an assemblage of evangelical churches, or an indiscriminate collection of communities practicing immersion?" Conservative Christians, like all orthodox Protestants, insist that saving faith involves definite doctrinal beliefs in the deity of Christ, his substitutionary death for sinners, his personal return, the reality of divine wrath, the integrity of the whole Bible, and such like. We deny that a person can be consistently Christian and reject these truths.

Cooperate For What?

We Baptists are united in a cooperative effort for the purpose of publishing our faith abroad in the world. A union of Baptists can fulfill the great commission more effectively than can individual Baptists working alone. But in any such union the indispensable condition is agreement on the doctrinal rule of faith. The Scriptures warn us frequently that the Church will be harassed by false teaching and heresy, especially toward the end (2 Peter 2:1). It is imperative that doctrinal error be dealt with and put out of the fellowship lest it eat like a canker (2 Tim. 2:17). One of the requirements for a faithful pastor, in addition to giving instruction in sound doctrine, is to be able "to confute those who contradict it" (Tit. 1:9). We have done but half our job if, when we have preached the whole counsel of God (Acts 20:27), we allow error in the denomination to go unchallenged. Paul understood that to permit doctrinal heresy would negate everything he had been building up (Gal. 2:2b). A union of churches tolerating the denial of clear Scriptural truths is displeasing to God, and believers have the unpleasant duty of dealing with it. The refusal to discipline false teachers is not charity, but stupidity, for it contains the seeds of our own destruction. The Convention is not an umbrella stretched to its limits to cover all possible shades of human opinion. It is (or was) a voluntary association of evangelical believers who hold to the norm of the infallible Word and wish to get on with the only job Christ gave us, to preach the unsearchable riches of the Gospel.

Peace At Any Price?

Peace at any price is not the mentality of the New Testament. Repeatedly the Apostles denounced error and dealt with false teachers. Loyalty to God's Word stands above any merely outward tranquillity of a church. The advantages gained in a denomination in a cooperative effort are carnal and spurious if they be gained at the expense of the clarity of the Gospel. Cancer requires surgery, and surgery is painful. Evangelicals have to consider before God whether they really care that much for the truth to pay the price for the purity of the Church. Most churches in America today refused outright to insist on Biblical truth against modernist theology, and their sickly condition is their deserved judgment. When men prefer a consensus of human opinion to the plain teaching of the oracles of God, the candlestick is taken away from that church. Which is more important to the Southern Baptist Convention today—denominational peace or doctrinal integrity? We are fast approaching the hour when we may be unable to cherish both. The day our churches consider belief in the fundamental doctrines of Scripture a private and nonessential matter, its death warrant will have been signed.

Freedom of Interpretation?

This principle [freedom of Biblical interpretation] is sanctimoniously invoked more than any other in Baptist circles to justify simple evasions of Biblical teaching. The principle, however, was never intended to lead in the direction of anarchy, relativism, and total flux in matters of faith. Nevertheless, it is used hypocritically to camouflage anti-Biblical positions. One influential Baptist leader understands the principle to mean that there is no universally agreed upon set of beliefs to which Baptists must adhere, and that each Christian is free to come to his own personal convictions in these matters without persecution. In a similar way the Sunday School Board defended Professor Elliot in a statement which read: "The Broadman Press ministers to the denomination in keeping with the historic Baptist principle of the freedom of the individual to interpret the Bible for himself, to hold a particular theory of inspiration of the Bible which seems most reasonable to him, and to develop his beliefs in accordance with his theory." Fortunately the subsequent Convention overruled this amazing and dangerous statement and officially at least our churches are not committed to such apostasy.

The freedom Christ gives us obviously does not include the freedom to disobey Him! The freedom of interpretation principle does not permit a Baptist to hold a low view of Scripture in glaring contradiction to the high view Christ held, and then to develop his egocentric theology in contradiction to what the Apostles taught. What the ego of the individual sees in its inner light is not normative over what the Bible says. This is worse than Roman Catholicism wherein the ego of the Pope is exalted over God's Word. The Christian who claims to know Christ and disobeys his commandments is a liar (1 John. 2:4). This great principle is used today as a tactic of evasion by those who are unfaithful to the historic Christ and the written Word. Its true significance pertains to the responsibility of each believer to heed and obey God's Word of his own volition. We have one Teacher (Matt. 23:8) and what He commands we will do. The opinions of men are not equal to the doctrines of Christ and his delegated Apostles.

On Facing The Issue

At present there are two divergent and diverging movements in the Southern Baptist Convention. There are those who see in the attempt to maintain doctrinal standards in our agencies and churches a dangerous tendency which will destroy the denomination and cost them their jobs. And there are others who believe that unless our churches keep true to the teachings of the entire Bible in its literal interpretation dissolutions of the union would be the best possible thing. We evangelicals are set as watchmen for the cause of Christ.... It is our duty to ask, and keep asking, why Biblical truths are not proclaimed and implemented at every level of our cooperative effort. There is no reason why the money of God's people should be squandered on an unorthodox and ineffective student movement, on Baptist colleges which show very little mark of standing for Biblical principles, on seminaries which indoctrinate students in the latest theological fads while ignoring historic evangelical thought, on a press and book stores which manifest considerable haziness about what a truly good Christian book is, on Sunday School materials which specialize in dilution, and on agencies which seem to prefer the antics of the radical left in the National Council of Churches to the mundane duty of preaching regeneration as the cure of social ills.

Lambs Or Tigers?

Observe how quickly a wild tiger committed to a zoo becomes docile. Down through history most people, once enslaved, have readily adjusted to their altered situations; their lot becomes the new normalcy and any break with it is upsetting and prompts resistance. We have so long become accustomed to the powerful domination of fuzzy-minded liberal theologians that we have come to accept it as a fact of life. Evangelicals must learn to swim in thick sand. It is time to break the status quo. Every year the problem of theological ambiguity grows larger. It is action, not slogans that we need, not the profession, but the practice of the truth. God is bypassing many of the great denominations today because they refused to maintain a pure testimony to the truth. If we do not wish to see our schools, presses, and buildings fall into the hands of men who bow to the spirit of our age, then we need to act now.

Pinnock Postscript: How My Mind Has Changed

Written in 1999 by Clark Pinnock for this book, specifically concerning the above selection that dates from 1968.

I do not like the tone of this piece I wrote in 1968. It presents the situation in the Southern Baptist Convention in the late 1960s as radically bifurcated, with true believers on one side and liberals and agnostics on the other. It seems to be saying that Baptists must adhere to a rigid rule of faith, composed of fundamentalistic interpretations, the denial of which puts one outside the true church. It is a tendentious depiction of the situation in the denomination and a call to ecclesiastical warfare and schism.

One sees here the bitter root of fundamentalist-evangelicalism manifesting itself: the militancy, the rationalism, and the doctrinalism. It reminds us where the roots of twentieth-century evangelicalism lie, and how hard it is to transcend them, however much one tries. After decades of reforming fundamentalism, the militant root stem refuses to die, but sends out new shoots. How at thirty years of age I fell into it, I am unsure. My own roots spiritually were warmly pietistic and my sympathies charismatic. I admired C. S. Lewis and I studied with F. F. Bruce, both of whom were men of generous instincts. Something triggered the militant root to manifest itself in me at this earlier time.

It may have been the heady mixture of Francis Schaeffer joined to my encounter with Baptist fundamentalism while I was at the seminary in New Orleans. At any rate, in the late 1960s I found myself heralded as a conservative voice, and I succumbed to the populist adulation. I advocated that Baptists give up their liberty and take on the yoke of credalism. True, there was a problem in the Southern Baptist Convention at the time, a disaffection between fundamentalist laity and educated elites, which needed to be addressed. But it did not justify fostering schism and not living in love with fellow believers. I am embarrassed about the attitude that is expressed here. I did not start out the Christian life in this spirit, and I am sorry for any harm that I did.

A Rich Selection of Christian Evidences

Original Source: Clark Pinnock
Reason Enough: A Case for the Christian Faith
(Downers Grove, Ill.: InterVarsity Press, 1980), pages 12-17.

I recognize that there are those who think that religion cannot and should not be supported by any rational means. Some hold this opinion because they have not yet been convinced that reasons for faith exist, and others because of the influence of existential styles of thinking. Faith, they hold, is void of all security, whether intuitive or intellectual, and any attempt to bolster it with reasoned argument is self-contradictory. But I don't think that faith can bypass the truth question so easily. Rather, I am committed to appealing to reason to try to persuade those yet unconvinced to make a decision for Jesus Christ. Faith according to the Bible does not involve a rash decision made without reflection and is not a blind submission in the face of an authoritarian claim. It is the act of wholehearted trust in the goodness and promises of the God who confronts us with his reality and gives us ample reason to believe that he is there.

It is perfectly in order before making such a faith commitment to scrutinize the alternatives and weigh all the issues. I see reasons for faith serving as a road map helping us determine where we wish to go and showing us how to get there. One of the things that makes the Christian message an option for us today is its ability to show us reason enough to be committed to Christ.

The Five Circles of Credibility

I have organized the argument of this book into what I call five circles of credibility, that is, five subject areas or categories of evidence which support in a complementary way the Christian understanding of reality and Christ's claim on our lives. All of them are referred to in the Bible, and all of them have been used with regularity in the literature of Christian persuasion for the past two thousand years. A brief summary of these five arguments and evidences will give an overview of the chapters that follow

1. Circle One. Circle one points to the practical value of the Christian faith and hence is called the *pragmatic* basis for faith. All of us need to believe that our lives have dignity and worth, and the gospel gives us the necessary basis for believing that they do. It satisfies a basic human need. The hunger after meaning is a deep existential drive within the human heart, and the gospel can satisfy that hunger by supplying the solid basis for confidence in the worthwhileness of life. Circle one is a basic argument for faith which does not presuppose a religious interest, but addresses the question which ordinary life always raises.

2. Circle Two. Circle two looks at the *experiential* dimension of religious and Christian faith. Although often downplayed as "subjective," the evidence of religious experience is universal and impressive, and cannot be left out of the evidential picture. There is a host of high quality reports and reporters, not the least of whom is Jesus himself, and the relevance of their testimonies to the fundamental desire of the human heart to be in touch with the creative ground of reality makes this circle crucial. Religious experience is a fact about our world which cannot just be swept aside and ignored. The offer of a vibrant relationship with a loving Father is central to the gospel and is an exciting possibility that deserves to be considered.

3. Circle Three. Circle three focuses on the *cosmic* (or metaphysical) basis for faith. Here we broaden the horizon of our investigation to consider the mystery of the universe itself over and above its strictly human dimension. Mankind has always been engaged in a quest after the intelligibility not only of his own existence but of the world, a world which is full of marvelous wonders that cry out to be accounted for. Circle three shows us that belief in God makes rational sense of the world and fulfills the deep human desire to explain and understand it. In my view science has not made belief any harder or unbelief any easier, but has if anything provided us with fresh evidences of the existence of God. As the psalmist says, "How clearly the sky reveals God's glory! How plainly it shows what he has done!" (Psalm 19:1).

4. Circle Four. Circle four, which deals with the *historical* basis for faith, is particularly important to our presentation for two reasons. First, the gospel is centrally concerned with God's intervention in the history of the world in the life of ancient Israel and especially in the career of Jesus of Nazareth. Second, circle four focuses precisely on the object of Christian faith, the person of Christ himself. The first three circles prepare us to take seriously what the gospel says. But they do not by themselves identify the gospel as the unique message of salvation that is historically mediated to us.

In an attempt to convince King Agrippa about the gospel of Christ, the apostle Paul reminded him that the facts underlying the message were not "hidden away in a corner" (Acts 26:26). They were capable of being investigated because they occurred on the stage of verifiable history. To the Athenians he even said, in discussing the coming judgment the whole world would one day face, that God "has given proof of this to everyone by raising that man Jesus from death" (Acts 17: 31). In the last analysis the decision to be a Christian will be a decision about the person and history of Jesus the Christ.

5. Circle Five. Circle five has to do with the way Jesus' followers have lived. A new human reality was created by the resurrection of Jesus and the outpouring of the Spirit. There is, therefore, a community basis for faith that calls attention to Jesus' promise of personal and social healing. Although the record of Christians is not flawless, there is good evidence that the gospel can create new community. The promise and the reality are there. Those who long to belong to the family of God should be drawn by this evidence.

The Christian Gospel Is "True"

A glance at the five circles of credibility will show that I believe the Christian gospel is "true" in various ways. It is the true end to the human quest for meaning and our quest for the intelligibility of the world, true to the religious longings of our heart, true to the biblical record, and true to the moral intuition that we need a new kind of human community on this groaning planet. The five circles together provide a comprehensive structure of evidence that goes a long way toward justifying Christianity's claim to truth. Since the Christian faith addresses so many aspects of human life, it only is natural that evidence for its truth will be found in a variety of settings and that these various circles will interact with each other in a complementary way, creating a cumulative effect on the mind. One circle appeals more to practical relevance and another more to intellectual comprehension, but both contribute to an adequate case for the gospel.

The image of the circle is not the only one possible. Circles designate broad areas which contain evidences of a specific kind. We could, however, speak of them as lines of argument directing our understanding to the true object of faith, or as points in a lawyer's presentation which are adduced to convince a judge and jury. Whatever image is used, the main point is that a rich selection of Christian evidences exists and that these various indicators of truth work together to lead us to a reasonable conclusion.

Pinnock Postscript: How My Mind Has Changed
Written in 1999 by Clark Pinnock for this book,
specifically concerning the above selection that dates from 1980.

One aspect of the rationalism native to fundamentalistic evangelicalism shows up in the inordinate interest such evangelicals have in apologetics. That love of evidences and arguments surfaced in two books of mine, *Set Forth Your Case* (1967) and *Reason Enough* (1980). How evangelicals savor the thought that conservative beliefs are not only biblical, but intellectually superior to those of liberal Protestantism. How we cheered James Gresham Machen when he held his own with the best of the modernists and secularists. How we loved it when Fuller Theological Seminary was established in 1948, when professors like Edward John Carnell and Carl F. H. Henry began to churn out the apologetics, and when Gleason Archer and Wilbur Smith would seem to answer every biblical difficulty.

The significance of the above text from my *Reason Enough* is its revelation of an epistemological shift which happened to a number of us when we tried "to set forth our case." The shift is visible in Bernard Ramm and Edward Carnell as well as in myself. While it is true that Carl Henry stuck to his rationalism to the end, not many others did. What we see is a shift from hard to soft rationality or, as we might say now, from modernity to postmodernity. It was a shift from maintaining that the Christian truth can be proven by the canons of logic to the view that the truth is better represented by a cumulative argument which makes an appeal to intuitive and ultimately to personal judgment.

On the one hand, the softer rationalism was a better apologetic approach which made a more effective appeal possible. But, on the other hand, it was more than an adjustment in epistemology. It also marked the shift from a more to a less rationalistic approach and from a more to a less militant frame of mind. In other words, it represented a softening of the categories of what we know for certain, and it took the older militancy down a notch. Soft rationalists are less hardline in their opinions and more open to dialogue. They are less likely to wield the truth as a weapon against others. My journey has taken me in a softening direction.

Biblical Inspiration and Authority

Original Source: Clark Pinnock
The Scripture Principle
(San Francisco: Harper & Row, 1984), pages 54-58.

The Bible does not give us a doctrine of its own inspiration and authority that answers all the various questions we might like to ask. Its witness on this subject is unsystematic and somewhat fragmentary and enables us to reach important but modest conclusions. It does support the central place of the "Scripture principle" in Christianity.... [The Scripture principle] means that the Bible is regarded as a creaturely text that is at the same time God's own written Word, and that we can consult his Word, which reveals his mind, and seek to know his will in it. It means that God has communicated authoritatively to us on those subjects about which Scripture teaches, whether doctrinal, ethical, or spiritual, and that we believers willingly subject ourselves to this rule of faith. More than merely human tradition and merely existential address, the Bible is the informative Word of God to the church. The text is not reduced to an expression of human experience and tradition, as in liberalism, but is a contentful language deposit that addresses, as it decides, with the authority of God.

The evidence suggests that it was God's will that written revelation in the form of Scripture should emerge out of the traditions of Israel and church to preserve the substance of the faith and make it available to believers. This appears most clearly in the way Jesus and the New Testament writers handle the Old Testament as the Word of God, and in

231

the way the apostles describe themselves as heralds and witnesses of the Word. What has been given is trustworthy and ought to be received obediently in a spirit of faith. Religious liberals cannot successfully deny what classical Christians have always believed concerning the divine gift of Holy Scripture as the inspired Word of God. Christianity without a Scripture principle is a figment of the liberal imagination, something that has never existed and was not meant to exist. The idea that the Bible is a collection of fallible human documents whose authority is on a par with other sources of information is a modern idea out of keeping with the nature of the texts themselves and the way they have always been seen. Without belaboring the issue, the Bible itself supports the view that Scripture is a product of divine revelation and to be gratefully received.

A second conclusion the evidence leads us to is the practical purpose of the Bible as a book that testifies to salvation in Jesus Christ. As the thirty-nine Articles say, the Bible gives us "all things necessary" to the life of faith: "Holy Scripture contains all things necessary to salvation, so that whatsoever is not read therein, nor may be proved thereby, is not to be required of any man, that it should be believed as an article of the faith, or be thought requisite or necessary to salvation" (VI). The Bible is basically a covenant document designed to lead people to know and love God. As such, it has a focused purpose and concentration. This is the kind of truth it urges us to seek in it, and this is the context in which its truth claims ought to be measured. Even though our Bibles in their present form are not flawless, and there are many things in them that are puzzling and admit of no obvious solution, the Bible is not prevented from carrying out its designated purpose. The Bible was "written for our instruction, that by steadfastness and by the encouragement of the Scriptures we might have hope" (Rom. 15:4). Their treasure and their wisdom are oriented to presenting Jesus Christ, the wisdom and the power of God. We should never define biblical authority apart from this stated purpose or apply to it standards of measurement that are inappropriate. God speaks through the Bible, not to make us scholars and scientists, but to put us in a right relationship with God and to give us such a religious understanding of the world and history that we can grasp everything else better. Citing 2 Timothy 3:16-17, the Second

Vatican Council was wise in asserting that the Scriptures teach "firmly, faithfully, and without error that truth which God wanted put into the sacred writings for the sake of our salvation" (*Dogmatic Constitution on Divine Revelation*, chap. 3).

The importance of grasping the purpose of the Bible is obvious once we consider that the interpreting of any book depends upon the kind of book it is, whether a novel or a cookbook or a dictionary. If the Bible is the covenant book of the people of God, then it exists for them and for their religious (in the broad sense) needs, not primarily for literary critics, historians, geologists, and text critics. It is the witness to the agreement we have with God through Christ. What we expect to learn from it is "teaching, reproof, correction, and instruction in righteousness" to make us the kind of mature disciples and servants of the Lord we want to be. Knowing how inspiration happened or whether the original texts were or were not free from what someone might regard as a flaw is not necessary for us, and the Bible does not tell us these things. What it does do is confront us with the living God and involve us in a relationship with him through our faith. About this, the Scriptures are clear and plain, and their profitability for the life of faith evident and empirical.

Another conclusion the evidence points to is the complex character of the Bible as the Word of God. It contains many kinds of literature and several levels of claim to authority. The truth appropriate in a psalm or a proverb, in situated command or a parable, is discerned by reference to the genre in question. We will want to notice whether the author claims to be delivering a prophetic oracle or a piece of advice, an apostolic commandment or an agonized question. Although God is the ultimate origin and we might say the "author" of the whole Bible, he is not the speaker of every line in it except in an ultimate sense, so that we must give thought to what he is saying to us in each place. What is God saying through the psalmist crying out in this way, or through the scribe arranging the narrative in this manner, or through Ecclesiastes giving expression to his doubts the way he does? We need to avoid being too simplistic when we utter slogans like "what the Bible says, God says," when a glance at almost any page will show how unsimple such a conviction is in practice. The simple thing we can say about the Bible from the testimony is that it is the text in which the Word of God can be heard and the will of God discerned. What is not simple is cashing in on this assurance. We have to take the portion we are reading in relation to the organic structure of revelation it is a part of and observe the kind of claim it is making on us.

A conclusion we can draw from the New Testament use of the Old Testament that has great bearing upon the interpretation of Scripture is the dynamic nature of our encounter with the text. Jesus and the apostles did not feel limited to every jot and tittle of the text as laid down. They accorded utmost respect to the smallest detail, but they also read the text in relation to the present context and sought for the will of God in the interaction between the text and their own situation.... Even in the case of Jesus' own words, the Gospel writers take some liberties, when they rephrase what he said and place his words in new contexts to bring out fresh meaning. It is not that the authority of the original is being denied in any way, but that the text means something different in the new context. The key point to learn is this: the Word of God is not to be found simply by staring at the text of the Bible or by searching one's own religious consciousness, but in the interaction between the two, from the coming together of revelation past and revelation present. There is a freedom permitted us in our reading of Scripture that was lacking in the Pharisaic and in the fundamentalist doctrine. God's Word is related to the situation to which it was addressed, and to understand it properly we need to search through it for the will of God for our own situation. God does not say exactly the same thing to every historical context, and we muzzle the power of Scripture when we refuse to ask how the Lord wants to use this Scripture in our hearing now. God has spoken in the Scriptures, but he also speaks through them today in ways that the original writer may not have intended. In saying this, we are simply confessing our faith in the Spirit as alive and active in bringing out from the Bible the ever-relevant Word of the Lord. Therefore, we study the text with the greatest care and also open our minds prayerfully to God's particular Word to us. In this way we do not exalt the letter over the Spirit or eliminate the written norms in favor of subjectivity, but allow the Word and the Spirit to function together.

Finally, what does the Bible teach in regard to the vexed question of errorlessness so vehemently debated, at least in North America? If God be the author of the Bible, does it not follow that the text must be free from any flaw and from all error? Can God lie? Did not Jesus use the Old Testament with such a total trust as to imply the total perfection of it?.... But the case for biblical errorlessness is not as good as it looks. Of course God cannot lie, but that is not the issue. God gave the Bible, not by mechanically dictating it (as all in this debate agree), but by transmitting through all manner of secondary authors. We cannot determine ahead of time what kind of text God would give in this way. We have to inquire into what it claims and what was produced.... God could have produced an errorless Bible, but we have to look and see if this is what he willed to do. What we might expect God to do is never as important as what he actually does. We might hope God would reveal the list of canonical books, or ensure the perfect transmission of the text, or give us a pope to make the meaning of the Bible plain, but he did not perform according to human expectations. From the affirmation of the inspiration of the Bible, we cannot deduce what the Bible must be like in detail.

This leaves us with the question, "Does the New Testament, did Jesus, teach the perfect errorlessness of the Scriptures?" No, not in plain terms.... It is not just that the term *inerrancy* is not used in the Bible. That would not settle anything. The point to remember is that the category of inerrancy as used today is quite a technical one and difficult to define exactly. It is postulated of the original texts of Scripture not now extant; it is held not to apply to round numbers, grammatical structures, incidental details in texts; it is held to be unfalsifiable except by some indisputable argument. Once we recall how complex a hypothesis inerrancy is, it is obvious that the Bible teaches no such thing explicitly. What it claims, as we have seen, is divine inspiration and a general reliability, with a distinct concentration upon the covenantal revelation of God. And when we examine the text in detail and note how the Gospels differ from one another, how freely the New Testament quotes from the Old Testament, and how boldly the chronicler changes what lay before him in Kings, this impression is strongly confirmed.

Why, then, do scholars insist that the Bible does claim total inerrancy? I can only answer for myself, as one who argued in this way a few years ago. I claimed that the Bible taught total inerrancy because I hoped that it did—I wanted it to. How would it be possible to maintain a firm stand against religious liberalism unless one held firmly to total inerrancy? Factors in the contemporary situation accounted for the claim, at least in my case. All I had to do was tighten up the case for inspiration one can find in the Bible and extend it just a little further than it goes itself. The logic of inspiration coupled with the demands of faith today were quite enough to convince me. Looking at the actual biblical evidence today, I have to conclude that the case for total inerrancy just isn't there. At the very most, one could say only that it is implicit and could be drawn out by careful argument, but this is disputable and not the basis for the dogmatic claims one hears for inerrancy. In the last analysis, the inerrancy theory is a logical deduction not well supported exegetically. Those who press it hard are elevating reason over Scripture at that point.

Pinnock Postscript: How My Mind Has Changed
Written in 1999 by Clark Pinnock for this book,
specifically concerning the above selection that dates from 1984.

Belief in the inspiration and authority of the Bible is basic to evangelicalism in every form. In the case of fundamentalistic evangelicalism, the category is raised to a very high level and posits the factual inerrancy of the Bible as well as its infallible teachings. The doctrine is hyped in order for it to fit with an overall rationalistic orientation. Any attempt to reform the thinking about it is bound to be opposed vehemently.

It never was my intention to create a problem within evangelical ranks. I had simply decided to take a closer look at the biblical witness to inspiration which, as I had argued earlier, undergirded the inerrancy doctrine (*Biblical Revelation*, 1971). But when I did so, I found it wanting. The prooftexts I had relied on do not actually yield what the doctrine of strict inerrancy requires. In effect, I found myself drawn back to the position of James Orr—which we had earlier dismissed. I was naive enough to think that this move would not be controversial, but actually would be welcomed as a sounder version of the "Scripture principle" we all loved. I thought that people would appreciate learning about the possibility of a more realistic doctrine of biblical inspiration and would be grateful to be freed from a host of unnecessary biblical difficulties. Some indeed were appreciative and freed, but many were not. In my opinion, the desire to have absolute truth is for many evangelicals stronger than their desire to accept the actual biblical witness.

Revising the Doctrine of God

Original Source: Clark Pinnock
"From Augustine To Arminius: A Pilgrimage In Theology,"
The Grace of God and the Will of Man, ed. Clark Pinnock
(1989, Minneapolis: Bethany House Publishers edition, 1995),
pages 23-26.

The course of my theological pilgrimage has taken me onto the territory of Christian theism itself. Although I had already come to a fresh understanding of the goodness and power of God, I realized in the early 1980s that there were still more implications to be drawn in the area of the divine attributes. It is understandable that they would dawn on me last rather than first, because God who is the mystery of human life is also theology's greatest and most demanding subject. But I could not finally escape rethinking the doctrine of God, however difficult.

The basic problem I had to cope with here is the fact that the classical model of Christian theism, shaped so decisively by Augustine under the influence of Greek philosophy, located the biblical picture of a dynamic personal God in the context of a way of thinking about God that placed high value on the Deity's being timeless, changeless, passionless, unmoved, and unmovable. The resulting synthesis more than subtly altered the biblical picture of God and tended to suppress some important aspects of it. In particular it resisted hearing the Bible's witness to a God who genuinely interacts with the world, responds passionately to what happens in it, and even changes his own plans to fit changing historical circumstances. Augustine's idea that God knows and determines all things in advance and never has to adjust his planning is one that stands in obvious tension with the Bible and yet is deeply fixed in historic Christian thinking. It is due to the accommodation made in classical theism to the Hellenistic culture.

Although the Bible itself presents a very dynamic picture of God and the world, the Greek world in which Christianity moved in the early centuries had a very negative view of historical change and the passage of time and therefore preferred to conceptualize the Deity in terms of pure actuality, changelessness, timelessness, and the like—ideas that negate the value of history and historical change. Curiously in this respect, at least modern culture, which values history so much, is closer to the biblical view than classical theism.

I soon realized something would have to be done about the received doctrine of God. I knew I would have to deal with the fact that God has made creatures with relative autonomy alongside himself and that I would have to consider what that implies for the nature and attributes of God.

1. First of all I knew we had to clarify what we meant by the divine immutability. I saw that we have been far too influenced by Plato's idea that a perfect being would not change because, being perfect, it would not need to change—any change would be for the worse. The effect of this piece of Greek natural theology on Christian thinking had been to picture God as virtually incapable of responsiveness. Creatures can relate to God, but God cannot really relate to them. Christian piety has always assumed a reciprocity between God and ourselves, of course, but the official theology had tended to undercut the assumption by declaring God to be unconditioned in every aspect of his being. The way forward, I found, was to speak of specific ways in which the God of the Bible is unchangeable—for example, in his being as God and in his character as personal agent—and also of ways in which God is able to change, as in his personal relationships with us and with the creation. It is not a question of God's changing in the sense of becoming better or worse, but of his pursuing covenant relationship and partnership with his people out of love for them, flexibly and creatively. Immutable in his self-existence, the God of the Bible is relational and changeable in his interaction with his creatures. The Word "became" flesh—praise God for his changing unchangeability!

2. Although thinking of God as timeless has some apparently positive advantages, I came to believe that it also posed a threat to the basic biblical category of God's personal agency. How could a timeless being deliberate, remember, or anticipate? How could it plan an action and undertake it? How could it even respond to something that had happened? What kind of a person would a timeless being be? I had known of these philosophical objections to a timeless deity for some time but had not previously given much thought to possible biblical objections. What I came to realize at this stage was how strongly the Bible itself speaks of God as operating from within time and history. He is always presented in the Bible as One who can look back to the past, relate to the present as present, and make plans for what is yet to happen. The alleged timelessness of God does not make a lot of sense to this way of portraying the deity. Of course I do not think God is threatened by time. He is the everlasting God, and his years have no end. But the Bible presents him as operating from within time. God is able to be inside time, and not only outside of it. If he were not able to be within time, he would not be able to be with us on our journey, or freely relate to what goes on, or make plans and carry them out, or experience the joy of victory or the anguish of defeat, as Scripture says God does. Everything would be completely fixed and settled, and novelty would be mere appearance and unreal.

3. Finally I had to rethink the divine omniscience and reluctantly ask whether we ought to think of it as an exhaustive foreknowledge of everything that will ever happen, as even most Arminians do. I found I could not shake off the intuition that such a total omniscience would necessarily mean that everything we will ever choose in the future will have been already spelled out in the divine knowledge register, and consequently the belief that we have truly significant choices to make would seem to be mistaken. I knew the Calvinist argument that exhaustive foreknowledge was tantamount to predestination because it implies the fixity of all things from "eternity past," and I could not shake off its logical force. I feared that, if we view God as timeless and omniscient, we will land back in the camp of theological determinism where these notions naturally belong. It makes no sense to espouse conditionality and then threaten it by other assumptions that we make. Therefore, I had to ask myself if it was biblically possible to hold that God knows everything that can be known, but that free choices would not be something that can be known even by God because they are not yet settled in reality. Decisions not yet made do not exist anywhere to be known even by God. They are potential—yet to be realized but not yet actual. God can predict a great deal of what we will choose to do, but not all of it, because some of it remains hidden in the mystery of human freedom. Can this conjecture be scriptural?

When I went to the Scriptures with this question in mind, I found more support than I had expected. Evidently the logic of Calvinism had worked effectively to silence some of the biblical data, even for me. I began to notice how the prophets in the Old Testament would present God as considering the future as something he did not already know fully. God is presented as saying, "Perhaps they will understand," or "Perhaps they will repent," making it sound as if God is not altogether sure about the future and what he may have to do when it reveals itself (Jer. 3:7; Ezek. 12:3). I also detected a strong conditional element in God's speech; for example, "If you change your ways, I will let you dwell in this place, but if not..." (Jer. 7:5-7). These are future possibilities that are seen to hang upon the people's amendment of their ways, and what God will do (and therefore knows) depends on these outcomes. God too faces possibilities in the future, and not only certainties. God too moves into a future not wholly known because it is not yet fixed. At times God even asks himself questions like "What shall I do with you?" (Hosea 6:4).

Most Bible readers simply pass over this evidence and do not take it seriously. They assume the traditional notion of exhaustive omniscience supported more by the old logic than by the biblical text. Of course the Bible praises God for his detailed knowledge of what will happen and what he himself will do. But it does not teach limitless foreknowledge, because the future will include as-yet-undecided human choices and as-yet-unselected divine responses to them. The God of the Bible displays an openness to the future that the traditional view of omniscience simply cannot accommodate.

Thus is has become increasingly clear to me that we need a "free will" theism, a doctrine of God that treads the middle path between classical theism, which exaggerates God's transcendence of the world, and process theism, which presses for radical immanence.

Pinnock Postscript: How My Mind Has Changed
Written in 1999 by Clark Pinnock for this book,
specifically concerning the above selection that dates from 1989.

In addition to rationalism and militancy, Calvinistic theology was part and parcel of fundamentalistic evangelicalism. The original movement was an alliance of the dispensationalists and the old Princeton Presbyterians (among others). Thus it was that, along with other problems, theological determinism came into the evangelical stream. This came to mean (at least for me) that the doctrine of the attributes of God would need rethinking, as well as epistemology and the doctrine of Scripture. My 1989 writing (above) is part of my testimony about how I got free from hyper-transcendence. Had I been a Wesleyan, I might have had an easier time of it.

It happened that in the early 1970s I was struck by the way in which the author of the book of Hebrews saw the human relationship with God in conditional and relational terms. I noticed how he said that the good news benefited people when it was mixed with faith, but not otherwise (Heb. 4:2). That simple observation released me to consider free-will theism, in which human relationships with God are bilateral and in which there is a give-and-take in the way God chooses to deal with us. It became clearer and clearer to me as the years went on that God is not a grand manipulator or a metaphysical iceberg, but the living, interacting, personal God of the Bible.

I suppose that the most controversial aspect of my re-thinking is my openness to thinking of divine knowledge as *present* knowledge, the view which affirms omniscience but not exhaustive *foreknowledge*. It is based on those biblical texts which show God sometimes being hesitant about the future and on the commonsense notion that truly free decisions (almost by definition) cannot be exhaustively foreknown because they have not been made yet. It is not a defect in God not to be able to know what cannot be known or for God not to be able to do what cannot be done (which everyone acknowledges). One does not have to take this view of present divine knowledge in order to be a relational theist, but at least the strength of it has merit. It means that the future really is open to what we will decide to do and what God will decide to do. What kind of freedom is it if God has to consult his foreknowledge to know what to do next?

High Christology
and a Pluralistic World

Original Source: Clark Pinnock, *A Wideness in God's Mercy*
(Grand Rapids: Zondervan, 1992), pages 74-80.

What disturbs people most is not high Christology itself but the thought that such a belief entails a narrowness in divine salvation and what this belief may say about our attitude to other people. It is this that causes pluralists to take extreme measures such as revising Christology downwards. Although most church members would not think this a right or practical thing to do, and are not attracted to any kind of relativism or syncretism, nevertheless they feel the same pressure pluralists feel and they want better answers from traditionalists than they have been getting. Church members understand what motivates the pluralists, even if they are uncomfortable with their proposed solutions.

What has to be said forthrightly is that a biblically based Christology does not entail a narrowness of outlook toward other people. The church's confession about Jesus is compatible with an open spirit, with an optimism of salvation, and with a wider hope. Sensitivity to religious pluralism does not require radical revision of our doctrine of Christ. God's decision to deal with humanity through the agency of Jesus does not mean or imply that his plan is lacking in universal implications. According to the New Testament, the work of redemption, which spans all ages and continents and comes to fullest expression at a particular point in history, also issues out again into universality. The pattern is certainly unusual and distinctive. If, as C. S. Lewis said, the Christian message were something we were making up, then we could have made it less surprising. Nevertheless, the salvation of the world through Jesus Christ is not an incoherent idea but something true, beautiful, and satisfying....

Wisdom of the Second Vatican Council

The spirit and wisdom of the Second Vatican Council [of the Roman Catholic Church, 1962-65] is worthy of commendation in these matters. The Council made clear that God's grace is global, and that the belief in the Incarnation complements and does not cancel that fact. Faith in the triune God gave the bishops the wide scope of their sympathies. If God be the Father, maker of heaven and earth, who identifies himself with humanity in the person of his son Jesus Christ who entered history for our sake and subsequently poured his Spirit out upon all flesh, then we are not dealing with a small operation in his plan of redemption. As stated in the preface to the Council's Decree on Missionary Activity, "The present historical situation is leading humanity into a new stage. As salt of the earth and light of the world, the church is summoned with special urgency to save and renew every creature. In this way all things can be restored in Christ and in him humankind can compose one family and one people."

The achievement of Vatican II was in showing Christians that it is possible to hold to the finality of Jesus Christ and at the same time give qualified recognition to the positive religious worth of other faiths. The bishops prove that it is not necessary, in order to recognize God's work among nations, to deny central elements of the Christian faith such as a high Christology or world missions. Instead, one can say that a high Christology "mandates both an openness to other religious traditions and a responsible ministry of evangelism on a worldwide scale."

The Vatican Council knows no other salvation than what God has given through Jesus Christ and no other hope than the hope of the Gospel, imperfectly embodied as it is in the church's life and message. It knows no other basis of hope for humanity than the hope founded in the work of Jesus Christ for sinners. But at the same time, the Council views the whole world as lying within the circle of God's grace and the object of his loving care. One may be "outside" the church, but one can never be "outside" God's love. The Council knows how to distinguish the ontological necessity of Christ's work of redemption from the epistemological situation of sinners. There is no salvation except through Christ, but it is not necessary for everybody to possess a conscious knowledge of Christ in order to benefit from redemption through him. The patriarch Job, for example, was saved by Christ (ontologically) without actually knowing the name of Jesus (epistemologically)....

The Triune God As Foundation

The basis of an open attitude to all peoples theologically is the doctrine of the triune God and of his prevenient grace. Let us review the matter briefly. First, we confess the lordship of God: "We believe in God the Father Almighty, Maker of heaven and earth." God, the Creator of the world and Lord of all history, is the mystery of our being and present everywhere. "For in him we live and move and have our being" (Acts 17:28). God is within and God is beyond all human structures and institutions. God is the unity in the midst of all the diversity. He is the gracious God, the God who loves the world so much that he sent his Son to be redeemer of the world. There are not two gods, an angry Father and a gracious Son, but one God, the Father of our Lord Jesus Christ. God the Father is present everywhere in his graciousness, not only where Jesus of Nazareth is named. God is present and at work in every sphere of human life, secular as well as sacred. He is free to act outside as well as inside ecclesiastical structures. We live in one world, which is the creation of the one God. There is no other source from which anyone draws life, and the mystery which surrounds us is the God who loves us in Jesus Christ. God has the whole world in his hands. He sees the sparrow fall. He sustains our life in the world. God is love.

The church also confesses: "We believe in Jesus Christ his only Son our Lord." The life of Jesus is the point in history where God's secret plan for the creation is disclosed, where what he has been doing hiddenly on a grand scale becomes visible and explicit. In Christ, the mystery hidden for ages is revealed and we are made aware of the gracious God who makes all things new. The Incarnation does not weaken but seals and strengthens our confidence in the universal salvific will of God. From the

Old Testament Scriptures we learn about God's global reach of grace, and through the Son we receive definitive confirmation of that grace. The Incarnation underlines and highlights the universal salvific will of God. Through our living Lord, now exalted in the heavens, and through the outpoured Spirit, God is working to make all things new. Although God is present everywhere in his graciousness, his purpose and will are not everywhere clearly perceived. The coming of Jesus, far from shutting the door to universality as some suppose, opens it widely and decisively. Now one can connect the light that has enlightened everyone coming into the world with a stronger light that has come with Jesus, the embodiment of the Logos which is at work in the whole world.

It is important to remember that the Logos, which was made flesh in Jesus of Nazareth, is present in the entire world and in the whole of human history. Though Jesus Christ is Lord, we confess at the same time that the Logos is not confined to one segment of human history or one piece of world geography. The second Person of the Trinity was incarnate in Jesus, but is not totally limited to Palestine. In a real sense, when the missionaries take testimony about Jesus to the world, they take the gospel to places where the Logos has already been active. They will discover noble insights and actions which are the result of God working among the peoples.

Evangelicals tend to be unitarians of the second person and often not fully trinitarian. We need to realize that our insisting that God is embodied and defined by Christ does not mean that God is exhausted by Christ or totally confined to Christ. God the Logos has more going on by way of redemption than what happened in first-century Palestine, decisive though that was for the salvation of the world. Recognizing the cosmic Christ is a way to balance the exclusive and the inclusive biblical texts and can be the key to broadening our Christian attitudes. Acknowledging the Logos at work in the wider world is the way to confess the Incarnation without it being a hindrance to openness.

We also confess: "We believe in the Holy Spirit, the Lord, the giver of life…who has spoken through the Prophets." The Spirit is the mysterious presence, the breath and vitality of God in the world. It is important for us to consider siding with the Eastern churches in an ancient dispute about the Spirit over the question of whether the Spirit proceeded from the Father and the Son (*filioque*), or from the Father only. Most people today may consider this a futile and useless question, but it is not when considered in this context. What makes it important in the context of religious pluralism is that, according to the Eastern view, the Spirit is not tied to the Christ-event exclusively, but rather can operate in the whole world, which is the Father's domain. This provides another way of thinking about God being active in the world at large. God is active by his Spirit in the structures of creation, in the whole of history, even in the sphere of the religions. The breath of God is free to blow wherever it wills (Jn. 3:8). The economy of the Spirit is not under our control, and certainly it is not limited to the church.

The triune God is a missionary God. The Father sends the Son and the Spirit into the world (Gal. 4:4-6). His heart reaches out to embrace it. He gives himself up in becoming human and thus moves history toward redemption. Here is the basis of the unity of humankind and the salvation of the world. There is no hint of the grace of God being limited to a single thread of human history.... A trinitarian theology supplies the broad and adequate basis we need for openness and hope. Those texts used to support pessimism and exclusivism are being read out of context. Of course there is no other name given to us by which to be saved (Acts 4:12), but Peter is referring to messianic salvation, including physical healing through Jesus' name. He is not denying premessianic occurrences of God's grace. Certainly Jesus is the way, the truth, and the life, and no one comes to the Father but by him (John. 14:6). No one else can show us the way to find God understood as Abba, Father. But in saying this, Jesus is not denying the truth about the Logos enlightening everyone coming into the world (John. 1:9). He is not denying God at work in the wider world beyond Palestine and before his own time.

God and the World's Religions

Why was Karl Barth, a great trinitarian theologian, not more open to general revelation, to prevenient grace, and to other religions? Why did he not recognize the meaning of the trinity for the wider work of God? It was due to what is called his Christomonism. A strong defender of the *filioque,* Barth could only see God reaching out to people in and through Jesus. To maintain this position, of course, he had to ignore a good deal of scriptural material. Barth is proof that a high Christology can be used to entail narrowness and justify pluralist fears in that regard. But it seems to me that a trinitarian theology does not point in the direction of narrowness.

These two axioms do not enable or require specific deductions with regard to the view we should take concerning other religions. For example, it does not require Karl Rahner's deduction. Although he is correct in saying that we may expect God to be seeking lost sinners, he may be mistaken to dogmatize about the role the world's religions play in this. We cannot know by way of deduction that religions will necessarily be the main sphere of life in which God deals with people. On the other hand, it does not require Karl Barth's deduction either. Although he is correct in insisting that God's grace comes to humankind in Jesus Christ (Rahner would agree with him), he may be wrong to state so dogmatically that religions as such are always negative. Why would God, who is present everywhere, absent himself so totally from the sphere of religion, the very realm in which people search for ultimate answers? These are sheer speculations, isolated from the scriptural data. The triune God is free to work out the application of his love and salvation for humankind in the ways he chooses....

Pinnock Postscript: How My Mind Has Changed
Written in 1999 by Clark Pinnock for this book,
specifically concerning the above selection that dates from 1992.

Overcoming determinism was not enough for me as far as re-thinking the doctrine of God was concerned. Not only the personal and dynamic divine nature, but the goodness of God is at stake on another front. For a theology to call itself evangelical, many of our traditions contain a considerable amount of bad news. One example of this is theological determinism. Another is restrictivism, a dark position which maintains that the majority of the human race will perish without God doing a thing to help.

I have always thought, how can this be? If God loves the world and Christ died for the human race, how can God be indifferent to the fate of the majority of humankind? The answer lies close at hand in the work of C. S. Lewis (a great favorite of evangelicals, although much more liberal in spirit than most of them) and in J. N. D. Anderson (an InterVarsity Christian Fellowship icon), both of whom take a wider-hope position on salvation than is typical of evangelicalism. In the case of Lewis, it proved to be an inclusivist model (akin to Vatican Council II of the Roman Catholic Church); in the case of Anderson, it was a generously exclusivist point of view. Realizing the need to present such insights to evangelicals, I decided to give the topic a book-length treatment, which had not been done to that time (a selection from this 1992 book is above).

I have been gratified by the reception (pro and con) to this book and believe that over time this approach will gain support, if only because restrictivism is so unbelievable evangelically. How can we possibly say that the God who loves the whole world has chosen to neglect providing any means of access to salvation for the majority of the human race? I cannot imagine it, and I wrote this book to offer people a more positive way of reading the biblical story. Fortunately, it was not too difficult to find a more hopeful hermeneutic. As Saint Paul says, "Where sin abounds, grace does much more abound" (Rom. 5:20).

On Theological Method

Original Source: Clark Pinnock, "The Conditional View,"
in *Four Views on Hell,* ed. William Crockett
(Grand Rapids: Zondervan, 1996), pages 158-166.[1]

Theological method is an important factor that comes into play whenever we debate any subject in theology. For our reflections to be profound, we need to pick up on some of these dynamics. Since there are four main sources that are regularly appealed to (Scripture, tradition, reason, and experience), let us run a check of them and see what is going on in this debate [about the nature of hell].

1. The Bible. Concerning the Bible as source, there are two elements to watch in relation to its authority and interpretation. First, as to its authority, defenders of the traditional view of the nature of hell will often argue thus: "We dislike this doctrine of everlasting torment, but we have to accept it because the Bible teaches it. Does this not just go to show how highly we regard biblical authority?" They claim that believing in everlasting conscious torment is proof of faith in biblical authority and questioning it is proof of the denial of the Bible. Though this might be true in the case of religious liberals, the reader knows by now that this is irrelevant in the present instance. I share this respect for the authority of the Bible with traditionalists and am only contesting their interpre-

---

[1]Another good Pinnock discussion of theological method is his "New Dimensions in Theological Method" in *New Dimensions in Evangelical Thought,* ed. David Dockery (Downers Grove, Ill.: InterVarsity Press, 1998), 197-208.

tation of an authoritative Bible. This is an issue of biblical hermeneutics, not biblical authority.

In relation to biblical interpretation, a key issue is how to interpret eschatological texts. My impression is that traditionalists selectively over-interpret and over-literalize biblical symbols of the future. I say selectively because most do not take the biblical language of perishing literally! Being overly literal is unwise because eschatology is an area of biblical teaching (like creation) that what we know by way of specific factual information is limited. The Bible is reserved about giving detailed information about the nature of heaven or hell; therefore, modesty in interpretation is called for. Jesus' sayings about hell for example, are addressed more to the conscience than to intellectual curiosity. Details such as the time (Mark 13:32), the circumstances (Acts 1:6-7), and the nature (1 John 3:1) of future events are not given to us. My impression is that the traditional view of hell milks a small number of texts for details to support a theory that the Bible does not teach.

2. Tradition. Tradition plays a major role in determining people's thinking about hell, so I will devote more space to this factor. Though scriptural support for hell as eternal conscious suffering is weak and objections against it are strong, tradition is a formidable argument for holding the traditional view. I do not feel at all comfortable contradicting the likes of Saint Anselm and John Calvin.

I agree that tradition is a valuable source of theology, though it needs correcting from time to time. The key issue here is whether it needs correcting on this detail of eschatology. Evangelicals are clearly not opposed in principle to changing traditions because they have done so regularly. For example, many of us reject infant baptism, double predestination, and the sacramentalism of the mass, all of which are ancient catholic traditions. Thus evangelicals are not in a position to oppose challenging the old view of the nature of hell just because it is an old tradition.

I think one has to look in other directions to explain evangelical stubbornness on this feature of the tradition. At this point, let me mention one such reason: They fear that a change on this would indicate they are going liberal. Many of them have decided that believing in everlasting conscious torment is a defining characteristic of evangelical belief. In a major conference in 1989 held to discuss what it means to be evangelical, it was seriously debated whether a person such as John Stott or Philip Hughes, who hold to hell as annihilation, should be considered evangelicals. They can be accepted when sprinkling babies but perhaps not when advocating a revision of the tradition on the nature of hell. The vote to exclude such theologians who hold this opinion failed only narrowly. Obviously, a lot of people are wrestling with the legitimate limits of diversity in evangelicalism.

There is a conundrum here. Why do evangelicals who freely change old traditions in the name of the Bible refuse so adamantly even to consider changing this one? Who do they insist on holding to the old position as stated here: "Hence, beyond the possibility of doubt, the Church expressly teaches the eternity of the pains of hell as a truth of faith which no one can deny or call into question without manifest heresy." There must be some factors other than Scripture or tradition driving the issue, factors that may show up when we review the remaining factors of theological method.

Before moving on, let me defend the option of making a change in the traditional doctrine of the nature of hell. All doctrines undergo a degree of development over time—issues such as Christology and soteriology get taken up at various periods in church history and receive a special stamp from intellectual and social conditions obtaining at the time. A variety of factors in society and thought impact the way in which issues are interpreted. All doctrinal formulations reflect to some extent historical and cultural conditions and have a historical quality to them.

Eschatology is not an exception to this principle but rather exemplifies it, having gone through so many changes over the years. Consider the change from the expectation in the New Testament and early church of the nearness of the second coming of Christ to the delayed expectation of latest orthodox theologians in regard to it; from a millennial belief in the early centuries to the belief of Augustine that sees God's rule in the world above and beyond history to expecting it at the moment of death; from an emphasis on the gloriously resurrected body to an emphasis on the naturally immortal soul, etc. Eschatology is a doctrine in which interpreters should be careful not to place uncritical confidence in what the tradition has said, since it has undergone several large changes and does not speak with a single voice.

With reference to the evangelical context, I realize that in interpreting hell as annihilation, I am adopting a minority view among evangelicals and placing myself at risk among them. Even though these same people permit dozens of differences to exist among themselves and have made many changes themselves to ancient traditions, somehow to propose this change is still forbidden. One can expect to be told that only heretics or near-heretics would think of denying the doctrine of everlasting conscious punishment and of defending annihilation. It seems that a new criterion of truth has been discovered which says that if Adventists or liberals hold any view, that view must be wrong. Apparently a truth claim can be decided by its associations and does not need to be tested by public criteria in open debate. Such an argument, though useless in intelligent discussion, can be effective with the ignorant who are fooled by such rhetoric. Thus, when a noted evangelical such as John W. Wenham shows himself open to hell as annihilation, it is put down to liberal influences in his publisher (InterVarsity Press) and to poor research on his part for thinking it. The same thing happened to me when *Christianity Today* published my view of hell as annihilation (March 20, 1987); Adrian Rodgers, then president of the Southern Baptist Convention, appealed to it to prove that my theology was going liberal.

But despite such tactics of harassment, the view is gaining ground among evangelicals. John R. W. Stott's public endorsement of it will certainly encourage this trend. In a delicious piece of irony, this is creating a measure of accreditation by association, countering the same tactics used against it. It has become all but impossible to claim that only heretics and near heretics hold the position, though I am sure some will dismiss Stott's orthodoxy precisely on this ground. Stott himself expresses anxiety lest he should become a source of division in the community in which he is a renowned leader. He writes:

I am hesitant to have written these things, partly because I have a great respect for longstanding tradition which claims to be a true interpretation of scripture, and do not lightly set it aside, and partly because the unity of the worldwide evangelical constituency has always meant much to me. But the issue is too important to suppress, and I am grateful to you (David Edwards) for challenging me to declare my present mind. I do not dogmatise about the position to which I have come. I hold it tentatively. But I do plead for frank dialogue among evangelicals on the basis of scripture. I also believe that the ultimate annihilation of the wicked should at least be accepted as a legitimate, biblically founded alternative to their eternal conscious torment.

He is right to feel anxious on this score because he is proposing to change what orthodoxy has claimed about the nature of hell. Some will insist that it is an essential doctrine which Stott should have defended against Edwards. They will agree with William Shedd, who wrote: "The common opinion in the ancient church was, that the future punishment of the impenitent wicked is endless. This was the catholic faith; as much so as belief in the Trinity." As long as evangelicals hold this view, persons suggesting change will have to be viewed as heretics.

I propose turning the tables on the whole issue of hell in the tradition. Rather than insisting that the view of hell as everlasting conscious torment remain a defining characteristic of orthodox doctrine, we should be throwing it over. In fact, the entire set of beliefs surrounding hell, including unending torture, double predestination, and the delight that the saints are supposed to feel at the pains of the damned, does orthodox theology absolutely no good. This set of dismal ideas should be dumped in the name of credible doctrine. Why should sound doctrine have such burdens to bear? If we would clean up our act, it might even be possible to save hell as an intelligible belief.

3. Reason. Reason is also a valuable source for theology. Everyone uses reason in assessing the meaning of texts, in constructing doctrines, and in striving to understand. As Anselm said: "Faith seeks understanding."

Reason enters theology on both sides of the debate over eternal torment versus annihilation. Both sides are trying to present their position on hell as coherent in the light of God's nature as just and good. We saw that when we reviewed the issues around the areas of mortality, justice, and metaphysics. On both sides, reasoning operates in a ministerial way, playing a role in deciding doctrinal questions. Though it is true that traditionalists appeal more often to mystery than annihilationists do, perhaps in order to get off the painful hook of some of the objections, the traditional view can be intelligently defended, and I leave the reader to decide which view is most reasonable.

4. Experience and Culture. Experience and culture is a fourth factor that affects theological judgment, as also appears on both sides of this debate. A lot of cultural and situational input enters into the discussion. We may even be on the track of the most important factor.

One can distinguish at least three such influences on the traditional side from experience and culture. First, there is the hellenistic belief in the immortality of the soul. As Swinburne says, "I suspect that one factor which influenced the Fathers and scholastics to affirm eternal sensitory punishment was their belief in the natural immortality of the soul." Here is a secular belief influencing theology. Second, it has been common to use hell as a moral deterrent. Pusey used the belief as a whip to keep people in line, and he was not alone in this. The orthodox often fear what will happen in society if the belief in everlasting torment were to decline. Would people not behave without moral restraint and the society devolve into anarchy? For such reasons William Shedd considered no doctrine more important than hell, given the increase of wealth and sinful excess he saw growing in the Western world. His reason for defending it, then, involves a strongly contextual factor. Third, Jonathan Edwards used hell to frighten people into faith, and he is not alone in this either. I have heard people oppose hell as annihilation on the grounds that is isn't frightening enough and would let the wicked off too easily. Everlasting conscious punishment is a huge stick that some people do not want to give up. It has always been used to promote the urgency of missions, and the strongest objection to any revision may well come from missionary agencies.

These three points are powerful and make me wonder whether the true strength of the traditional view of hell does not lie in experience and culture rather than in Scripture, tradition, or reason. If so, the irony would be that the traditionalists are operating in the case of hell out of an essentially liberal methodology that makes primary use of contextual factors in respect to doctrine.

But are annihilationists perhaps in the same situation with the experience-culture factor dominating their view as well? There is some evidence of this. The reader will have detected, for example, strong emotion in my rejection of the traditional view. Obviously, I am rejecting the traditional view of hell in part out of a sense of moral and theological revulsion to it. The idea that a conscious creature should have to undergo physical and mental torture through unending time is profoundly disturbing, and the thought that this is inflicted upon them by divine decree offends my conviction about God's love. This is probably the primary reason why people question the tradition so vehemently in the first place. They are not first of all impressed by its lack of a good scriptural basis (that comes later) but are appalled by its awful moral implications. This process shows that along with Scripture, they are drawing on moral intuitions in their theological reflection, just as their opponents are doing in theirs. Both sides clearly draw upon the resources of subjectivity and relevance, though my judgment is that the traditionalists are more affected by it than annihilationists.

I conclude that the traditional belief that God makes the wicked suffer in an unending conscious torment in hell is unbiblical, is fostered by a hellenistic view of human nature, is detrimental to the character of God, is defended on essentially pragmatic grounds, and is being rejected by a growing number of biblically faithful, contemporary scholars. I believe that a better case can be made for understanding the nature of hell as termination—better biblically, anthropologically, morally, judicially, and metaphysically.

But whatever hell turns out to be like, it is a very grim prospect. Though annihilationism makes hell less of a torture chamber, it does not lessen its extreme seriousness. After all, to be rejected by God, to miss the purpose for which one was created, to pass into oblivion while others enter into bliss, to enter nonbeing—this will mean weeping and gnashing of teeth. Hell is a terrifying possibility, the possibility of using our freedom to lose God and destroy ourselves. Of course, we do not know who or how many will be damned, because we do not know who will finally say "No" to God. What we do know is that sinners may finally reject salvation, that absolute loss is something to be reckoned with. I do not think one needs to know more about hell than that.

In the current situation, given the difficulties that attend the traditional view of the nature of hell, I think it is possible that changing our view would be a wise step. Rather than threatening the doctrine of hell, it may actually preserve it. The fact is that the tradition of everlasting conscious torment is causing more and more people today to deny hell altogether and accept universal salvation in order to avoid its sadistic horror; on the other hand, the view of the nature of hell that I am proposing does not involve sadism, though it does retain belief in the biblical category of the second death. In any case, the objections to the traditional view of the nature of hell are so strong and its supports so weak that it is likely soon to be replaced with something else. The real choice is between universalism and annihilationism, and of these two, annihilation is surely the more biblical, because it retains the realism of some people finally saying "No" to God without turning the notion of hell into a monstrosity.

Pinnock Postscript: How My Mind Has Changed
Written in 1999 by Clark Pinnock for this book,
specifically concerning the above selection that dates from 1996.

The above selection from my writing in 1996 reveals a couple of things. First, it reveals evangelicalism opening up more to the Wesleyan theological tradition, which always has been present in the coalition but has not always been respected as a participant. In this case, the text shows an openness to the Wesleyan quadrilateral way of understanding theological method—which is so rich and fruitful for hearers of God's Word. Second, it puts the method to work on a controversial subject, the nature of hell.

Before being asked to write about hell for a "four views" book on the subject, I had not thought that much about the nature of hell. Therefore, I welcomed the invitation because the interactive format of such a project is fruitful for delving into issues. The format also shows how pluralistic evangelicalism is theologically, contrary to its own self-promotion. I knew that someone needed to test the traditional view of the nature of hell as everlasting conscious punishment. It is embarrassing to see how our theologies so often end on a sadistic note.

One point of revision was easy enough. If God is relational, hell must be voluntary and locked only on the inside. It is not God's will that people go there. I knew that the majority of evangelicals already believed that and that even the hardliners can hardly bring themselves to say what they ought to say based on their own theological premise—that God predestines sinners for hell to display divine justice. The second point for revision was more difficult. Even if hell were freely chosen, the question remains. Is it sadistic punishment? Does God actually torture people endlessly in hellfire?

Putting to work the theological method of the quadrilateral featured in the above selection of my writing, I was surprised at how well it operated. Taking the position that the nature of hell was a second death could be defended very plausibly. In more recent reflection, I have added the insight that everyone, Christians and non-Christians alike, pass through and are tried by fire (1 Cor. 3:13). For faithful disciples, the fire affects a purging and cleansing while for the finally impenitent, the fire leaves nothing and they perish.

APPENDIX G

The Evangelical Big Tent

Original Source: Clark Pinnock,
"Evangelical Theologians Facing the Future:
Ancient and Future Paradigms," *Wesleyan Theological Journal*
33:2 (Fall 1998), pages 7-28.

Let me speak about the evangelical big tent and the appropriateness of doing theology under its shade. Many theologians work under this umbrella. It is not a space constituted by a confession, but is a loose coalition made up of a great variety of believers who feel religious kinship. Some like myself were "born again" into it through the influences of Billy Graham, the Canadian Keswick Conference, Youth for Christ, InterVarsity Christian Fellowship, and so forth, and it was natural for such people to identify with it and work within it. We prefer its broad spaces to the more restrictive quarters of the denominations. We benefit from the fruitful interaction of a confluence of traditions....

An Informal Alliance

Theologians today (like Christians at large) are not as strongly attached to a single tradition or denomination as they once were. We live in an increasingly post-denominational world. God is bringing the church together. Many like myself found faith in the context of evangelicalism (where else are you likely to find it?). Though Baptist (or whatever), we value our evangelical associations more than any denominational ones and derive more stimulation from them, in much the same way as others savor mainline/ecumenical spaces. The rise of the postwar evangelical movement has created a rare opportunity for theologians not to work only in narrow confines, unenriched and ecumenically challenged, but in larger fields and wider rivers which make possible a theology-in-dialogue stimulated by the plurality of a new ecclesial situation....

Evangelicalism is informally constituted by people who feel a sense of kinship and enjoy working together for common goals. Early on it was city evangelism under Billy Graham which brought people together in large numbers, not on the basis of theology, but for the purpose of winning others to Christ. It was and remains an informal alliance. Theologically, it is surely a patchwork quilt, kept together more by vital religious experience and commitment to mission than by theological confession. There are doctrinal boundaries, but they are fluid and not closely drawn. The coalition is not without a theological character, but it is more like an ethos—specifically, a post-fundamentalist and anti-liberal ethos. This identity has proved to be a winning ticket in attracting all sorts of people into its sphere, believers who, despite sectarian differences, agree on the importance of defending Christianity against liberal theological innovations.

When it gets right down to it, evangelicalism is more like a distinctive spirituality than a precise theology and it finds it unity in a few basic commitments: fidelity to the biblical message as the supreme norm, belief in a transcendent personal God who interacts with creation and acts in history, belief in the transforming grace of God, and commitment to the mission of bringing the goodness of Jesus Christ to the whole world. There is space here for both theological common ground and rich diversity. On the one hand, there are controls stemming from a conservative theological ethos; on the other hand, there are wide-open spaces....

Problems To Be Addressed

My thesis is that evangelical theology can contribute to the renewal of theology under circumstances of reform. There needs to be an improvement in theological method and in the doctrine of God. I think we need to move to a larger concept of method (as represented by the Wesleyan quadrilateral) and to a more dynamic model of the nature of God (as intimated also in Wesley's thinking).[1]

---

[1]See, for instance, the excellent work of Barry L. Callen in his systematic theology titled God As Loving Grace (Nappanee, Ind.: Evangel Publishing House, 1996).

The basic problem in evangelical theology is the rationalist/ propositional method. What an irony that what was seen initially as its trump card is in fact detrimental to sound theology. The old guard represented by Carl F. H. Henry would suppose that evangelical theology was born with a solidly rational method that has since been placed in danger. In fact, it was born with a birth defect which is at long last beginning to be corrected. At first, in reaction to liberal theology, the rational method seemed necessary and effective, but now it appears as an obstacle which stands in the way of doing better quality work. The appeal of evangelicalism never was its method or excellence in theology; its appeal derived from its being consonant with a mood which was pro-classical and anti-liberal. It always had the potential of being fruitful theologically, but the potential was something that would take time to be realized....[2]

Evangelicals have to get over their fears born in the fundamentalist/ modernist controversies. The specter of liberalism has kept us long enough from celebrating new possibilities and has robbed us of confidence in our imaginations. It has made us suspicious of new suggestions and even grumpy and mean-spirited at times. A new idea often gets greeted with fear-filled phrases like: "This is a dangerous trend" or "Does this cross over the line?" We seem to have lost the ability to believe that in some respects theology might actually move closer to the truth in our day. The fear of timeliness is debilitating and frustrates the ability to engage our generation. I am not advocating exegetical relativism or attempting to introduce worldly ideas into theology. I want to see us do better work and have deeper biblically-based convictions. With a little methodological maturation, there would be fewer failures and more achievements....[3]

---

[2]Stanley J. Grenz was one of the first to identify this problem in his *Revisioning Evangelical Theology: A Fresh Agenda for the 21st Century* (Downers Grove, Ill.: InterVarsity Press, 1993).

[3]The best methodology in my opinion, and the one toward which I have been drawn over the years, is called the "Wesleyan quadrilateral." See Donald A. D. Thorsen, *The Wesleyan Quadrilateral* (Grand Rapids: Zondervan, 1990) and W. Stephen Gunter et al., *Wesley and the Quadrilateral: Renewing the Conversation* (Nashville: Abingdon Press, 1997).

Conclusion

A great opportunity exists for fruitfulness in theology and evangelical theologians can certainly contribute to it. If thus far their contributions have been minimal, were they to correct certain of their weaknesses, they would be in a strong position to help. Distancing ourselves from rational/propositionalism and theological/omni-causalism would take us far in the direction of wider engagements and larger visions.[4] What is required is that we grow as hearers of the Word of God and accept the sometimes painful consequences of growing up. I love the evangelical heritage, but have been burdened by its difficulties my whole life. They have set me off on tangents and prevented me from doing the quality of work that I would have wished. Fortunately, a whole new generation of evangelicals is rising which recognizes these problems and will be able to transcend them ever more effectively. Theology is an unfinished task and a venture in hope. May it be that our vision of truth will be continually enlarged through interaction with others on the way to fullness of life in the future of God.

Pinnock Postscript: How My Mind Has Changed
Written in 1999 by Clark Pinnock for this book,
specifically concerning the above selection that dates from 1998.

I was converted in the context of the North American fundamentalist-evangelical movement following World War II, and I am appreciative of its witness. Along with uncounted others, I met God there and, even though I would have a lot of growing to do as a hearer of God's Word in this context, I greatly enjoy its ecumenical breadth. Despite all of its shortcomings, the evangelical coalition (which I affectionately call "the big tent") is a vital, interdenominational coalition.

---

[4]Were I to add a third area of reform, it would be to make the Holy Spirit as central in theology as it is in biblical thinking. Perhaps it will be the pentecostals in the ranks of the new pietists who will improve this matter. In the meantime, I have had some thoughts. See my *Flame of Love: A Theology of the Holy Spirit* (Downers Grove, Ill.: InterVarsity Press, 1996).

It may not use the word "ecumenical" because of certain negative associations, but it does practice it and enrich its members thereby.

Furthermore, the quality has been improving as the coalition has been enlarging. As the movement has grown it has added more color and diversity to its ranks, which makes it an even better locale to contact other believers and work shoulder to shoulder with them. Not everyone will agree with me on this, but occasionally I like to get outside the limiting atmosphere of my own denominational context and partake of the greater richness of the church at large.

I know that for many evangelicals the debates that are going on under this umbrella spell decline, but I do not agree. I believe that the ferment is creative and a sign of health and vitality, and I believe that the best days for us evangelicals may yet lie ahead. Of course, I am not blind to the bad aspects—the biblicism, the sectarianism, sometimes even the meanspiritedness and so on, but I also see arising a company of the best quality of theologians that we have ever had, men and women who are developing compelling understandings of the gospel for our day. For my part, it is no time to vacate the big tent. Rather, it is time to work vigorously for needed reform.

Afterword

by
Clark H. Pinnock
Written August 10, 1999, after reading the draft of this manuscript.

My general response to this manuscript about me and my theological career is as follows. Dr. Callen has created a convincing interpretation of my work, and I do not challenge it in any way. It is very well done, very sensitive to my concerns, and free of any kind of slips. I am grateful that he worked so hard on the project and for his being so discerning and appreciative.

As I look back upon my life, I am not happy with everything that I see. Nevertheless, I am (paradoxically) grateful for all that has happened, both good and bad, because God has always been with me. Everything that has happened in my life (and in the lives of all of us) has contributed to bringing us to the place where we now stand, and we should respond to the mercies of God with thankful hearts. Of course, there are things in my life that I am happy about and things which I wish had not happened, but I remember the whole story with gratitude. Just as St. Peter's denials of our Lord did not paralyze him but, once forgiven, became a source of fresh commitment, so I trust that my failures can be redeemed and that I can be an inspiration to others. Even if some of my ideas do not prove finally convincing, maybe my life as a theologian before God will nonetheless encourage and edify.

As for my contribution to evangelical theology, such as it is, I see it in constructive and not deconstructive terms. Even though I have had to chip away at a number of barnacles that cling to the good ship of

269

evangelicalism's theology, I have always seen this task positively, part of the work that all evangelical theologians share, the task of reforming fundamentalism. After all, was the evangelical coalition following World War II not formed precisely for that reason? Was there not the goal of ridding the fundamentalist mindset of certain characteristics and patterns which were thought to be detrimental to the work of the gospel? Among these characteristics are rationalism, biblicism, sectarianism, traditionalism, otherworldliness, anti-intellectualism, and the ghetto mentality. We all knew that there was a lot of work to do (even more than the original leaders like Carl Henry imagined); nevertheless, reforming fundamentalism has been an exhilarating and fruitful task and one which holds for the future the promise of a more mature and transforming evangelical witness.

I have always seen myself as one among many workers in search of a wiser and more generous Christian orthodoxy. I have been sensitive to the painful side of having to suggest some significant theological changes as part of the creative ferment. My journey certainly does reveal changes in my orientation and substance. This dynamism does not sit well with those evangelicals who prefer that theologians exhibit greater consistency of thought. I understand this concern and even feel a little envious of my critics.

Why did my setting and temperament not make following a straight and smooth path possible for me? How did those theologians who have held firm to a network of opinions for decades manage without changing? Is it because they lucked out by finding the truth right away when they were young so that they did not need to change anything, or were they just more stubborn than I in holding to positions even when they became open to major challenges? I do not have the answer, but I hope that the experience of one like myself, struggling as Jacob did with the self-revelation of God, might convey useful lessons. Certainly, Christian theology is a continuing search for the truth of God made known in Jesus Christ. There is no other possibility for me than to be a pilgrim without permanent residence or certain destination. I cannot be content with unexamined beliefs just because they are traditional. I feel compelled to face up to hard questions, even if there are more questions than easy answers.

Speaking further to the issue of changing one's mind, I observe that there is a darker side. Some evangelical leaders call attention to changes in my views over the years in order to discredit my opinions. They say that Pinnock is unstable and a loose canon. But scratch the surface and one finds out that it is not the changing they are really concerned about, but the direction of the change. Ask yourself this. Had I been a liberal who had found his way through great difficulty back to the standard evangelical ideas, would these observers have criticized my changing? No, they would have celebrated the direction of the change and excused the movement itself as something necessary. They would have said, as in the case of responses to Thomas Oden, that it is better to arrive at the truth through changing than not to have found it at all.

My change in theology is not itself the cause of the offense that some take in my work. The offense has more to do with the direction of some of my theological change, specifically, the move to liberation from certain hard facets of fundamentalist evangelical thought which are placed off limits by some of the influential opinion makers. One thinks of the soteriological restrictivism challenged in my *A Wideness in God's Mercy*, the rationalism and scholasticism critiqued in my *The Scripture Principle* and *Tracking the Maze*, and the theological determinism disputed in *The Openness of God*. In other words, I have included in the list of matters to be looked at critically items which some interpreters strongly hold should be considered beyond the need of reforming. Thus, I have gotten myself into trouble with certain of the gatekeepers of evangelical theology for not leaving supposedly irreformable issues alone.

It is acceptable, we are told, to reform fundamentalist evangelicalism in certain respects, but not in others. To be more precise, the old Princeton orthodoxy was a major factor in the formation of fundamentalist evangelicalism in the 1920s. Some stalwarts of this Reformed theology oppose suggestions that it can be improved upon. Opposition to my work on this score has been especially strong, in large part because early in my career I myself advocated paleo-Calvinism and thus now have come to pose a special threat to its continuing defenders. Without intending it, my life experience has placed me in a position to help people become free of paleo-Calvinism, if they should want to, of course. My work in effect says to evangelicals that they do not have to remain in this problematic position. After all, I found a way out and have even explained the escape route. It is hardly surprising then that, for every person who is grateful for my work, there is another who is appalled.

I bear no malice. This continuing discussion between Augustinians and Arminians is familiar and can be conducted amicably. It is part of the ongoing search for the fuller truth of God's Word. St. Paul tells us to welcome those with different opinions. Remember, there are many interpreters, each with a distinctive history to deal with (Romans 14:1). So I proceed with the work of reforming fundamentalism and of bringing to light more of the glorious mysteries of Christ's everlasting gospel. I see the task of evangelical theology to be one of assisting the church in its renewal through faithfulness to God's Word, all on behalf of a timely witness.

Select Clark H. Pinnock Bibliography

Doctoral Dissertation of Clark Pinnock

1963. "The Concept of the Spirit in the Epistles of Paul," University of Manchester, England. Mentor: Dr. F. F. Bruce.

Books Authored by Clark Pinnock

1967. *Set Forth Your Case: Studies in Christian Apologetics.* Nutley, N.J.: Craig Press. Reprint, Chicago: Moody, 1971.

1967. *A Defense of Biblical Infallibility.* Philadelphia: Presbyterian and Reformed Pub. Co.

1968. *A New Reformation: A Challenge To Southern Baptists.* Tigerville, S.C.: Jewel Books.

1969. *Evangelism and Truth.* Tigerville, S.C.: Jewel Books.

1971. *Biblical Revelation: The Foundation of Christian Theology.* Chicago: Moody Press. Reprinted, with "Foreword" by J. I. Packer, Phillipsburg, N.J.: Presbyterian and Reformed, 1985.

1972. *Truth On Fire: The Message of Galatians.* Grand Rapids: Baker Book House.

1972. *Live Now, Brother.* Chicago: Moody Press. Reprinted as *Are There Any Answers?*, Minneapolis: Bethany, 1976.

1980. *Reason Enough: A Case for the Christian Faith.* Downers Grove, Ill.: InterVarsity Press. Reprinted as *A Case for Faith*, Minneapolis: Bethany, 1985.

1984. *The Scripture Principle.* San Francisco: Harper & Row.

1985. *Three Keys to Spiritual Renewal.* Minneapolis: Bethany Fellowship. In Canada, *The Untapped Power of Sheer Christianity.* Burlington, Ont.: Welch, 1985.

1990. *Theological Crossfire: An Evangelical/Liberal Dialogue.* Grand Rapids: Zondervan. With Delwin Brown.

1990. *Tracking the Maze: Finding Our Way Through Modern Theology from an Evangelical Perspective.* San Francisco: Harper & Row.

1992. *A Wideness in God's Mercy: The Finality of Jesus Christ in a World of Religions.* Grand Rapids: Zondervan.

1994. *Unbounded Love: A Good News Theology for the 21st Century.* Downers Grove, Ill.: InterVarsity Press. With Robert C. Brow.

1996. *Flame of Love: A Theology of the Holy Spirit.* Downers Grove, Ill.: InterVarsity Press.

2001. Forthcoming: *The Most Moved Mover: Beholding God's Fair Beauty.* Grand Rapids: Baker Books (U.S.) and Paternoster Press (U.K.). The Didsbury Lectures, Nazarene Theological College, Manchester, England, October 2000.

Books Edited by Clark Pinnock

1971. Editor, with David F. Wells. *Toward a Theology of the Future.* Carol Stream, Ill.: Creation House. Chapter, "Prospects for Systematic Theology," 93-124.

1975. Editor. *Grace Unlimited.* Minneapolis: Bethany Fellowship.

1989. Editor. *The Grace of God, the Will of Man: A Case for Arminianism,* chapter "From Augustine To Arminius: A Pilgrimage In Theology." Grand Rapids: Academic Books, Zondervan. Reissued, Minneapolis: Bethany House Publishers, 1995.

1994. *The Openness of God* (participated in the editorial process, with no specific editor identified; see detail below).

2000. Editor, with John B. Cobb, Jr., *Searching for an Adequate God: A Dialogue Between Process and Free Will Theists.* Grand Rapids: Eerdmans, forthcoming (title as projected).

Book Chapters Contributed by Clark Pinnock to Books Edited by Others

1966. "On the Third Day," in *Jesus of Nazareth: Savior and Lord*. Ed. Carl F. H. Henry. Grand Rapids: Eerdmans, 145-155.

1968. "The Inspiration of the New Testament," in *The Bible: The Living Word of Revelation*. Ed. Merrill C. Tenney. Grand Rapids: Zondervan, 143-164.

1971. "The Philosophy of Christian Evidences," in *Jerusalem and Athens: Critical Discussions on the Theology and Apologetics of Cornelius Van Til*. Ed. E. R. Geehan. Presbyterian and Reformed, 1971, 420-427.

1974. "Limited Inerrancy: A Critical Appraisal and Constructive Alternative," in *God's Inerrant Word*. Ed. John Warwick Montgomery. Minneapolis: Bethany, 143-158.

1974. "The Inspiration of Scripture and the Authority of Jesus Christ," in *God's Inerrant Word*. Ed. John Warwick Montgomery. Minneapolis: Bethany, 201-218.

1977. "Three Views of the Bible in Contemporary Theology," in *Biblical Authority*. Ed. Jack B. Rogers. Waco: Word Publishers, 45-73.

1979. "The Need for a Scriptural, and Therefore a Neo-Classical Theism," in *Perspectives on Evangelical Theology*. Ed. Kenneth S. Kantzer and Stanley N. Gundry. Grand Rapids: Baker, 37-42.

1984. "A Pilgrimage in Political Theology: A Personal Witness," in *Liberation Theology*. Ed. Ronald Nash. Milford, Mich.: Mott Media, 103-120.

1985. "How I Use the Bible in Doing Theology," in *The Use of the Bible in Theology: Evangelical Options*. Ed. Robert K. Johnston. Atlanta: John Knox, 13-34.

1986. "God Limits His Knowledge," in *Predestination and Free Will*. Ed. David and Randall Basinger. Downers Grove, Ill.: InterVarsity Press, 141-162.

1986. "Schaeffer on Modern Theology," in *Reflections on Francis Schaeffer*. Ed. Ronald Ruegsegger. Grand Rapids: Zondervan, 173-193.

1986. "Biblical Authority and the Issues in Question," in *Women, Authority, and the Bible*. Ed. Alvera Mickelsen. Downers Grove: InterVarsity, 51-58.

1987. "Between Classical and Process Theism," in *Process Theology*. Ed. Ronald Nash. Grand Rapids: Baker, 309-327.

1988. "The Finality of Jesus Christ in a World of Religions," in *Christian Faith and Practice in the Modern World*. Ed. Mark A. Noll and David F. Wells. Grand Rapids: Eerdmans, 152-168.

1988. "The Pursuit of Utopia," in *Freedom, Justice, and Hope: Toward a Strategy for the Poor and the Oppressed*. Ed. Marvin Olasky. Westchester, Ill.: Crossway, 65-83.

1988. "Baptists and the 'Latter Rain'," in *Costly Vision: The Baptist Pilgrimage in Canada*. Ed. Jarold Zeman. Burlington, Ontario: Welch Publishing Company, 258-265.

1990. "Bernard Ramm: Postfundamentalist Coming To Terms With Modernity," in *Perspectives on Theology in the Contemporary World: Essays in Honor of Bernard Ramm*. Ed. Stanley Grenz. Macon, Ga.: Mercer University Press, 15-26.

1990. "Defining American Fundamentalism," in *The Fundamentalist Phenomenon*. Ed. Norman J. Cohen. Grand Rapids: Eerdmans, 38-55

1991. "Acts 4:12: No Other Name Under Heaven," in *Through No Fault of Their Own*. Ed. William Crockett and James Sigountos. Grand Rapids: Baker Book House.

1994. "Systematic Theology," in *The Openness of God*. Downers Grove, Ill.: InterVarsity Press, 101-125.

1994. "Holy Spirit as a Distinct Person in the Godhead," in *Spirit and Renewal*. Ed. Mark Wilson. Sheffield: Sheffield Academic Press, 34-41.

1995. "An Inclusivist View," in *More Than One Way? Four Views on Salvation in a Pluralistic World*. Ed. Dennis Okholm and Timothy Phillips. Grand Rapids: Zondervan, 95-123.

1995. "The Great Jubilee," in *God and Man: Perspectives on Christianity in the 20th Century*. Ed. Michael Bauman. Hillsdale, Mich. : Hillsdale College Press, 91-101.

1996. "The Conditional View," in *Four Views On Hell*. Ed. William Crockett. Grand Rapids: Zondervan, 135-166.

1998. "New Dimensions in Theological Method," in *New Dimensions in Evangelical Thought*. Ed. David S. Dockery. Downers Grove, Ill.: InterVarsity Press, 197-208.

1998. "Evangelical Theology in Progress," in *Introduction to Christian Theology*. Ed. Roger Badham. Louisville: Westminster John Knox Press.

1999. "The Holy Spirit in the Theology of Donald G. Bloesch," in *Evangelical Theology In Transition: Theologians in Dialogue with Donald Bloesch*. Ed. Elmer M. Colyer. Downers Grove, Ill.: InterVarsity Press, 119-135.

Select Journal Articles, Lectures, and Book Reviews by Clark Pinnock

1970. "The Harrowing of Heaven," *Christianity Today* (June 19), 7-8.

1971. "A Truce Proposal for the Tongues Controversy," *Christianity Today* (Oct. 8), 6-9. With Grant Osborne.

1973. "The New Pentecostalism: Reflections by a Well-Wisher," *Christianity Today* (Sept. 14), 6-10.

1974. "Baptists and Biblical Authority," *Journal of the Evangelical Theological Society*, vol. 17:193-205.

1976. "Liberation Theology: The Gains, the Gaps," *Christianity Today* (Jan. 16), 13-15.

1976. "A Call for the Liberation of North American Christians," *Sojourners* (Sept.), 23-25.

1978. "Evangelicals and Inerrancy: The Current Debate," *Theology Today* 35:1 (April), 65-69.

1979. "An Evangelical Theology: Conservative and Contemporary," *Christianity Today* (January 5), 23-29.

1981. "Opening the Church to the Charismatic Dimension," *Christianity Today* (June 12), 16.

1982. "I Was a Teenage Fundamentalist," *The Wittenburg Door* (Dec. 1982-Jan. 1983), 18.

1986. "Catholic, Protestant, and Anabaptist: Principles of Biblical Interpretation in Selected Communities," *Brethren In Christ History and Life* (December), 264-275.

1989. "Climbing Out of a Swamp: The Evangelical Struggle To Understand the Creation Texts," *Interpretation* 43:2 (April), 143-155.

1990. "Toward an Evangelical Theology of Religions," *Journal of the Evangelical Theological Society* 33:3 (Sept.), 359-368.

1990. "The Destruction of the Finally Impenitent," *Criswell Theological Review* 4, 243-259.

1991. "Desert Storm.... A Just War?" *The Canadian Baptist* (March), 17-18, 20.

1993. "The Role of the Spirit in Interpretation," *Journal of the Evangelical Theological Society* (December).

1995. "Assessing the Apologetics of C. S. Lewis," *Canadian C. S. Lewis Journal* (May).

1996. "God's Sovereignty In Today's World," *Theology Today* 53:1 (April), 15-21.

1996. Review of Gordon Fee, *God's Empowering Presence: The Holy Spirit in the Letters of Paul* (Hendrickson, 1994), in *Pneuma* 18:2 (Fall), 230-234.

1998. "Does Christian Unity Require Some Form of Papal Primacy?" in *Journal of Ecumencial Studies* 35:3-4 (Summer-Fall), 380-382.

1998. "Evangelical Theologians Facing the Future: An Ancient and a Future Paradigm," *Wesleyan Theological Journal* 33:2 (Fall), 7-28.

1999. "Divine Relationality: A Pentecostal Contribution to the Doctrine of God," Azusa Street Lecture, Regent University, April 20 (forthcoming in *Journal of Pentecostal Theology*).

1999. "Biblical Texts: Past and Future Meanings," *Wesleyan Theological Journal* 34:2 (Fall), 136-151.

1999. "Toward a More Inclusive Eschatology," paper presented at the Evangelical Theological Society, Boston (November), unpublished.

1999. "Response to Daniel Strange and Amos Yong," *The Evangelical Quarterly* 71:4 (October), 349-357.

Select Writings About Clark Pinnock

1982. Nielsen, Glenn, "Clark Pinnock," unpublished research paper, Southern Baptist Theological Seminary.

1985. Orser, Alan, "An Interpretation of Dr. Clark H. Pinnock and His Contribution to the Baptist Convention of Ontario and Quebec, 1977-1985," unpublished research paper, Acadia Divinity College.

1988. Price, Robert M., "Clark H. Pinnock: Conservative and Contemporary," *Evangelical Quarterly* 60:2, 157-183.

1989. High, Mary, "The Development of Clark Pinnock's Concept of Biblical Authority," M.A. thesis, Southern Baptist Theological Seminary.

1990. Brown, Delwin, "Rethinking Authority from the Right: A Critical Review of Clark Pinnock's *The Scripture Principle*," *Christian Scholar's Review* 19:1, 66-78 (including Pinnock's response).

1990. Rakestraw, Robert V., "Clark Pinnock: A Theological Odyssey," in *Christian Scholar's Review* 19:3, 252-70.

1990. Rakestraw, Robert V., "Clark Pinnock," in *Baptist Theologians*. Ed. Timothy George and David Dockery. Nashville: Broadman Press.

1990. Roennfeldt, Ray C. W., *Clark Pinnock on Biblical Authority*, Ph.D. Dissertation, Andrews University.

1992. Randy L. Maddox, "Clark Pinnock on World Religions: Evangelical Precedents?" *Proceedings of the Wheaton Theology Conference*, 208-215.

1993. Johnston, Robert K., "Clark H. Pinnock," in *Handbook of Evangelical Theologians*. Ed. Walter Elwell, Baker Books.

1999. Strange, Daniel. "The Possibility of Salvation Among the Un-evangelised: An Analysis of Inclusivism in Recent Evangelical Theology," doctoral dissertation, University of Bristol, England.

1999. Strange, Daniel. "Clark H. Pinnock: The Evolution of an Evangelical Maverick," in *The Evangelical Quarterly* 71:4 (October), 311-326.

1999. Yong, Amos. "Whither Theological Inclusivism? The Development and Critique of an Evangelical Theology of Religions," in *The Evangelical Quarterly* 71:4 (October), 327-348.

2001. Chris Sinkinson and Tony Gray, eds. A forthcoming collection of essays on the work of Clark Pinnock, to be published by Paternoster Press.

Also, some of the works listed below on "Evangelicalism Generally" include discussions of Clark Pinnock (e.g., the 1998 works by Dorrien, Erickson, and Olson).

Select Works on Free-Will Theism
(pro and con, and other than by Clark Pinnock)

1985. Rice, Richard. *God's Foreknowledge and Man's Free Will.* Minneapolis: Bethany House.

1996. Basinger, David. *The Case for Free-Will Theism: A Philosophical Assessment.* Downers Grove, Ill.: InterVarsity Press.

1996. Callen, Barry L. *God As Loving Grace: The Biblically Revealed Nature and Work of God.* Nappanee, Ind.: Evangel Publishing House.

1996. Carson, D. A. *The Gagging of God: Christianity Confronts Pluralism.* Grand Rapids: Zondervan Publishing House.

1996. Wright, R. K. McGregor. *No Place for Sovereignty: What's Wrong with Freewill Theism.* Downers Grove, Ill.: Inter-Varsity Press.

1997. Boyd, Gregory. *God At War: The Bible and Spiritual Conflict.* Downers Grove, Ill.: InterVarsity Press.

1998. Sanders, John. *The God Who Risks: A Theology of Providence.* Downers Grove, Ill.: InterVarsity Press.

1998 Hasker, William, and Alfred J. Freddoso, "The Openness of God," a symposium, in *Christian Scholar's Review* 28:1 (Fall), 111-139.

1999. Boyd, Gregory. *The God of the Possible.* Published privately.

1999. Geisler, Norman. *Chosen But Free: A Balanced View of Divine Election.* Minneapolis: Bethany House Publishers.

Select Works on Evangelicalism Generally

1967. Henry, Carl F. H., *Evangelicals at the Brink of Crisis.* Waco, Texas: Word Books.

1971. Henry, Carl F. H., *A Plea for Evangelical Demonstration.* Grand Rapids: Baker Books.

1974. Quebedeaux, Richard, *The Young Evangelicals: Revolution in Orthodoxy.* San Francisco: Harper & Row.

1976. Henry, Carl F. H., *Evangelicals in Search of Identity.* Waco: Word Books.

1976. Lindsell, Harold, *The Battle for the Bible.* Grand Rapids: Zondervan.

1979. Lindsell, Harold, *The Bible in the Balance.* Grand Rapids: Zondervan.

1979. Johnston, Robert, *Evangelicals at an Impasse.* Atlanta: John Knox Press.

1980. Bruce, F. F., *In Retrospect: Remembrance of Things Past.* Grand Rapids: Eerdmans.

1983. Hunter, James, *American Evangelicalism: Conservative Religion and the Quandary of Modernity.* New Brunswick, N. J.: Rutgers University Press.

1984. Abraham, William J., *The Coming Great Revival: Recovering the Full Evangelical Tradition.* San Francisco: Harper & Row.

1984. Marsden, George, ed., *Evangelicalism and Modern America.* Grand Rapids: Eerdmans.

1984. Schaeffer, Francis, *The Great Evangelical Disaster.* Westchester: Crossway Books.

1985. Marsden, George, "Reformed and American," in *Reformed Theology in America,* ed. David F. Wells. Grand Rapids: Eerdmans, 1-12.

1986. Henry, Carl F. H., *Confessions of a Theologian: An Auto-biography.* Waco: Word Books.

1987. Hunter, James, *Evangelicalism: The Coming Generation.* Chicago: University of Chicago Press.

1989. Bebbington, D. W., *Evangelicalism In Modern Britain.* London: Unwin Hyman.

1989. Robert Morey, *Battle of the Gods: The Gathering Storm in Modern Evangelicalism.* Southbridge, Mass.: Crown.

1991. Dayton, Donald, and Robert Johnston, eds., *The Variety of American Evangelicalism.* Knoxville: University of Tennessee Press.

1993. Stackhouse, John G., Jr., *Canadian Evangelicalism in the Twentieth Century.* Toronto: University of Toronto Press.

1993. Grenz, Stanley, *Revisioning Evangelical Theology: A Fresh Agenda for the 21st Century.* Downers Grove, Ill.: InterVarsity Press.

1993. Land, Steven J., *Pentecostal Spirituality: A Passion for the Kingdom.* Sheffield, England: Sheffield Academic Press.

1994. Noll, Mark, *The Scandal of the Evangelical Mind.* Grand Rapids: Eerdmans.

1994. Maddox, Randy L., *Responsible Grace: John Wesley's Practical Theology.* Nashville: Kingswood Books, Abingdon Press.

1996. McGrath, Alister, *A Passion For Truth: The Intellectual Coherence of Evangelicalism.* Downers Grove, Ill.: InterVarsity Press.

1997. Erickson, Millard, *The Evangelical Left: Encountering Post-conservative Evangelical Theology.* Grand Rapids: Baker Books.

1997. Knight, Henry III, *A Future for Truth: Evangelical Theology in a Postmodern World.* Nashville: Abingdon Press.

1997. McGrath, Alister, *J. I. Packer: A Biography.* Grand Rapids: Baker Books.

1998. Dorrien, Gary, *The Remaking of Evangelical Theology.* Louisville, KY: Westminster John Knox Press.

1998. Abraham, William J., *Canon and Criterion in Christian Theology.* Oxford: Clarendon Press.

1998. Dockery, David, ed., *New Dimensions in Evangelical Thought.* Downers Grove, Ill.: InterVarsity Press.

1998. Erickson, Millard, ed., *Postmodernizing the Faith: Evangelical Responses to the Challenge of Postmodernism.* Grand Rapids: Baker Book House.

1998. Olson, Roger, "The Future of Evangelical Theology," *Christianity Today* (February 9), 40-50.

1999. Callen, Barry L., *Radical Christianity.* Nappanee, Ind.: Evangel Publishing House.

1999. Colyer, Elmer M., ed., *Evangelical Theology In Transition: Theologians in Dialogue with Donald Bloesch.* Downers Grove, Ill.: InterVarsity Press.

1999. Olson, Roger, *The Story of Christian Theology: Twenty Centuries of Tradition and Reform.* Downers Grove, Ill.: InterVarsity Press.

1999. Webber, Robert E., *Ancient-Future Faith: Rethinking Evangelicalism for a Postmodern World.* Grand Rapids: Baker Book House.

Interviews Conducted For This Biography

1998. Clark Pinnock, interviewed by Barry Callen (April 18).

1998. Anthony Campolo, interviewed by Barry Callen (April 18).

1998. Clark Pinnock, interviewed by Barry Callen (April 19).

1998. John Sanders, interviewed by Barry Callen (September 21).

1998. Clark Pinnock, interviewed by Barry Callen (November 21).
1998. Roger Olson, interviewed by Barry Callen (November 22).
1999. Grant Osborne, interviewed by Barry Callen (January 26).
1999. Clark Pinnock, interviewed by Barry Callen (July 15 to August 13).

In addition to the above, from 1997 to 1999 there were numerous e-mail exchanges with Clark Pinnock and with the series of scholars whose endorsements appear with the finalized book.

Index

A

Abraham, William J., 83, 2812-283

Adventism, 21, 256

Alley, Robert S., 81

American Prophetic League, 19

American revivalism, 185

amillennialism, 119

Anabaptism, 68, 109, 114, 116, 176, 278

Anderson, Sir Norman, xi, 24

annihilationism, xxii, 155, 163-164, 167, 190, 193, 255-260

Anselm, 254, 257

apologetics, xxi-xxii, 5, 23, 26-27, 37-38, 46-47, 49, 51, 63, 77, 79, 103, 106, 123, 188, 199, 205, 228-229, 273, 275, 278

Aquinas, Thomas, 143

Archer, Gleason Jr., 87

Armerding, Carl, 62

Arminian theology, xv, 19, 95, 99, 101-102, 116, 128-129, 138, 142, 182, 205

Arminius, Jacob, 129, 142

Asbury Theological Seminary, 137-138

Aslan, 169

atonement, 129, 133, 162, 212

attributes, of God, 92, 240, 243

Augustine, 6, 8, 15, 22, 25, 70, 87, 92, 100, 103-105, 115, 120, 128, 130, 140, 143, 152, 164-165, 171, 212, 239, 255, 274

autographs, of the Bible, 53, 61, 65, 68, 81

Azusa Street Lecture, 100, 154, 196, 278-279

B

Badham, Roger, xxii, 91, 134, 188, 277

Baptists, 16-18, 26, 36, 38, 46, 48, 54, 59, 67, 69, 72-73, 78, 117, 179, 201-202, 205, 219, 221, 223, 273, 276-277

Baptist Union, 219

Baptist Convention of Ontario and Quebec, 178, 279

Baptist General Conference, 158-159

Barnhouse, Donald Grey, 19

Barr, James, 57, 60-61, 65

Barth, Karl, 74, 144, 176, 200, 249-250

Basinger, David, 25, 140, 156-157, 275, 280

Basinger, Randall, 25, 140, 157, 275

Beegle, Dewey N., 58

believers baptism, 219

Believers Church tradition, 180

Bible, 2, 5, 15, 17-18, 25, 30, 35, 39, 41-44, 46, 48-50, 52-54, 57-61, 64, 66-74, 78, 82, 85, 92-93, 96, 98-99, 101, 103-105, 108-109, 117, 122-124, 129-131, 133-135, 137, 139, 143, 146, 149-150, 154, 165-168, 170-171, 178, 181, 183-184, 191, 205, 207-211, 213, 216, 219, 221-222, 225-226, 231-236, 239-243, 253-255

Bloesch, Donald, xxi, 69, 83, 91, 123, 161, 191-192, 207, 277, 283

Boettner, Loraine, 157

Bonhoeffer, Dietrich, 108

Boyd, Gregory A., 104, 153, 281

Brackney, William, 180

Broadman Press, 10, 48, 51, 67, 72, 79, 139, 194, 221, 279

Brethren tradition, 26, 63

Brown, Delwin, xix, 5, 66, 96-98, 135, 139, 147, 196, 198, 274, 279

Bruce, F. F., xv, 5, 12, 24, 26, 28, 31, 35, 54, 57-58, 60, 62, 64, 72, 197, 223, 273, 281

Brümmer, Vincent, 103

Buckley, William Jr., 195

Bultmann, Rudolf, 46, 58, 98

Butler, Trent, 42

C

Callen, Barry L., xiv-xv, 4, 10, 12, 23-24, 28, 37, 49-51, 58, 63, 75, 77, 80, 88, 109-110, 113, 116, 118-119, 147, 157, 160, 163, 179-181, 189, 195, 199-200, 204, 206, 210, 264, 269, 280, 283

Calvin, John, 25, 93, 99, 102, 104, 123, 154, 254

Calvinism, 22, 25, 35, 74, 89-90, 93-94, 99-100, 102-103, 105-106, 109, 120, 124, 138, 142-143, 145, 158, 176, 182, 186-187, 212, 241-242, 271

Campolo, Anthony, xix, 283

Canada, xiii, xx, 4-5, 13, 16-18, 22-23, 27, 35, 56, 62, 112-113, 164, 178-179, 201-202, 204, 273, 276

Canadian Evangelical Theological Association, 189

Canadian Keswick Bible Conference, 19

Canal Street Presbyterian Church (New Orleans), 77

Canons of Dort, 90

capitalism, 107, 110, 115, 117-118, 205

Carnell, Edward, 229

Carson, D. A., 149, 190, 280

charismatics (see Pentecostal)

Christian socialism, 110, 113

Christianity Today, 4, 7, 11, 28, 36, 42, 45-47, 50-51, 57-58, 61, 65, 71, 79, 81, 95, 100, 109, 112, 114, 132, 164, 167, 191, 193-194, 204, 256, 277-278, 283

christology, 131, 161, 216, 245-246, 250, 255

circles of credibility, 122, 226, 228

Claremont School of Theology, 57, 87, 94, 122, 148, 195, 205, 215

Clark, Gordon, 20, 100

classical theism, 82, 115, 129, 131, 133, 137, 143, 145-147, 150, 154-155, 193, 205, 240, 243, 275-276

Cobb, John B. Jr., 148, 274

Cohen, Norman, 19, 28, 39, 117, 276

Collins, Gary, 87

Colyer, Elmer M., xix, 191, 277, 283

communist, 112-113

Conference on Biblical Inerrancy (1978), 10, 48, 51-52, 67, 72, 79, 194

Conservative Baptist Theological Seminary, 142

Crockett, William, 165-166, 253, 276-277

Cross, Terry L., 12, 80, 147, 168, 175, 215

culture, 6, 27, 29-30, 38, 55, 66, 75, 85, 88, 92, 95, 110-111, 113-114, 116-117, 121, 124, 131, 135, 138, 146, 200, 203, 240, 258-259

D

Dallas Theological Seminary, 37, 52, 108

Davis, Stephen, 56, 61-62

Day, Dorothy, 110

DeSmidt, Diane, 82

Dead Sea Scrolls, 31

deconstructionism, 90

Decree on Missionary Activity, 246

Desert Storm, 119-120, 278

determinism, 92, 102, 154, 157, 168, 183, 186, 202, 211, 241, 243, 250, 271

dispensationalism, 52

Dockery, David, 44, 74, 79, 131, 139, 253, 277, 279, 283

doctoral dissertation (C. Pinnock's), 26, 33, 51, 80, 273

Dorrien, Gary, xix, 74, 125, 172, 205, 283

Dulles, Avery, 161

Dunning, H. Ray, 129, 183

E

Eastern Christianity (Orthodoxy), xi, 83, 101, 128, 142, 178, 180-183, 185

"ecumenical evangelical," xv

Eddleman, H. Leo, 36, 84

Edwards, David, 164, 257

Edwards, Jonathan, 258

election, divine, 89, 93, 104, 281

Elliott, Frank, 18

England, xiii, 4-5, 12-13, 18-19, 24, 26-27, 31, 35-36, 38, 50, 54, 58, 62-64, 81, 88, 161, 182, 197, 273-274, 280, 282

Enlightenment, 90, 134, 198

epistemology, 28, 53, 75-76, 81, 92, 122, 125, 162, 229, 243, 247

Erickson, Millard, 4, 80-81, 96, 137, 153, 171, 283

eschatology, 15, 108, 119, 127, 160-161, 170, 254-256, 279

evangelicalism, xiii, xv, xix, xxi-xxii, 3-4, 7, 13, 15-16, 19-25, 28, 31, 34-36, 46, 62, 64, 74, 79, 83-84, 90-92, 94, 96-97, 99-101, 106-107, 122, 124-125, 127-128, 131, 134, 136, 138-140, 142, 159, 161, 169, 172, 181, 184, 187, 192, 194, 196, 199, 201-202, 204-206, 214, 223, 228, 236, 243, 251, 255, 260-261, 263-265, 270-271, 280-283

evangelical "big tent," 21, 35, 94-95, 263, 266-267

evangelical-liberal dialogue, 97-98, 139, 147, 274

evangelical-process dialogue, 57, 87, 94, 122, 148, 195, 205, 215

Evangelical Theological Society, 7, 17, 42-43, 50, 59, 68, 78, 85, 128, 161, 163, 181, 189, 209, 213, 277-279

evangelism, 21, 23, 38, 47-48, 50, 79, 83, 99, 112, 116, 246, 264, 273

existentialism, 29

F

Fackre, Gabriel, 132, 143

Faith Seminary, 30

Falwell, Jerry, 28, 116

Farley, Edward, 61

Fee, Gordon, 32-33, 278

filioque, 249-250

First Things, 115

foreknowledge, of God, 143, 153, 156-160, 241-244, 280

foundationalism, 57, 90, 94, 122

free will, 25, 99, 105-106, 130, 138, 140, 148, 155-157, 183, 186, 242, 275, 280

free-will theism, xxii, 103, 128-129, 137, 144, 148, 150, 154, 159, 243, 274, 280

Frei, Hans, 214

Fuller Theological Seminary, 27, 65, 100, 163, 229

fundamentalism, 10, 17, 19-20, 24-25, 28-29, 37-39, 52, 57, 76, 84, 90, 98, 106, 108-109, 117, 124-125, 132, 184, 187, 202, 205, 214, 223, 234, 264-266, 270-272, 276, 278

Fuller, Charles, 19

G

Gasque, Ward, 62

gehenna, 166

Geisler, Norman, 67, 89-90, 106, 153, 159, 281

generous orthodoxy, 180, 214, 270

George, Timothy, 4, 79, 95, 139, 279

Gerstner, John, 20, 100

Gish, Arthur, 110

grace, xvi-xvii, xxii, 6, 15, 17, 34, 43, 56, 75-76, 83, 87, 92-93, 99, 101-102, 105, 114, 117, 119, 127-129, 133, 140, 151-152, 154, 157, 161-162, 165, 167-172, 179, 182-187, 189-190, 199-200, 210-212, 214, 216, 239, 246-251, 264, 274, 280, 282

Graham, Billy, 19-20, 107, 263-264

Greek philosophy, 130, 164, 239

Grenz, Stanley J., xix, xxi, 36, 38, 73, 76, 81, 90, 96, 125, 132, 136, 167, 188, 191, 194, 265, 276, 282

Grider, J. Kenneth, 91

Grounds, Vernon, 106

Gundry, Robert, 52

H

Hartshorne, Charles, 145

Hebrews, book of, 102, 243

hellenization, 32, 136

Henry, Carl F. H., 8, 20, 22, 24, 36, 49, 52, 65, 83, 100, 108, 164, 194, 214, 229, 265, 270, 275, 281-282

hermeneutics, 68, 109, 135, 209, 253-254

hermeneutic of hopefulness, 168

Holloman, Henry, 42

Holy Spirit (see Spirit of God)

Houston, James, 62

Hughes, Philip, 164, 255

I

Iliff School of Theology, 147

illumination, 75, 80, 206, 209-211

immortality, 163-164, 167, 258

inclusive language, 149

inerrancy, biblical, 5, 10, 26, 37, 41-43, 46, 48, 50-54, 56-58, 60-61, 64-70, 72-75, 79, 81, 83, 89-92, 100, 102, 108, 112, 181, 184-185, 191, 194, 205, 211, 235-237, 275, 277

inspiration, of the Bible, 28, 41, 50, 53-54, 57, 59-60, 64, 71-73, 75, 79-81, 84, 92, 101, 112, 130, 132, 184, 209-210, 221, 231, 233, 235-237, 269, 275

InterVarsity Christian Fellowship, 4, 20-25, 33-34, 49, 88, 251, 263

InterVarsity Press, xviii, xxi, 3, 22-23, 25, 44, 48, 74, 95, 103-104, 106, 119, 121, 124-125, 127, 130-131, 136, 140-143, 145, 157, 159-161, 164, 168, 183, 188, 191-192, 197, 199, 207, 212, 225, 253, 256, 265-266, 273-277, 280, 282-283

J

James, Robison, 46

Jennings, Theodore Jr., 145

Jesus, xviii, 13, 24, 30, 32, 34, 36-37, 43, 46, 48, 51, 60-61, 66, 73, 76, 98, 105-108, 111-112, 118, 121, 133, 142, 149, 155-156, 161-172, 177, 180, 186, 189, 201, 203, 205, 208-209, 212-213, 216, 225-227, 231-232, 234-235, 245-250, 254, 264, 270, 274-276

Jewett, Paul, 20

John XXIII, Pope, 198

John Paul II, Pope, 198

Johnston, Robert, 61, 108, 110, 275, 280-282

journey, xiv-xix, xxi-xxii, 1-4, 8, 10-13, 15-16, 18-19, 21, 24, 27, 33, 39, 43, 67, 69, 74, 76, 80, 82, 84-85, 89, 91, 99, 101, 115, 118-120, 124-125, 129-130, 133, 139, 159, 172, 176-178, 180, 183, 185-186, 190, 198-199, 201, 206, 211-213, 216-217, 229, 241, 270

just war, 119-120, 278

K

Kantzer, Kenneth, 20, 52, 85, 87, 275

Keswick (England), 19, 161

Klein, William W., 103

Knight, Henry H., III, 176, 283

Koivisto, Rex A., 7, 50

Kostlevy, William, xix

Kraft, Robert, 26

L

L'Abri Fellowship, 27-30, 50, 72, 116

Ladd, George Eldon, 52

Land, Steven J., 282

Lausanne Covenant, 69

Leon Morris Lecture, 164

Lewis, C. S., xv, 23-24, 28, 58, 169-170, 200, 223, 245, 251, 278

Lewis, Edwin, 138

liberal theology, xv, 29, 48, 51, 154, 159, 163, 208, 256, 265

liberalism, 19, 30, 35, 51, 58, 66, 70-71, 96-97, 99, 134, 136, 179, 202, 204-205, 214, 231, 236, 265

liberation, theology of, 60, 118, 132

Lindsell, Harold, 52, 57-58, 92, 281

Lints, Richard, 125

Lloyd-Jones, Martyn, 20

Luther, Martin, 2

M

McClendon, James Jr., 8

McGrath, Alister, 63, 164, 168, 176, 283

McIntire, Carl, 30

McMaster Divinity College, 17-18, 44-45, 60, 63-64, 139, 160, 178-179, 192

Macarius, 101

Macchia, Frank, 152, 217

Machen, J. Gresham, 29

Maddox, Randy L., xvi, 172, 279-280, 282

Marshall, I. Howard, 60, 102-103

Marxism, 117, 200

Martin, Ralph, 27

materialism, 51, 115, 121, 200

Meadows, Philip R., xix, 156, 182

Mennonite community, 113

Methodism, 2, 16, 91, 95, 145, 178, 186

Mikolaski, Samuel, 48

millennialism, 52, 114, 119

mission, xvii-xxii, 2, 5-6, 8-10, 12, 17-19, 31, 33, 39, 42, 72-73, 80-81, 83-84, 94, 120, 125, 160, 169, 171-172, 185, 188, 192, 200, 205, 264

modernity, 5, 9, 16, 36, 38, 42, 57, 66, 73, 125, 146, 150, 229, 276, 281

Moltmann, Jürgen, 15-16, 39, 200

Montefiore, Hugh, 146

Montgomery, John Warwick, 24, 47, 87, 275

Morey, Robert, 159, 282

Mother Teresa, 113

Muller, Richard, 155

Murray, John, 20

N

Narnia, 169

Nash, Ronald, 82, 108, 143, 193, 275-276

National Assoc. of Evangelicals, 138

National Council of Churches, 222

Neuhaus, Richard John, 113

neo-orthodoxy, 29, 37, 49, 74, 78

New Orleans, La., 13, 36-38, 48-49, 51-52, 77, 84-85, 195, 199, 223

New Orleans Baptist Theological Seminary, 36, 48

Nicole, Roger, 57, 61, 65, 191, 194

Nigeria, 16-17

Noll, Mark, 46, 168, 276, 282

Novak, Michael, 113

O

Oden, Thomas, 4, 91, 95, 271

Olson, Roger, xviii-xix, 2, 5, 11, 94, 132, 136, 284

omniscience, divine, 95, 153, 156-158, 193, 241-243

Ontario, Canada, 16-17, 19, 27, 45, 60, 62-63, 85, 139, 160, 178, 201-202, 276, 279

openness of God, 10-11, 95, 127, 131, 136, 141, 143-144, 149-150, 153, 157, 159, 271, 274, 276, 281

optimism of salvation, 245

original sin, 183, 186

Orr, James, 237

orthodoxy, xiv, 4-5, 29, 37-38, 49, 52, 79, 83, 98, 101, 125, 128, 130, 132, 140, 142, 158, 178, 180-181, 183-184, 189, 192, 202, 204, 211, 214, 217, 256-257, 270-271, 281

Orthodox tradition (see Eastern Christianity)

Osborne, Grant, xix, 88, 182, 277, 284

P

pacifism, 109, 111

Packer, James I., 20, 24-25, 29, 46, 54, 63, 88, 160-161, 163-164, 170, 193, 214, 273, 282

para-church organizations, 4, 19-21, 84

Park Road Baptist Church, 17

Patterson, Paige, 52, 194

Payton Lectures, 65, 163

Pentecost, 203

Pentecostalism, xiv-xv, xxi-xxii, 4, 6, 21, 33, 77-81, 91, 100, 103, 124, 176-178, 185, 196, 198-199, 201, 204-205, 217, 223, 266, 277-278, 282

Peoples Christian Coalition, 108, 112

Peoples Church (Toronto), 19

perseverance of saints, 87, 102

Pietism, 2, 28, 34, 63, 76, 79-80, 84, 91, 107, 124-125, 142, 178, 223, 266

pilgrim, xix-xxi, 7, 25, 122, 132, 270

Pinnock, Dorothy, xx

Pinnock, Harold, 16

Pinnock, Madora, 16

Pinnock, Mable Clark, 18

Pinnock, Samuel, 16, 25

Pinnock, Sarah, 36

Piper, John, 158

Plato, 168, 240

pluralism, 90, 113, 160, 163, 167, 169, 188, 206, 245, 249, 280

pneumatology, xv, 31, 33, 114, 131, 188, 216-217

political radicalism, 107, 132

post-Christian, xvii

postconservative, 5, 80, 96, 137, 282

post-modern, xvii, 123

postmodernism, 4, 90, 283

postmillennialism, 119

Post American, 109, 112

premillennialism, 108, 119

prevenient grace, 101, 105, 161, 169, 171-172, 186, 247, 249

Price, Robert, 8, 76, 82, 177, 279

Princeton tradition, 25

process theism, 82, 133, 143, 146, 148, 150, 193, 243, 276

process theology, 82, 133, 143, 146-150, 159, 187, 193, 276

providence, of God, 107, 115, 127, 141, 156-157, 159-160, 183, 280

Puritans, 28, 184

Q-R

quadrilateral (see Wesleyan quadrilateral)

Qumran, 31, 33

Rakestraw, Robert, 78, 279

Ramm, Bernard, 36-37, 73, 96, 194, 229, 276

Reagan, Ronald, 113

reason (critical thought), 36, 70, 75, 96, 122-123, 135, 154, 225, 236, 253, 257-259

reciprocity, 100-106, 114-115, 145, 150, 161, 240

Reformed scholasticism, 5, 7, 90, 143, 154

Reformed theology, xiv, 2, 90, 100, 134, 161, 271, 282

Regent College (Vancouver), 56, 60, 62, 112, 130, 160

Regent University (Virginia), 100, 154, 196, 278-279

relativism, 43, 47, 53, 74-75, 221, 245, 265

religious experience, xxi, 82-83, 200-201, 226, 264

restrictivism, 162-163, 250-251, 271

resurrection, of Jesus, 37, 48, 156, 227

revelation, divine, xv, xxi, 3, 9, 16, 35, 41, 43-47, 49-51, 54, 56, 58, 60, 62, 64-66, 69-71, 74-75, 77, 80-81, 83, 93-94, 96, 98-99, 121, 123-124, 129, 134, 149, 162, 165-166, 168-169, 171-172, 175, 180, 191, 201-202, 207, 209, 229, 231-236, 249, 270, 273, 275

Rice, Richard, 156-157, 280

Ritschl, Albrecht, 46

Rockwood, Perry F., 19

Roennfeldt, Ray C. W., xix, 54, 60, 73, 76, 90, 101-102, 194, 279

Rogers, Adrian, 10, 52

Rogers, Jack, 57, 275

Roman Catholicism, 161, 170, 221, 246, 251

Ryrie, Charles, 24, 52

S

sacramental presence, 43, 114

Sacred Feathers, 170

salvation, xv, 66, 68-69, 81, 84, 91, 93, 99, 101, 105, 112, 114, 116, 129, 133, 147, 151, 154, 158-159, 161-164, 167-172, 176, 178, 180, 183-184, 187, 208, 212, 215, 227, 232-233, 245-251, 260, 276-277, 280

Sanders, John, xix, 103, 141, 153, 157, 160, 162, 179, 189, 204, 206, 281, 283

satisfaction theory (atonement), 129

Scaer, David, 52

Schaeffer, Francis, 5, 23, 27-30, 35, 42, 47, 54, 57, 72, 77, 107, 116, 197, 200, 223, 275-276, 282

Schaeffer, Franky, 116

Schleiermacher, Friedrich, 46, 76, 82

Schloss Mittersill (Austria), 199

scholasticism, 5, 7, 20, 90, 94, 127, 143, 154, 191, 196, 271

Scripture principle, 41-43, 57, 61, 65-67, 69, 75, 92, 123, 147, 184, 191, 193-194, 197, 207, 231-232, 237, 271, 273, 279

Shank, Robert, 104

Shedd, William, 257-258

Sider, Ronald J., 116

Sire, James W., 142

Smith, Oswald J., 19

Smith, Timothy L., 185

social Trinity, 144, 147

Sojourners, 30, 60, 107, 109-112, 132, 277

sola Scriptura, 70, 133

soteriology, 205, 216, 255

Southern Baptist Convention, 5, 36, 38, 48, 51-52, 70, 222-223, 256

Southeastern Baptist Theological Seminary, 52

speaking in tongues (*see* tongues)

Spirit, of God, xv, xviii-xx, xxii, 7, 12, 19, 31-34, 51, 57, 67, 73, 80-81, 92, 100, 108, 114, 118, 129-130, 135, 145-146, 152, 160-161, 168-169, 173, 177-178, 182, 185-186, 191-192, 197-199, 201-204, 206-207, 210, 212-213, 216-217, 248, 266, 274, 276-278

spirituality, xxi, 22, 57, 78, 81, 112, 125, 160, 200, 264, 282

Sproul, R. C., 158

Spurgeon, 219

Stackhouse, John Jr., 23, 62, 282

Stott, John R. W., 21, 256

Strange, Daniel, xxii, 162, 176, 215, 280

Strong, Douglas, xix, 181

Switzerland, 4, 13, 27, 30, 38, 50

T

"The Hour of Decision," 19

"The Old Fashioned Revival Hour," 19

theism, 82, 95, 101, 103, 115, 128-131, 133, 137, 139, 143-151, 154-155, 158-159, 181, 192-193, 196, 205, 239-240, 243, 275-276, 280

Theological Studies Fellowship, 88-89

Thompson, Claude, 138

Thorsen, Donald A. D., 265

Tillich, Paul, 29, 49

tongues, 77, 79, 197, 199, 204, 277

Toronto Blessing, 199, 202-203

Toronto, Ontario, 17-20, 27, 31, 63, 137, 202, 204

transcendence, of God, 92, 136, 145, 148, 150, 243

Trinity, 144, 146-147, 151, 248-249, 257

Trinity Evangelical Divinity School, 47, 55-56, 62-63, 69, 85, 87-89, 92, 102, 105-110, 112, 128, 130, 141-142, 182, 192

Trueblood, D. Elton, 1

TSF Bulletin, 88

U-V

unevangelized, 162-163, 171-172, 189

universalism, 105, 163-164, 168, 172, 260

University of Manchester, 12, 26, 31-32, 36, 62, 64, 197, 273

University of Toronto, 20, 23, 25, 31, 33, 62, 170, 282

Van Til, Cornelius, 20, 103, 275

Vatican Council II, 251

Vietnam, 109, 113

Vineyard Fellowship, 202

W

Wallis, Jim, 108

Warfield, B. B., 28-29, 54, 74, 93

Wells, David F., 55, 274, 276, 282

Wenham, John, 164, 256

Wesley, John, xv, 75, 78, 83, 101, 105, 128-129, 145, 151, 156-157, 161, 171, 181-184, 186-187, 282

Wesleyan/Holiness tradition, 4, 138

Wesleyan quadrilateral, 70, 96, 181, 260-261, 264-265

Wesleyan theology, 129, 181

Wesleyan Theological Society, xvi, xxi, 91, 128, 181

Western Christianity, 128, 200

Westminster Confession, 91, 140, 176

Westminster Seminary, 30

Westmount Baptist Church (Hamilton, Ontario), 139

wideness in God's mercy, 160-161, 163-164, 168, 170-171, 245, 271, 274

Williams, Colin, 186

Wimber, John, 79

World Congress on Evangelism (1966), 48

World Council of Churches, 30

Wright, R. K. McGregor, 103, 105-106, 130, 191-192, 281

Wycliff Bible Translators, 20, 25

Wynkoop, Mildred Bangs, 182

X-Y-Z

Yoder, John Howard, 107, 109-110, 112

Yong, Amos, xxii, 161-162, 176, 215

Young, Edward, 52

Youth for Christ, 19, 263

Zeman, Jarold, 179, 201, 276